The Roots of Terrorism in Indonesia

SOLAHUDIN is a researcher and journalist, and a leading expert on the *jihadi* movement in Indonesia. He commenced research on jihadism after the October 2002 Bali bombings, in part out of a desire to uncover the genealogy of the movement behind the attacks. His book on the Indonesian *jihadi* movement, presented in translation herein, is an Indonesian bestseller and has generated widespread discussion in that country among the media, academic and religious communities. He worked as principal researcher with a Lowy Institute team on the 2011 Lowy Institute Paper, *Talib or Taliban? Indonesian Students in Pakistan and Yemen.* In 2013, he also joined the Indonesia Strategic Policy Institute (ISPI) to establish a data-base of extremist violence in Indonesia. He also researches political and religious movements in Papua, as well as the history of Islam there. Solahudin has worked for more than a decade as a journalist and an activist for freedom of the press, including holding the position of Secretary-General of the Alliance of Independent Journalists (AJI) from 2001 to 2003. His advocacy in cases of violence against journalists includes successfully acting as a mediator in the release of two Belgian journalists held hostage in Papua in 2001. He was also a member of the mediation team that nego-tiated the release of one of the Indonesian journalists held by the Free Aceh Movement (Gerakan Aceh Merdeka – GAM) in 2004.

DR DAVE McRAE is a research fellow in the East Asia Program at the Lowy Institute for International Policy. He has researched conflict, poli-tics, democratisation and human rights issues in Indonesia for well over a decade. He was Lead Researcher for the World Bank's Conflict and Development Team in Indonesia between 2008 and 2010 and worked for the Jakarta office of the International Crisis Group from 2004 to 2006, researching and writing reports on most of Indonesia's major conflict areas. Dave holds a Bachelor of Asian Studies (Specialist – Indonesian) degree with Honours and University Medal from the Australian National University, and a Ph.D. in Southeast Asian Studies. He is the author of *A Few Poorly Organised Men: Interreligious Violence in Poso, Indonesia* (2013).

The Roots of **Terrorism** in Indonesia

From Darul Islam
to Jema'ah Islamiyah

Solahudin

Translated by Dave McRae

Foreword by Greg Fealy

Cornell University Press
Ithaca and London

Published in 2013 by Cornell University Press

Printed in the United States of America

© Solahudin, in the original text in Bahasa Indonesia, 2013
© The Lowy Institute for International Policy, in the translation by Dave McRae

First published in Indonesia in Bahasa Indonesia in 2011 under the title
NII Sampai Ji: Salafy Jihadisme di Indonesia by Komunitas Bambu, Depok

First published in Australia by UNSW Press, an imprint of UNSW Press Ltd.

First printing, Cornell Paperbacks, 2013

Library of Congress Cataloging-in-Publication Data

Solahudin, author.
　　[NII sampai JI. English]
　　The roots of terrorism in Indonesia : from Darul Islam to Jema'ah Islamiyah /
Solahudin ; translated by Dave McRae, foreword by Greg Fealy.
　　　pages cm
　　Includes bibliographical references and index.
　　ISBN 978-0-8014-5292-5 (cloth : alk. paper)
　　ISBN 978-0-8014-7938-0 (pbk. : alk. paper)
　　1. Jihad. 2. Terrorism—Religious aspects—Islam. 3. Islamic fundamentalism—
Indonesia. 4. Darul Islam (Organization) 5. Jamaah Islamiyah (Indonesia)
I. McRae, Dave, 1977– translator. II. Fealy, Greg. III. Solahudin.
NII sampai JI. Translation of: IV. Title.
　　BP182.S63513　2013
　　363.325'1109598—dc23　　　　2013031793

Cover images: Students line up to greet Militant cleric Abu Bakar Bashir at Al Mukmin Islamic School in Solo, Indonesia, June 2006. AP Photo/ © 2006/ Dita Alangkara.

Cloth printing　　　　10 9 8 7 6 5 4 3 2 1
Paperback printing　　10 9 8 7 6 5 4 3 2 1

Contents

Preface

Initially it was a question, then it became an answer. Two questions particularly disturbed me when I witnessed the repeated acts of terror in the name of *jihad* which began in 2000. First, what sort of interpretation of Islam was it that justified a *jihad* to kill children, women, the elderly and even Muslims themselves? Where did this interpretation originate from, and how and why was it able to develop in Indonesia? Second, what were the origins of the *jihadi* movement in Indonesia? Why and how did these groups come to adopt and practice an interpretation often associated with Al-Qaeda ideology?

As these two questions were genealogical in nature, I looked for the answer in the literature on the history of Islam in Indonesia, in particular the history of Islamic movements that had chosen *jihad* as their path of struggle. My research focused on the Darul Islam movement, which has actively called for *jihad* to establish an Islamic state in Indonesia. It turned out, though, that the books which discussed this movement, which Sekarmadji Maridjan Kartosuwirjo founded, were not completely satisfactory. There were only a few texts that were useful in understanding this movement, which had actively confronted the state from the late 1940s through to the early 1960s. These texts include Cees van Dijk's *Rebellion Under the Banner of Islam* and Holk H. Dengel's *Darul Islam dan Kartosuwirjo: Angan-Angan yang Gagal*. Although they were useful, these two books only touched on Kartosuwirjo's interpretation of *jihad*. To address this gap, I then researched Darul Islam documents such as *Pedoman Darma Bakti* and *Qanun Azasi*, as well as various of Kartosuwirjo's works such as *Sikap Hijrah 1* and *2*, *Daftar Usaha Hijrah* and *Haluan Politik Islam*, as well as his articles in the *Fadjar Asia* daily.

The search for an answer became most difficult, however, when I began to study the history of Darul Islam following its defeat in 1962. Difficult, because there was barely even a single text that could explain what happened to Darul Islam after this defeat. This was despite there having been various subsequent clashes between Darul Islam activists and the Indonesian state, such as the Komando Jihad episode in the 1970s, as well as Warman's Terror and the *usroh* movement, both in the 1980s. It was here that the real challenge began. I gradually gathered various court documents, primarily interrogation depositions, for suspects in the cases, from Komando Jihad through to the Bali bombings. To deepen my understanding of Darul Islam's teachings and dynamics after 1962, I also gathered various internal documents produced by the *jihadi* movement, from the SPUI (*Sejarah Perjuangan Umat Islam – History of the Struggle of the Islamic Community*) to the MTI (*Manhaj Taklimat Islamiyah – Islamic Briefing Material*). I also collected and read as many books as I could that had been published in Indonesia between the 1950s and the 2000s on an Islamic state and *jihad*.

From the outset, I have been aware of the need for caution in reading these documents and books. Efforts to reconstruct history can be misleading when the author makes mistakes in sorting through details which are often mutually contradictory, particularly in the case of court documents, or misinterprets these documents and books. Consequently, I then looked for people I could ask questions to help verify all of the information that I obtained from the various court documents, internal documents, and books on *jihad* and an Islamic state. Fortunately, I was able to meet and interview a number of former perpetrators of violence in the name of *jihad*, as well as their associates in the same groups. For example, to confirm the information on Komando Jihad that I obtained from court documents, I held intensive discussions with the late Uci Enong, a figure in Darul Islam Fillah, the late Ridwan, one of the first post-1962 Darul Islam cadres, and with the late Gaos Taufik, alias Aki, a Komando Jihad figure from Sumatra.

Through people such as Aki and Uci and Ridwan, I had the opportunity to verify all of the information from the various documents and books. Only then did I attempt to reconstruct events. In undertaking this reconstruction, I also held intensive discussions with Sidney Jones. Her various criticisms and input greatly assisted me in achieving a more solid reconstruction of the history of the *jihadi* movement and *jihadi* ideology in Indonesia.

I present this reconstruction of history in this book, which provides a history of Salafi Jihadism in Indonesia. This ideology is frequently associated with Al-Qaeda, but Darul Islam members in earlier times in fact followed a similar ideology. This book also presents a history of the *jihadi* movement in Indonesia, from Darul Islam through to Jema'ah Islamiyah.

My efforts to reconstruct this history took a long time, and certainly involved other people. I thank my interviewees, who were willing to share information with me. I owe a special debt of gratitude to Sidney Jones, as a friend in debate and also as a friend who always gave encouragement. Thanks also to Komunitas Bambu press, who published the Indonesian language edition. Nor should I forget to thank Greg Fealy, who contributed a foreword for both the Indonesian and English editions of the book.

Specifically for the English edition, I would like to thank Bill Paterson, without whose assistance it would have been difficult to publish this work in its English edition. I also owe a debt of gratitude to Dave McRae, who translated the text into English. Thanks also to Anthony Bubalo for his hard work in editing the translation to adapt it for readers outside of Indonesia, and to UNSW Press for publishing the manuscript.

Finally, happy reading.

Solahudin
Depok

Translator's note

When my colleague Anthony Bubalo approached me with the idea for the Lowy Institute to produce an edited translation of Solahudin's *NII Sampai JI: Salafy Jihadisme di Indonesia*, I was delighted to take on the task of translation, with Anthony editing. I have a long familiarity with Solahudin's unique work through my own study of post-authoritarian violence in Indonesia. Introducing a leading expert on Indonesian jihadism to an English-speaking audience fit with the Lowy Institute's goal of shedding light on this important subject. It was also a continuation of the Institute's work on Indonesia more broadly, as well as of more specific research on Islamist connections between the Middle East and Indonesia. A grant from the Department of Foreign Affairs and Trade made the translation and its publication possible, as did the willingness of UNSW Press to partner with the Lowy Institute on the project.

The translation is not a direct replica of the Indonesian-language book, which was written for an audience with an altogether different level of familiarity with Indonesia and Islam. With the author's agreement, we were keen to make this edition of the book as accessible as possible to a new audience, while remaining true to the original. To that end, the text in translation has been edited and shortened, with some changes to the chapter structure. Solahudin has also added a new epilogue for this edition. The text in translation omits a portion of the detailed discussion of *jihadi* doctrine found in the original, but preserves what I think is a rich portrait of a movement that has continued to regenerate, despite internal divisions and repeated setbacks in the face of moves against it by the Indonesian state. Through Solahudin's extensive use of primary sources, including interviews with those involved in the events under discussion, the text presents a fascinating glimpse of the mindset and thinking of some of the key actors in the Indonesian *jihadi* movement.

This translation retains the conventions used by the author in the original book when it comes to Indonesian names. In accordance with Indonesian practice, the text uses an individual's first name after the first complete mention for most Javanese and Sundanese names. For example, Aceng Kurnia becomes Aceng, Mursalin Dahlan becomes Mursalin. The one exception is Ajengan Masduki, where Masduki is used because Ajengan is an honorific. When Muhammad in any of its various spellings is the first name, the second name becomes the standard shortened form. Thus Muhammad Jabir becomes Jabir and Mohammad Sanusi becomes Sanusi. For individuals of Arab descent, the surname is generally used for the shortened form, thus Abu Bakar Ba'asyir and Abdullah Sungkar become Ba'asyir and Sungkar. There are a few other cases where, because of common usage, the surname is also used – for example, Kartosuwirjo, and Moertopo as the shortened form of Ali Moertopo. I have omitted most honorifics from names mentioned in the text.

Additionally, Islamic terms that used the Indonesian transliteration in the Indonesian text use the Arabic transliteration here, unless they appear as part of the name of an organisation. Some names of people and organisations appear in the form most familiar to an English-speaking audience, such as Osama bin Laden and Al-Qaeda.

I would like to thank Solahudin for his collaboration and co-operation in the production of this edition. Special thanks also to Sidney Jones for her valuable input on the translation and edits, and to Greg Fealy for advising on various points of translation. Tricia Dearborn ably copyedited the text, and Phillipa McGuinness and Uthpala Gunethilake have been a pleasure to work with at UNSW Press.

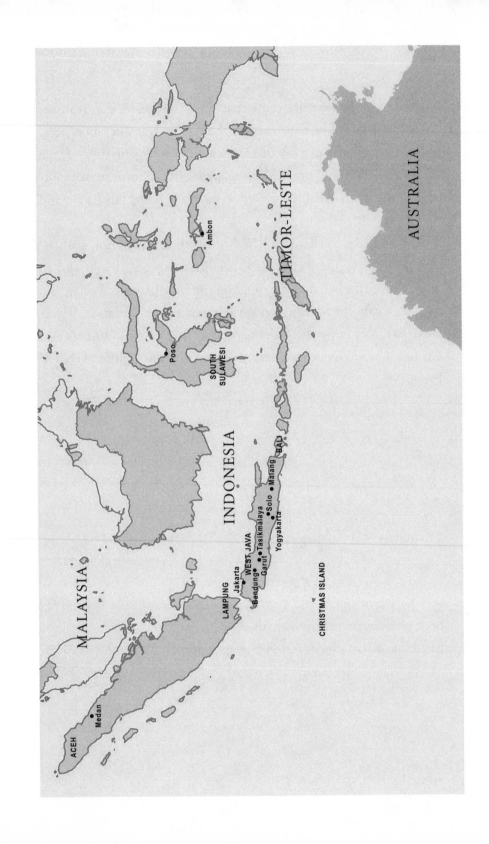

Foreword

Militant jihadist movements have been part of Indonesian history since the first years of independence. Some aspects of this history have been extensively researched and are quite well understood, but many others remain vague or neglected. The early years of the Darul Islam movement, from its inception in the late 1940s to its 'defeat' in insurgency in 1962, have been the subject of numerous books and articles, including some of high scholarly value, such as van Dijk's *Rebellion under the Banner of Islam* (1981) or Holk Dengel's *Darul Islam dan Kartosoewirjo* (1995). Similarly, the short-lived but high-profile Laskar Jihad (2000–02) has been extensively studied, resulting in a number of well-regarded academic works, most notably Noorhaidi Hasan's *Laskar Jihad* (2006). Most recently, Jema'ah Islamiyah (1993 to present) has attracted close scholarly scrutiny, though the number of rigorously researched publications on it remains surprisingly small. Aside from Sidney Jones's groundbreaking International Crisis Group reports on Jema'ah Islamiyah (2002–12) and writings from a handful of other scholars such as Ken Ward (2008) and Muhammad Haniff Hassan (2006), the literature on JI is much thinner than for other major jihadist organisations elsewhere in the world.

By far the most neglected aspect of Indonesian jihadism is that period from 1962 till the fall of Suharto's New Order regime in 1998. Only a small number of serious scholarly works have dealt with this period, including Martin van Bruinessen's 'Genealogies of Islamic Radicalism' (2002) and Quinton Temby's 'Imagining an Islamic State in Indonesia' (2010). There have also been some interesting, but not always reliable, accounts from activists and writers close to Darul Islam, such as al-Chaidar (2008) and Umar Abduh (2002).

Solahudin's *The Roots of Terrorism in Indonesia* is the first work to provide a comprehensive account of jihadism from the early years of the Darul Islam rebellion till the Jema'ah Islamiyah terrorist bombings in the early 2000s. The historical description of these jihadist movements is rich in detail, particularly regarding Suharto's New Order (1966–98). This is a difficult period for which to piece together a reliable narrative. Not only did the regime often engage in deliberate misinformation, but the jihadists themselves operated covertly and relatively few have been willing to speak candidly about their activities and motivations. Little was written down in jihadist circles, for fear of detection by the security services, so primary source documents are scarce. Moreover, a good deal of the available written and oral data is contradictory, perhaps because those producing the information have failing memories or an incomplete grasp of what was happening, or because they sought deliberately to mislead in order to justify their own actions or discredit others.

Solahudin's account of the 1970s to the early 1990s illuminates a critical period in the development of Indonesian jihadism, revealing how key individuals and groups changed their thinking, strategies and organisational forms in response to increasingly heavy state repression and ideological stimulus from abroad. He looks closely at the revival of Darul Islam in the early 1970s, examines the role played by both the Siliwangi Division and BAKIN in co-opting and mobilising Darul Islam members, and maps the deepening divisions between senior Darul Islam leaders throughout the 1970s and 1980s.

Of special interest is the description of disputes between Darul Islam figures on how to interpret (or perhaps, more accurately, reinterpret) the legacy of Kartosuwirjo, Darul Islam's revered founder, in the context of Suharto's Indonesia. Should Darul Islam members continue to undertake violent struggle to create (or in their minds, maintain) an Islamic state, or should they pursue, at least for the short term, non-violent means of consolidating their movement and popularising the Islamic state concept? Should they cooperate with the regime and its security services as a means of protecting and covertly rebuilding Darul Islam or should they avoid the taint of contact with a secular and 'anti-Islamic' state? Moreover, who had the greater claim to Darul Islam leadership: those who had surrendered to the Republic and sworn allegiance to the religiously neutral state doctrine of Pancasila in the early 1960s or those who had remained underground and never capitulated? Solahudin shows how ideological, and sometimes personal, differences on these issues produced recurring fissures and occasional bloody violence between protagonists. Thus, for much of the New Order, Darul Islam proved unable to provide unified and effective central leadership, especially after the ongoing arrests of members from the late 1970s. Solahudin also captures the complexity of the relationships between the regime and key Darul Islam figures, with both sides engaging in double games and deception. Many of the Darul Islam leaders who accepted money and business opportunities from their military or intelligence 'patrons' continued to plan for subversive activity, while regime figures regularly manipulated the jihadists for their own political purposes.

Even though Darul Islam was factionalised for much of this period, with its main groups often subject to shifting alliances, the movement nonetheless continued to generate ongoing jihadist ferment. Solahudin explores connections between the original pre-1962 Darul Islam generation and subsequent operations, such as the so-called 'Teror Warman' murders in the late 1970s, the aborted assassination attempt on Suharto in 1982, the Bank Central Asia and Malang church bombings of 1984, the Borobudur bombing in 1985, the Christmas Eve 2000 church bombings and the 2002 Bali bombings. In total, such jihadist attacks have probably cost the lives of more than 350 people over the past thirty-five years.

Solahudin's text is also valuable for the way that it traces the growing internationalisation of Indonesian jihadism from the late 1970s. Darul Islam activists received funding from, and training in, Libya during the latter part of that decade and were also inspired by the 1979 Iranian Revolution, which, among other curious outcomes, led to the emergence of a Shi'ite group within Darul Islam that continues to exist until the present time. Most important of all was the training of hundreds of Indonesian *mujahideen* in Afghanistan from the mid-1980s till the early 1990s, most of whom came from Darul Islam ranks. This not only greatly enhanced the military and organisational capabilities of many jihadists but also had a major impact on their doctrinal thinking. Among other things, Afghanistan sharpened the differences between the more Islamically traditionalist Darul Islam leaders, such as Ajengan Masduki, and the more puritan and pan-Islamist leaders such as Abdullah Sungkar and Abu Bakar Ba'asyir. These disagreements would eventually cause a split within Darul Islam's ranks in late 1992, with Sungkar establishing Jema'ah Islamiyah early the following year. From the mid-1990s, new Darul Islam and Jema'ah Islamiyah training operations took place in Mindanao, in the southern Philippines; Jema'ah Islamiyah's linkages to the Moro Islamic Liberation Front (MILF) and the Abu Sayyaf Group continue to this day. When sections of Jema'ah Islamiyah undertook major terrorist operations such as the 2002 Bali bombing, they gained substantial funding from Osama bin Laden's al-Qaeda.

Perhaps the most controversial aspect of the book is its ideological analysis. Solahudin places Indonesian jihadism in a Salafi Jihadist framework. He does not argue that Indonesian jihadists have always been Salafi Jihadist, but rather that since the late 1940s Darul Islam's ideology shared a number of important elements with later Salafi Jihadism, even though Kartosuwirjo seemingly developed his thinking based on a somewhat idiosyncratic understanding of classical jihadism, rather than on an awareness of contemporary Middle Eastern discourses. This 'common ground' between traditional Darul Islam doctrine and the emerging Salafi Jihadist ideology of the late 1960s and 1970s helped to facilitate the spread of the latter within Indonesian Islamist circles from the late 1970s. This mixing of 'indigenous' with external influences is a major theme of the book. The Indonesian-language version of this book, published in 2011, aroused considerable debate among jihadists and scholars about the degree to which parallels can be drawn between Darul Islam doctrine of 50 years ago and contemporary Salafi Jihadism. If nothing else, Solahudin has helped to generate discussion on important ideological issues and typologies that previously have been the preserve of a small number of jihadist intellectuals.

Scholars of Indonesian terrorism will also gain much from the examination of divergent ideological trends within Jema'ah Islamiyah, especially the debate regarding the conditions under which extreme forms of violence – including suicide bombing and the attacking of civilians – can be undertaken, and who has the authority to approve such operations. Solahudin describes the impact Osama bin Laden's 1998 *fatwa* calling for attacks upon the United States and its allies had upon the most militant sections of Jema'ah Islamiyah based in the First Regional Command (Mantiqi I). Though the majority of Jema'ah Islamiyah rejected bin Laden's *fatwa* as not pertinent to Indonesia, key Mantiqi I leaders such as Hambali and Mukhlas regarded it as a timely and valid summons to war. They were further inspired by the 'success' of the 11 September 2001 attacks on New York and Washington and were determined that Indonesian jihadists should also strike a blow for the global Islamic struggle. The discussion of these ideological differences is insightful, and helps to redress widespread misconceptions that Jema'ah Islamiyah was doctrinally monolithic.

I have no hesitation in recommending this book to you. It offers a thorough and dispassionate account of Indonesian jihadism and adds greatly to our understanding of terrorist groups. Unlike many other writers on this subject, Solahudin eschews glib moralising and emphasises explanation over normative opinion. It will have great value as a reference work, such is the detail of its description of jihadist movements, ideologies and events, as well as being a contribution to the scholarly debate about jihadist motivations and rationale.

Greg Fealy
College of Asia and the Pacific
The Australian National University, Canberra

Introduction

Akhi [my brother], fill your life with the murder of *kuffar* [the unbelievers]. Has not Allah ordered you to kill them all, as they have killed our fellow Muslims? Aspire to be an executioner of unbelievers. Teach your grandchildren to become executioners and terrorists for all unbelievers. Truly *akhi*, this designation is better for us than to be a Muslim who pays no attention to the blood of his fellow Muslims murdered by the cursed unbelievers … If you hate and oppose the titles bestowed on us by the enemies of Allah, then by what other path will we enter heaven?

— Imam Samudera

On Saturday night, 12 October 2002, bombs exploded in two of the busiest nightspots in Bali. Two hundred and two people perished and more than 300 people were wounded, in what is generally regarded to be the largest terror attack in South-East Asia's history. One of the perpetrators, Abdul Aziz – better known by his alias, Imam Samudera – did not dispute that his actions constituted terrorism. In fact, he described his deed as terror in the name of *jihad*.[1] This notion of *jihad* contradicted the mainstream view held by most Muslims in Indonesia, who typically considered *jihad* to be war on a battlefield in which Muslims were under direct attack and in which it was forbidden to kill women, children and the elderly. Imam Samudera, however, saw terrorism as a path to heaven.

What understanding of Islam did Imam Samudera and the other perpetrators of the Bali bombings hold? Another of the conspirators, Ali Ghufron, known more widely by his alias, Mukhlas, described himself as a Salafi Jihadi.[2] The Bali bombings made many suddenly aware that this seemingly new ideology had taken root in Indonesia. Where did it originate? Why and how did its teachings spread in Indonesia? Why did a range of radical Islamic groups in Indonesia adopt and practice a doctrine that also formed the basis of al-Qaeda's ideology? This book is an attempt to answer these questions.

• • •

Salafi Jihadism and Indonesia

Indonesia has a long history of rebellions by Islamic groups that have struggled to establish an Islamic state and considered their war against the Indonesian government to be a *jihad*. One Islamic group has played a central role in many of these rebellions: Darul Islam, also known by the name Negara Islam Indonesia (NII – Islamic State of Indonesia). An Islamic insurgency, it fought its first major revolt against the new Indonesian government in the 1950s in West Java, inspiring other revolts in Aceh and South Sulawesi. Its leader and founder, Sekarmadji Maridjan Kartosuwirjo, formulated a doctrine of *jihad* that was similar to that of Salafi Jihadism, even though that ideology would not arrive in Indonesia until several decades later. Darul Islam considered a government that did not implement Islamic law to be apostate, and for war against it to be obligatory. Darul Islam also considered terrorism against civilians who did not support their movement to be legitimate. This group was the forerunner of the Salafi Jihadi movement in Indonesia, although Darul Islam in the 1950s was in no sense a Salafi movement in terms of its religious views (a detailed explanation of Salafism is given below). Kartosuwirjo and his followers in West Java were traditional Muslims, and Kartosuwirjo himself was a believer in Islamic mysticism – practices and ideas that are anathema to Salafi teachings.

The Indonesian army defeated the rebellion in West Java in 1962 and in South Sulawesi in 1965; in Aceh the revolt ended in 1962 with a negotiated truce. Former Darul Islam figures revived the movement in the 1970s, however, inspired by Kartosuwirjo's final message, in which he said that the struggle was entering a phase that he named '*Hudaibiyah*'. In the history of the Prophet Muhammad's struggle, *Hudaibiyah* was the name of the ceasefire reached between Muhammad's followers and the rival Quraish tribe before Muhammad's ultimate conquest of the city of Mecca. Kartosuwirjo's final message encouraged the movement's members to think that history would repeat itself and that, as for the Prophet Muhammad, Darul Islam victory was close at hand. Former Darul Islam members in Java, Sumatra and Sulawesi reorganised, and appointed Daud Beureueh as their new spiritual leader. This new Darul Islam movement adopted a structure intended for war against the Indonesian government. They sought funds and weapons from Libya, but the security forces got wind of their efforts. In early 1977, there was a major round of arrests of the movement's members.

Several senior Darul Islam figures evaded capture and instructed other senior figures to flee. Again they drew upon Kartosuwirjo's teachings and saw parallels between their flight from the authorities and the Prophet Muhammad's flight (*hijrah*) from Mecca to Madina. Kartosuwirjo considered *hijrah* a precondition for political victory, as the Prophet's experience had shown. His teachings inspired Darul Islam's leaders to move to a more secure area in West Java and establish a base from which they thought they would return, victorious. They also transformed Darul Islam into a clandestine movement based upon a system of cells, and conducted robberies to fund the organisation. The crimes, however, brought them to the attention of the authorities. In 1981, Darul Islam suffered another body blow when almost all of its leaders were arrested.

During this period, Darul Islam recruited and trained new members to regenerate the organisation. As a part of this effort, Aceng Kurnia, a Darul Islam commander and former aide to Kartosuwirjo, led a process of ideological renewal. Central to this was the movement's analysis of the political implications that flowed from the doctrine *tauhid*, or oneness of God, which made it clear that only Allah held the right to govern and formulate laws. Whoever infringed upon that right was seen as an unbeliever and a target for *jihad*. Aceng drew upon the ideas of radical Islamic thinkers, notably the Egyptian Muslim Brotherhood's ideologue, Sayyid Qutb, and the Pakistani thinker Abul Ala Maududi, as Salafi Jihadism would also eventually do.

Most of Darul Islam's recruits in this period came from an Islamic modernist background. Many came from the large modernist movement Muhammadiyah, or were sympathisers of Masyumi, two organisations that in the 1950s had been rivals of Darul Islam, though they shared a common goal: to uphold Islamic law in Indonesia. The difference was that they believed this goal could be achieved through participation in the secular political system, including through the Indonesian parliament. The political situation changed in the 1960s, however, when the New Order regime under President Suharto took power. Masyumi and Muhammadiyah figures were sidelined from the political stage and Islamic parties were emasculated. Some of their supporters thus joined Darul Islam to pursue their goals outside of formal politics.

Two such recruits were Abdullah Sungkar and Abu Bakar Ba'asyir, teachers from the Al Mukmin Islamic boarding school (*pesantren*) in Ngruki, Sukoharjo, Central Java – men who went on to play central roles in radical jihadist activism. Both had been activists in al-Irsyad, an association of Indonesians of Arab descent that had a strong Salafi component, and they promoted Salafi ideas among their students. It was a group of their students from Central Java who took over the leadership of Darul Islam after the arrests of its leaders in the early 1980s. A particular focus of Sungkar's group was purifying Indonesian society and politics from what it saw as examples of idolatry. This included saluting the Indonesian flag and singing the national anthem, as well as accepting Pancasila, the five founding principles of the Indonesian state, as the state ideology.

Despite this Salafi outlook, Sungkar's circle in Darul Islam took inspiration from a variety of sources. It adopted a system of organisation based on *usroh* – 'family units' that had been developed by the Muslim Brotherhood in Egypt. In the 1980s, Darul Islam members were exposed to Muslim Brotherhood members who lived in Indonesia, many of them teachers at the Saudi-linked Arabic Language Education Institute (LPBA) in Jakarta. Like other radical Islamic movements, Sungkar's group was influenced by the 1979 Iranian revolution. Indeed, its members saw great opportunity for a similar revolution in Indonesia at the time, as broad opposition to the New Order began to emerge. Islamic opposition to Suharto had grown primarily because of several New Order policies that were seen as anti-Islamic. These included the decision to incorporate Javanese mysticism (*aliran kepercayaan*) into the 'Broad Outlines of State Policy' (GBHN – Garis Besar Haluan Negara), issued by the Indonesian parliament, as one of Indonesia's acceptable religions, and Suharto's efforts to establish Pancasila as the sole basis for political parties and mass organisations.

It was in this climate that a small group of Darul Islam members around Sungkar, who came to be known as the '*usroh* group', working with other opponents of Suharto, sought to foment a popular revolution along Iranian lines. But their plans failed and they refocused on recruiting and training new members. Other Islamic groups continued their opposition to the New Order regime, however. In 1984 a large number of Muslim protestors were killed in clashes with security forces in the Tanjung Priok area of Jakarta. Several extremists sought revenge through terror attacks, including the bombing of the Borobudur temple in Central Java and attacks on several churches in 1985. The security forces responded with another round of repression.

In 1985, Sungkar and his associates took refuge in Malaysia, where they established contact with *mujahideen* leaders in Afghanistan and set up a training academy on the Pakistan–Afghan border for Darul Islam cadres. Their aim was not to fight the Soviet army, but to acquire military skills for use in Indonesia. More than 200 cadres received training there between 1985 and 1991, mostly Indonesian but Malaysians and Singaporeans as well. In addition to military training, these cadres also received religious instruction from international *jihadi* figures, including Abdullah Azzam, the Palestinian cleric who was an early mentor of Osama bin Laden. It was there that the Darul Islam cadres became more deeply imbued with the principles of Salafi Jihadism, abandoning some of their own religious doctrine where it conflicted with the new ideas. It was this experience in Afghanistan that established Salafi Jihadism as a new school of religious thought within Darul Islam.

These new ideas created problems within the movement, however, triggering a split. This arose when Sungkar and many of the movement's Afghan veterans began to criticise Darul Islam's newly appointed leader, Ajengan Masduki, who adhered to a traditionalist view of Islam. The Afghan veterans considered Masduki's beliefs to be deviant, and when Masduki and his followers took offence at their criticism, Sungkar and his associates left to form a new movement that would come to be known as Jema'ah Islamiyah. Established on 1 January 1993, the movement adopted the Salafi Jihadi ideas its members had learned in Afghanistan, but also incorporated the ideas of other radical movements, in particular the Egyptian militant movement al-Gama'ah al-Islamiyah. Up until 1998, the focus of this new movement's struggle was against the Indonesian government. But in February of that year, Osama bin Laden issued his famous declaration of war on America and its allies. This led to a debate within Jema'ah Islamiyah over whether it should continue to focus its struggle on the Indonesian government, or heed bin Laden's call for a *jihad* against America and its allies. The controversy was never resolved, but without the knowledge of many of its leaders, some members of the movement committed themselves to bin Laden's *jihad*. It was this commitment that ultimately resulted in the 2002 Bali bombings.

Salafism and Salafi Jihadism

So what were these Salafi Jihadi ideas that made such an impact on extremist activism in Indonesia? To understand the history and doctrine of Salafi Jihadism, one must first understand the history and the teachings of the distinct Salafi movement. Salafism refers to a purifying movement in Islam that seeks a return to the religious philosophy of the *salaf as-salih* – the first three generations of the Islamic community after the founding of Islam by the Prophet Muhammad. Salafis consider these first three generations to be unrivalled in their understanding of Islam because they learned either from the Prophet himself, the Prophet's companions or from the companions' students. As a result, one of the main characteristics of Salafism is the rejection of all innovations in Islam (*bid'ah*). Because Salafis see Islam as perfect in its founding revelation, any additions of faith and practice are seen to be unwarranted. For example, the late Saudi Sheikh and leading Salafi figure Abdullah bin Baz argued that commemoration of the birthday of the prophet Muhammad, a common practice throughout the Muslim world, was *bid'ah* because the Prophet himself provided no example of such worship.

Another key characteristic of Salafism is its firm opposition to anything that might compromise Islam's concept of the oneness of God, or *tauhid*. For example, Salafis sternly criticise Sufi worship practices such as *tawassul*, in which Sufis position Muslim saints as intermediaries in prayer or in seeking blessings from Allah. For Salafis, practices such as these, or other Sufi practices such as pilgrimages to the tombs of saints, are examples of idolatry (*shirk*). Such idolatrous actions negate a person's status as a Muslim, reverse his good deeds and condemn him to an eternity in hell.[3]

A key historical figure for Salafis, but also Salafi Jihadis, is the 13th-century Islamic scholar Taqi ad-Din Ibn Taymiyah. Born in Harran, Syria in 1263, he was a professor of *hadith* (the traditions of the Prophet) and Islamic jurisprudence by the age of nineteen. In a prolific career, he wrote more than 350 books. His followers granted him the title 'Sheikh al-Islam' in recognition of the breadth of his knowledge. His thoughts remain influential in the 21st century, and both Salafis and Salafi Jihadis quote his ideas and writings. Historian Richard Bonney argued that 'no other Muslim writer, medieval or contemporary, has exercised as much influence on the modern radical Islamist movement as Ibn Taymiyah.'[4]

Ibn Taymiyah presented himself as a true defender of orthodox Sunni Islam. He invited Muslims to return to the Qu'ran and the Prophet's *Sunnah* (his path and practices). He emphasised the purity of an Islam uncontaminated by various innovations. An adherent of the Hanbali school of Islamic jurisprudence, he opposed the view held by some Islamic scholars of his era that rational methods such as philosophy were necessary to understand the Islamic faith. Ibn Taymiyah considered this akin to saying that the Prophet Muhammad did not understand the verses of the Qu'ran handed down to him by Allah. In his view, the tenets of faith must derive from the Qu'ran and authoritative *hadith* (sayings of the Prophet), not from logic.

As well as being a professor of theology, Ibn Taymiyah was a leading propagandist of *jihad*. He lived in chaotic times, when the Islamic world was under attack from European Crusaders and Mongol invaders. To elevate the *jihadi* spirit of the Muslim community of the time, Ibn Taymiyah issued a *fatwa* (religious opinion), setting out the centrality of *jihad*, arguing that it was more important than the pillars of the faith like the *hajj* (the annual pilgrimage to Mecca), fasting and prayer.[5] To confront the threats facing the Muslim community, he advocated a defensive *jihad*, in which, he argued, it was obligatory for all Muslims to participate.

Among these external enemies at the time, the Mongols were the most terrifying. Ibn Taymiyah himself had the bitter personal experience of being forced to flee to Damascus with his family at the age of seven during one of their attacks. The event coloured his stance toward the Mongols, and as he grew older his hatred of them increased.[6] For him it did not matter that Mahmud Ghazan, the 13th-century Mongol ruler, had converted to Islam. In fact, Ghazan's pragmatic conversion led Ibn Taymiyah to issue what would become one of the most important *fatwa* used by Islamic movements in rebelling against their political leaders. Ibn Taymiyah argued that because the Mongol rulers had not established Islamic law as the basis of their government, they were effectively apostate – and *jihad* against apostate rulers was obligatory.

While Ibn Taymiyah is today considered among the most influential of the medieval Islamic scholars, in his own time his influence and fame was more limited. One of the most important revivers of Ibn Taymiyah's ideas was the 18th-century Islamic scholar Muhammad bin Abdul Wahhab (1702–1791), whose ideas, commonly referred to as Wahhabism, would form the basis of the modern Saudi state. Also an adherent of the Hanbali school, and originally from Najd (in present day Saudi Arabia), Abdul Wahhab was greatly impressed by Ibn Taymiyah's written works, finding in them the answer to the problems of 18th-century Arab society. In particular, he was scandalised by what he saw as the decline of Islamic belief, pointing to practices such as the pilgrimages that people made to the tombs of the Prophet Muhammad and his companions, and the worship of objects such as rocks and trees believed to hold mystical powers. As Abdul Wahhab saw it, the religious practices of contemporary Islamic society were full of innovation and idolatry, and required purification.[7]

Abdul Wahhab's teachings received support from Muhammad bin Saud, a tribal leader in the Dari'yah area of Najd. Their alliance brought together two interests: Muhammad bin Abdul Wahhab needed the ruler's support to spread his teachings; Muhammad bin Saud sought to legitimise the *jihad* that he was waging against the Ottoman Caliphate in order to establish his own independent state in Arabia. Abdul Wahhab issued a *fatwa* declaring the Ottoman Caliphate to be a *kafir* (unbeliever) state, using Ibn Taymiyah's earlier decree against apostate rulers as a reference. In Abdul Wahhab's view, the Ottomans were the equivalent of the Mongol rulers of Ibn Taymiyah's era, undermining Islam from within while pretending to be true Muslims.[8] The partnership formed in 1744 between

Muhammad bin Abdul Wahhab and Muhammad bin Saud conquered large parts of Arabia, and led to the establishment of the first Saudi state. That state would eventually be reconquered by Ottoman forces from Egypt, but the ideas upon which it was based proved to be resilient. On 8 January 1926, descendants of Abdul Wahhab and Muhammad bin Saud once again combined to found the second Saudi state, today known as the Kingdom of Saudi Arabia.

Salafism's strict, literal interpretation of Islam and its focus on the purification of Islamic belief are all important parts of the Salafi Jihadi worldview. But Salafi Jihadism should not be confused with Salafism per se. What distinguishes the two is the former's overwhelming emphasis on the importance of *jihad*. While Salafi Jihadism draws inspiration from Islamic scholars such as Ibn Taymiyah and Muhammad Abdul Wahhab, its ideas on *jihad* were also a product of particular historical circumstances, specifically the war in Afghanistan against the Soviet Union in the 1980s. Both the Saudi government and the religious establishment backed the war against the Soviets, funnelling billions of dollars of aid and men to the war. Among the recipients of that largesse was a man who, perhaps more than any other individual, laid the intellectual foundations of Salafi Jihadism: Abdullah Azzam.

Abdullah Azzam

In 1983, the Saudi, American and Pakistani governments began pursuing the idea of bringing Muslim volunteers to Afghanistan to join the war against the Soviet Union.[9] Initially it was not an easy idea to sell to Muslims around the world. Even militant groups were more focused on waging *jihad* against the apostate governments of their own countries.[10] In 1984, Abdullah Azzam (1941–1989), a Palestinian member of the Muslim Brotherhood, arrived in Afghanistan and sought to change the situation. He had joined the Palestinian struggle for statehood in 1973, but grew disillusioned with it. He moved to Saudi Arabia, where he taught at King Abdul Azziz University in Jeddah and entered the circles of Saudi Salafi scholars. After learning of the conditions in Afghanistan from a visiting Afghan *mujahid*, he decided to visit. He was captivated by his introduction to *mujahideen* figures and by his experiences on the front lines. In 1984 he decided to commit totally to *jihad* in Afghanistan.[11]

Azzam founded Maktab al-Khidamat, an institute designed to facilitate the arrival of volunteers from Islamic countries. He travelled the Islamic world promoting the Afghan *jihad* and raising funds for the struggle. He wrote books and pamphlets and published a monthly magazine, *al-Jihad*, filled with stories of epic battles and the heroism of the *mujahideen*. By 1986 an estimated 12 000 non-Afghan *mujahideen* – who came to be known as the Arab-Afghans – were in the country waging war. If humanitarian volunteers were included, the number of foreigners rose to some 25 000.[12] They came from various countries and included individuals, but also activists from established Islamist movements such as the Muslim Brotherhood, the militant Egyptian groups al-Gama'ah al-Islamiyah and Tanzim al-Jihad, as well as the Indonesian group Darul Islam. Among the foreigners was a young and wealthy Saudi named Osama bin Laden, who became a key funder and board member of Maktab al-Khidamat.

It was in these conditions that the ideas of Salafi Jihadism were born. In truth, Abdullah Azzam did not set out to formulate a religious doctrine for a new movement. Indeed, the term Salafi

Jihadism (in Arabic, *Salafiyya Jihadiyya*) was not used while Azzam was still alive. His ideas were designed mainly to justify the *jihad* in Afghanistan. Only later did these ideas become central to Salafi Jihadi groups worldwide. Azzam had a very specific interpretation of *jihad*. For many Muslims *jihad* does not just mean 'war'. In Arabic it literally means to surrender all of one's energy and capacity to achieve something one desires or loves. Consequently, *jihad* is often interpreted to mean all forms of hard work in the course of doing good deeds, including seeking knowledge or making a living. In Islamic terms, *jihad fisabilillah* – *jihad* in the path of Allah – is often interpreted to mean everything from the struggle to be a good Muslim to the military defence of Islam and the Muslim community. Azzam, however, interpreted *jihad* as *qital*, or physical battle.

According to Azzam, *jihad* was a form of worship and had to be understood in terms of Islamic law. He gave the example of prayer (*salat*). In Arabic, *salat* simply means prayer. In Islamic law, by contrast, *salat* is a set of specific movements and expressions that begins with the *takbiratul ikhram* (raising both arms and saying 'Allahu Akbar') and ends with the *salam* (saying 'Assalamualaikum'). In Azzam's view, a person can only be said to be performing *salat* if his or her prayer fulfils the Islamic legal requirements.[13] The same applied to *jihad*. For Azzam, the Afghan *jihad* was also *fard al-ain*, or obligatory for every Muslim. He claimed that to abandon the *jihad* in Afghanistan carried the same punishment for Muslims as abandoning prayer or the fast. Like Ibn Taymiyah before him, Azzam saw *jihad* as an even a greater priority than prayer or fasting. Should an unbeliever control even one plot of land in a Muslim territory, he argued, then *jihad* became obligatory for every Muslim living there.[14] And should local residents fail to drive out their enemies, then this obligation extended beyond local Muslims to the entire Muslim community worldwide. Azzam also held a very broad definition of Muslim lands, including not just majority Muslim countries but those that had been controlled by Muslim governments in the past – for example Granada, now part of Spain. According to Azzam, the obligation to wage *jihad* only ended when Muslims had retaken all these lands.[15]

One of Azzam's views on *jihad* that would cause controversy later was the idea that it was permissible to carry out terrorist acts during a *jihad*. According to Azzam, the Qu'ran contained an order for Muslims to perpetrate terrorism against unbelievers, specifically in Al-Anfal 60: 'And prepare against them whatever you are able of power and of steeds of war by which you may terrify the enemy of Allah and your enemy and others besides them whom you do not know [but] whom Allah knows.'

According to Azzam it was even permissible under certain circumstances to target civilians.

Azzam's ideas were not the only ones swirling around in this melting pot of militant ideology and activism in Afghanistan. Militant Egyptian Islamists in Afghanistan promoted the idea of *hakim-iyah* – the notion developed by the Pakistani Islamist thinker Abul Ala Maududi and the Egyptian ideologue Sayyid Qutb that political sovereignty can only rest with Allah. Muhammad Abdulsalam Faraj, one of the leading ideologues of Islamic Jihad, the Egyptian group responsible for the assassination of President Anwar Sadat, argued that any ruler of a Muslim country that rejected Islamic law was rejecting Allah's *hakimiyah*. He based his view on Ibn Taymiyah's *fatwa* that deemed the Mongol rulers of the time to be unbelievers. In Islamic jurisprudence, declaring a Muslim to be apostate and therefore a legitimate target of attack is known as *takfir*. It is tantamount to a death sentence and normally applied only in the most extreme circumstances. Faraj and other radical Islamists of his era applied it more liberally and came to be known as *takfiris*.

The ideas of Azzam and others concerning *jihad* were spread among foreign *mujahideen* in various ways. Religious and ideological instruction was a regular part of military training programs conducted by Azzam and other leading *jihadi* figures such as Abdul Rasul Sayyaf. Azzam held regular religious study sessions in the evening at his training camp for foreign fighters in Saada, on the Pakistan–Afghan border.[16] The sessions were recorded, and by 1989 Maktab al-Khidamat had distributed some 300 audiocassettes and 50 videos of Abdullah Azzam's lectures – many of which found their way to Indonesia.

As foreign fighters returned home, many established organisations that reflected the ideas they had learned in Afghanistan. While there were a number of reasons why these ideas spread, the most important was the success of the *jihad*. When the Soviet Union withdrew from Afghanistan, the foreign *mujahideen* could claim to have defeated one of the world's superpowers. The volunteers were convinced that *jihad* could defeat any enemy of Islam.

The Soviet defeat in Afghanistan did, however, raise questions among the foreign fighters about what they should do next. Two schools of thought emerged. One was that *jihad* must target 'foreign unbelievers' (*kafir ajnabi*) who had occupied Islamic lands such as Palestine, Mindanao in the Philippines and Kashmir, among others. Abdullah Azzam was of this view. Others, like Egyptian Islamic Jihad leader Ayman al-Zawahiri, were of the view that the post-Afghanistan *jihad* should target 'local unbelievers' (*kafir mahaly*) such as the 'apostate rulers' governing Muslim countries of the Middle East. The differences between the two sides were exacerbated by personality clashes. Proponents of the fight against 'local unbelievers' such as al-Zawahiri thought Azzam would obstruct their plans because Azzam was grateful to these governments for supporting the effort in Afghanistan. Even Azzam's long-time ally, Osama bin Laden, leant towards the views of the Egyptian radicals. In 1988, when bin Laden formed a new organisation, which he had called al-Qaeda, several central figures in Islamic Jihad became office holders, including al-Zawahiri.

It was against this background that, on 24 November 1989, Azzam was assassinated in Peshawar in a move some believe was orchestrated by the al-Zawahiri camp. Although it was unclear who had killed him, the *mujahideen* were convinced that America had been responsible.[17]

Al-Qaeda

By the time Osama bin Laden returned home to Saudi Arabia at the end of 1989, he had become a widely respected figure. His life in Saudi Arabia would, however, change dramatically on 2 August 1990, when Saddam Hussein invaded Kuwait. Worried that Saddam would also invade Saudi Arabia, the Saudi government turned to the United States for help. Thousands of US troops poured into the Kingdom. The Saudi government sought and received religious sanction for this controversial move from the Saudi Council of Islamic Scholars.

Bin Laden, however, saw Iraq's invasion of Kuwait as an opportunity to mobilise the *mujahideen* anew. He approached Saudi officials with a proposal to expel Iraq's army from Kuwait using Afghan veterans, and advised the Saudi rulers not to seek assistance from America on the grounds that bringing in American troops would be a violation of Islamic principles that regarded all of Saudi Arabia – the land of Islam's two holiest cities – as a religious sanctuary. Bin Laden also saw the American military moves in the region as an effort to control the oil-rich Arab world. The Saudi authorities rejected his offer.[18]

Bin Laden's stance against the American military presence was strongly influenced by the thinking of a number of Saudi religious scholars who were also critical of the government's decision, including Safar al-Hawali, a lecturer at Umm al-Qura University in Mecca. In March 1991, al-Hawali and more than 400 other religious scholars submitted a letter to the Saudi king protesting the continued presence of American forces in the Kingdom, but also demanding political reforms. The Saudi government responded by throwing a number of the signatories, including al-Hawali, into prison. Other opposition figures fled overseas.[19] Bin Laden fled to Sudan in 1991, which at the time was under the control of a military regime strongly influenced by Hasan Turabi, a Sudanese Muslim Brotherhood leader. The regime welcomed Bin Laden's arrival, as he brought capital with him to open new businesses in Sudan. He did not stay long, however. In November 1995 a bomb exploded in a Saudi National Guard Training facility in Riyadh, killing seven people, including five Americans. The Saudi and American governments accused bin Laden of involvement. Eventually, under international political pressure, the Sudanese government expelled him and his associates, and in 1996 he returned to Afghanistan.

It was from Afghanistan, the place that bin Laden had originally found fame, that he launched a new *jihad*. On 23 August 1996, he issued a 'Declaration of War Against America' but also against the Saudi regime. In February 1998, Bin Laden relaunched his campaign, but this time focused it more narrowly on America. His new declaration was issued in the name of the World Islamic Front. The signatories included Ayman al-Zawahiri (Islamic Jihad, Egypt), Rifa'i Ahmad Taha (al-Gama'ah al-Islamiyah, Egypt), Sheikh Mir Hamzah (Secretary of Jamiat al-Ulama, Pakistan) and Fazlur Rahman (Jihad Movement, Bangladesh). The objective was made very plain:

> To kill the Americans and their allies – civilians and
> military – is an individual duty incumbent upon every
> Muslim in all countries, in order to liberate the al-Aqsa
> Mosque and the Holy Mosque from their grip, so that their
> armies leave all the territory of Islam, defeated, broken, and
> unable to threaten any Muslim. This is in accordance with
> the words of God Almighty: 'Fight the idolater at any time,
> if they first fight you. Fight them until there is no more
> persecution and until worship is devoted to God. Why
> should you not fight in God's cause and for those oppressed
> men, women, and children who cry out "Lord, rescue us
> from this town whose people are oppressors! By Your grace,
> give us a protector and a helper!"' With God's permission
> we call on everyone who believes in God and wants reward
> to comply with His will to kill the Americans and seize
> their money wherever and whenever they find them. We
> also call on the religious scholars, their leaders, their youth

and their soldiers, to launch the raid on the soldiers of
Satan, the Americans, and whichever devil's supporters are
allied with them, to rout those behind them so that they
will not forget it.[20]

The declaration represented a further evolution of Salafi Jihadi thinking. It positioned America and its allies as the main enemy against whom war must be waged. Bin Laden also refined Salafi Jihadism's doctrine of terrorism in the service of *jihad*. Although Abdullah Azzam had formulated this doctrine in Afghanistan, it had never truly been implemented. The Afghanistan war had largely been between the *mujahideen* and the Soviet army. Bin Laden's new declaration not only permitted but mandated the killing of civilians (linked to the US).

Starting in 1998, bin Laden and his associates began to put their words into action. In August 1998, they bombed the United States embassies in Kenya and Tanzania, killing 231 people and injuring more than 4000 people, most of whom were locals. In 2000, they launched an attack on an American destroyer, the USS *Cole*, in Aden, Yemen, killing seventeen sailors and wounding dozens more. But it was on 11 September 2001 that bin Laden and his organisation achieved their ultimate infamy, crashing hijacked planes into the World Trade Centre in New York and the Pentagon in Washington, killing some 3000 people.

It was an attack that resonated around the world, including in Indonesia. Already imbued with Salafi Jihadi ideas from their time in Afghanistan, the events of September 11 inspired Indonesian extremists to mount their own assault on America and its allies. Just over a year later, in Bali, they did so. But the history of militant *jihadi* activism in Indonesia did not begin with the Bali bombings, or even with the events of September 11. The historical roots of Salafi Jihadism in Indonesia are far deeper, and it is to this history that we now turn.

1
Darul Islam

Although Salafi Jihadism as an ideology did not arrive in Indonesia until the 1990s, radical movements in Indonesia going back to at least the 1950s held similar ideas. Of these groups the most important was Darul Islam, the Islamic insurgency that emerged in the last year of Indonesia's war of independence against the Dutch. Darul Islam condemned Muslims who rejected Islamic law as apostates and declared *jihad* against the Indonesian government to be *fard al-ain* – an obligation incumbent upon each and every Muslim. Yet this group was not born out of the Salafi religious tradition: most of Darul Islam's founders and followers were traditionalist Muslims, adherents of the Shafi'i school of Islamic jurisprudence. Moreover, Sekarmadji Maridjan Kartosuwirjo, the group's leader, followed Sufi teachings that were, and remain, anathema to most Salafis.

Kartosuwirjo became a proponent of establishing an Islamic state in Indonesia at the end of the 1920s when he joined Partai Syarikat Islam (the Islamic Union Party). He developed his notion of *jihad*, however, during Indonesia's struggle for independence against the Dutch between 1945 and 1949. Kartosuwirjo was not alone. A number of Islamic groups had called for a holy war against the Dutch and issued *fatwa*s declaring *jihad* to be *fard al-ain* for all Muslims in Indonesia. When the struggle for independence was over, many of these groups turned to formal politics to pursue their aims. Kartosuwirjo and his associates, though, continued their *jihad* against the government of the newly established Republic of Indonesia. In fact, it was this war against the Indonesian government that led Darul Islam's philosophy of *jihad* to become even more extreme.

· · ·

From Padris to modernists

Salafi religious ideas found their way to Indonesia a little over a decade after the death of their great Arab revivalist, Muhammad bin Abdul Wahhab. In 1803, three ethnic Minangkabau pilgrims from West Sumatra, Haji Miskin, Haji Sumanik and Haji Piobang, returned to Indonesia from Mecca imbued with Salafi teachings. They formed a group called Padri, a word derived from Pidie, the Acehnese port from which most pilgrims from West Sumatra left for Mecca, and disseminated these teachings in the Minang lands.[1] Intent on cleansing the local community of innovation (*bid'ah*) and idolatry (*shirk*), they applied their stricter version of Islamic law in local villages. The Padri forbade alcohol, opium, tobacco, betel nut, gambling and cockfighting. They forbade making ritual visits to graves wearing golden jewellery and silk, and required everyone to pray five times a day. Women were required to cover their faces, whereas men had to wear white clothes with their trousers above their ankles and allow their beards to grow.[2]

They also advocated *jihad* against Muslims who rejected their teachings, including Sufis, killing many and burning their prayer houses to the ground. As a result, a civil conflict broke out in the midst of Minangkabau society. The main enemies of the Padris were local aristocrats and the followers of local customary law (*adat*). These groups sought help from the Dutch, offering to surrender the Minangkabau Kingdom to them if they would intervene against the Padri. The Dutch stepped in and by the 1830s the Padri were defeated.[3]

At the beginning of the 20th century, a number of socio-religious organisations were formed in Indonesia that were inspired by the need to return to the purity of Islam and rid it of various doctrinal and cultural accretions that it had acquired over the years. In Yogyakarta, Muhammadiyah was founded in 1912, focusing its preaching in urban areas.[4] In Jakarta, al-Irsyad was formed in 1914, as an association for Indonesians of Arab descent.[5] In Bandung, Persatuan Islam (Persis – Islamic Unity) was formed in 1923 and actively disseminated Salafi philosophy in West Java.[6] All of these movements promoted a return to 'the Qu'ran and the *Sunnah*', and sought to eradicate unwarranted innovation and idolatry in the Indonesian Muslim community. Their religious philosophy was strongly influenced by the ideas of the famous Egyptian Islamic reformer, Muhammad Abduh.[7]

Traditionalist Sunni Muslims typically follow one of the four major schools of Islamic jurisprudence – the Hanbali, Hanafi, Malaki or Shafi'i. Modernists attacked this practice on the ground that blind faith in the legal interpretations of a particular school (known as *taqlid*) could impede Muslims from the correct practise of Islam. In Indonesia, modernists rejected certain traditionalist religious practices that had incorporated local customs, such as *talkin*, reminding the dead during burial of key elements of the faith so they will remember them when asked by angels. Like the Padri before them, organisations like Muhammadiyah condemned *tawassul*, praying to Allah through an intermediary, and pilgrimages to the tombs of Islamic saints to obtain blessings. To defend themselves from the modernists, the traditionalists organised their own movement, Nahdlatul Ulama (NU), which was established in 1926 in Surabaya.[8]

From the outset, the modernists aspired to establish an Islamic state in Indonesia. But Indonesia's secular nationalists opposed this idea, believing that to achieve independence and establish a strong Indonesian state they would need to separate religion and the state and limit the role of religion to individual worship and beliefs. From the 1920s until Indonesia's declaration of independence in 1945, there was a fierce debate between Islamic and secular groups over this question.

Indonesia's first president, Sukarno, and his Indonesian National Party (PNI – Partai Nasional Indonesia) thought it would be dangerous and divisive to make Islam the state ideology. Non-Muslims would not support a state that only benefited Muslims, and made them second-class citizens.[9] Modernists felt that since most Indonesians were Muslims it was both logical and fair that the future state should be based on Islam. In their view there would be greater injustice if a minority were to determine a form of state that was detrimental to the majority. They argued that in an Islamic system, adherents of other religions would in any event be granted freedom of religion.[10] This debate came to a head in the 1945 sessions of the Body to Investigate Efforts to Prepare for

Independence (BPUPKI – Badan Penyelidik Usaha-Usaha Persiapan Kemerdekaan) – a forum created by the Japanese occupiers of Indonesia in the dying months of World War II to prepare for an independent Indonesia.[11] Both modernists and traditionalists pushed the concept of an Islamic state with some success. Sukarno sought a compromise in the so-called Jakarta Charter which identified 'belief in God, with the obligation for Muslims to implement Islamic law' as one of the five basic principles of the state.

Non-Muslim groups accepted this compromise reluctantly. But a day after Indonesia declared its independence on 17 August 1945, Protestants and Catholics who were dissatisfied with the Jakarta Charter threatened that they would form their own state in eastern Indonesia if this Islamic principle became part of the 1945 Constitution. In a sudden meeting on 18 August 1945, Vice-President Muhammad Hatta urged Islamic figures to change the Constitution. A Muhammadiyah leader, Bagus Hadikusumo, was among the Muslim representatives most firmly opposed to the change, but he wavered at the urging of another Muhammadiyah member, Kasman Singodimedjo. Singodimedjo argued that with the Netherlands lying in wait to invade Indonesia to reimpose colonial rule once the Japanese left, national unity was the more urgent requirement. He convinced Hadikusumo that once the situation became secure, they could again work for inclusion of the Jakarta Charter. In the end, Hadikusumo agreed.[12] The deadlock ended with the Islamic community representatives agreeing to remove the offending sentence from the 1945 constitution.[13]

The opportunity to strive anew to make Islam the foundation of the state came in October 1945, when the Indonesian government appealed to its people to form political parties. To channel

27

their political aspirations, the modernists joined the political party Masyumi, an acronym for the Consultative Council of Indonesian Muslim Associations that was established on 7–8 November 1945. This provided an important formal channel for modernist political ambitions, and was a key reason why they did not choose to pursue more subversive methods.

Kartosuwirjo

Masyumi was not just a party of modernists however. One of its board members was the traditionalist Sekarmadji Maridjan Karto-suwirjo. Kartosuwirjo was born on 7 January 1907 in Cepu, a small town between Blora and Bojonegoro, near the border of East and Central Java. In contrast to other Islamic figures, his background was not in religious education. It was Kartosuwirjo's good fortune to be formally educated in the Dutch system: his father's position as a Dutch colonial government official in the opium distribution system meant his parents could put him through Dutch schools. He completed high school at the Europeesche Legere School (ELS) in Bojonegoro. Subsequently, from 1923 he studied medicine at the Nederlandsch Indische Artsen School (NIAS). He took prepara-tory classes for three years before commencing lectures in medicine in 1926. Kartosuwirjo was to take lectures for only a year, however, as he was expelled from NIAS for possessing Socialist and Commu-nist books. The colonial government at the time was very sensitive to the threat from Communism, because of the 1926 Communist rebellion.[14]

Kartosuwirjo obtained these books from his uncle, Marko Kar-todikromo, a journalist and historian who was also a renowned

Communist figure, and who helped spur his nephew's political awareness. Kartosuwirjo was already active in political movements in 1923 when he joined Jong Java, a nationalist organisation for Javanese youth, in Surabaya. Then in 1925 he moved to Jong Islamieten Bond (JIB), an Islamic youth organisation in Java, and not long afterwards became head of the JIB branch in Surabaya. It was here that he got to know important Islamic leaders of the Indonesian nationalist movement such as Agus Salim and Oemar Said Tjokroaminoto, the leaders of an important Muslim political party, Partai Syarikat Islam (PSI). After he left school in 1927, he was offered a job by Tjokroaminoto, the party chair, as his personal secretary. Not long afterwards, when Tjokroaminoto moved to Cimahi, Bandung, Kartosuwirjo went with him. In 1927, Kartosuwirjo was appointed general secretary of the party at its congress in Pekalongan.

PSI's key aim was 'that Islamic law be in force, in the broadest and most perfect sense of the word, following the real example and model set in the *Sunnah Rasulullah* [the path and practices of the Prophet]'.[15] PSI itself did not just aspire to establish an Islamic state in Indonesia; it was also an adherent of pan-Islamic ideas that sought to unite the entire Islamic community worldwide in a caliphate, and initially strove quite seriously for this aim. In this framework, the struggle of the Indonesian Islamic community in Indonesia was part of a bigger effort by the global Islamic community to free itself from colonial domination. After the Ottoman Caliphate fell in 1924, PSI formed a caliphate committee to struggle for its restoration, although its enthusiasm for pan-Islamic goals soon faded.[16]

It was when he became active in the PSI that Kartosuwirjo began to study Islam, mostly through Dutch-language books, as he did not speak Arabic. While convalescing in 1930 from beriberi in Malangbong, Garut (in West Java), he studied with several religious scholars who were also PSI activists, including Ardiwisastera, who was to become his father-in-law, Yusuf Taudjiri, Mustofa Kamil and Ramli. All of his teachers were from traditionalist backgrounds.[17] He also studied Sufi teachings, possibly becoming a follower of the Qadariyah Tarekat, a Sufi order.[18] His understanding of Islamic mysticism would greatly influence his later thinking.

PSI's struggle for an Islamic state inspired Kartoswirjo.[19] As his religious knowledge grew, he became increasingly convinced of the importance of a state where Muslims could implement Islamic law, both in its personal and its social elements.[20] He was also convinced that an Islamic state, which he called Darul Islam – literally, 'abode of Islam' – could increase the Indonesian nation's dignity and prestige. He argued:

> In Islamic teachings, an Indonesian or a nation or religious
> community can only rise in the view of Allah and of people
> if it carries out the laws of Islam according to the orders of
> Allah and the *Sunnah* of the Prophet. Conversely, a people
> or nation can only go down in the view of Allah and of
> people because it disregards and lies about Allah's religion
> as handed down to His final prophet, Muhammad.[21]

Kartosuwirjo was the first person in modern Indonesian history to equate the term 'Darul Islam' to an Islamic state.

Kartosuwirjo's time in PSI underlined his uncompromising nature. When he joined the movement, PSI was enthusiastically applying a policy of non-cooperation with the Dutch colonial government. In 1936 an internal PSI dispute broke out between a faction led by Agus Salim, which argued for ending this policy because it was hurting the party, and PSI's new leader, Abikusno, who insisted on continuing it. Kartosuwirjo sided with Abikusno's faction, which eventually prevailed and forced Salim and his followers out of PSI.[22] Three years later, it was Kartosuwirjo's turn to enter into a dispute with Abikusno. He rejected the party leadership's decision to join the Indonesian Political Federation (GAPI – Gabungan Politik Indonesia), a grouping of Indonesian political parties formed in 1938. To Kartosuwirjo, GAPI's demand that the Dutch government establish a local parliament was tantamount to cooperation with the colonial authorities. Because of his opposition, Kartosuwirjo was dismissed from the party in 1939.[23]

PSI activists in Garut like Yusuf Taudjiri and Kamran, who had been Kartosuwirjo's teachers and friends, agreed with his stance. Following his expulsion Kartosuwirjo moved back to Malangbong. With Taudjiri and Kamran he established the PSI Committee for Defence of the Truth, which used PSI's rules of association and its constitution. In 1940, he formed the Suffah Institute, an unrealised PSI program intended to be 'a place of education, teaching and training for party leaders to implement the law and commands of Islam'.[24] This Institute was set up in the style of a traditional Islamic boarding school. Students were taught general knowledge, religion and politics. Education lasted for four to six months, with 30 to 50 students in each class. Some of the alumni of the Suffah Institute would go on to become loyal followers of Kartosuwirjo when he established Darul Islam.[25]

Kartosuwirjo's understanding of *jihad*

The Suffah Institute was closed down by Japanese forces when they invaded Indonesia in 1942. The Japanese occupation of Indonesia brought misery, but it also created an opportunity for Kartosuwirjo. The Japanese had permitted members of the Muslim community to form militias to assist in fighting the Allies, and the community responded with enthusiasm. Islamic groups promptly formed Islamic militia called 'Hizbullah' and 'Sabililah'. Kartosuwirjo also took advantage of this opportunity. He had long awaited the chance to form his own military organisation, and in 1945 reactivated the Suffah Institute to arm and train youths who had joined Hizbullah.[26]

Kartosuwirjo and his associates continued to train the militia after Indonesia became independent on 17 August 1945, precisely three days after the Japanese surrender in World War II. Kartosuwirjo had rightly calculated that an armed struggle would follow the declaration of independence. In September 1945, British forces came to Java to supervise the withdrawal of Japanese forces. The Netherlands Indies Civil Administration (NICA) came with the British to assume authority for civilian government. The Dutch army accompanied the NICA, in an effort to re-establish Dutch colonial rule.

The Muslim community strongly resisted the arrival of the Dutch and the British army. It was no ordinary resistance – the community declared a holy war. On 21–22 October 1945, representatives from NU branches throughout Java and Madura gathered in Surabaya. Hasyim Asy'ary, then NU chairperson, led the meeting, which produced a *fatwa* to the effect that war to preserve independence was *jihad fi sabilillah* (*jihad* in the path of Allah) and was *fard al-ain*, obligatory for all Muslims. The *fatwa* became popularly known as the Jihad Resolution (*Resolusi Jihad*). Immediately, religious scholars and their students mobilised the Hizbullah and Sabilillah militias.[27] On 10 November 1945, a fearsome three-week war erupted between them and the British forces. A number of other Islamic organisations then issued similar *fatwa*s. In its Yogyakarta session on 12 November 1945, Masyumi issued a *fatwa* on the obligation of Muslims to defend independence and to wage *jihad fi sabilillah*. Several handbooks on *jihad* were written in Indonesian at the time. Among them were *Guide to Holy War (Penuntun Perang Sabil)* by Arsjad Lubis, a religious scholar from Medan, and *Military and State Defence Science in Islam (Ilmu Pertahanan Negara dan Kemiliteran dalam Islam)* by Muhammad Hasbi Ashshiddiqiy, a religious scholar from Aceh.

In his book, Lubis explained that *jihad* became obligatory when an enemy entered Muslim lands. He said this obligation did not apply only to locals but also to others in the vicinity, who must help until the enemy was driven out. If the enemy was not driven out, then Muslims further away must assist until the enemy was evicted. This obligation applied to everyone, including women, the elderly and children. The Dutch were deemed to be unbelievers who had come to colonise a Muslim land:

> Anyone who takes part in this war with sincere intentions,
> with the intention of elevating the Word of God
> (*kalimatullah*), the intention to strive for Allah's blessings
> and rewards, and to exterminate the enemies of Allah, then
> they are waging war in Allah's path (*sabilillah*) and if they
> are killed, they have died as martyrs (*shahid fi sabilillah*), and
> heaven will be their place.[28]

This enthusiasm for *jihad* in the Muslim community was relatively new. Such calls for *jihad* had not been heard when the Dutch had ruled Indonesia, before Japan's occupation. Prior to independence, Kartosuwirjo had himself avoided discussing violent *jihad*. He said that equating *jihad* to war was a Western effort to discredit Islam. He argued that the West says 'that *jihad* is war or a holy war or murder or some such similar to that meaning. The result in the end is that they believe that Islam is only spread by the sword!'[29] In his view *jihad* had a broader meaning than just war; it meant genuine efforts in the path of Allah. War was merely the lesser *jihad*, whereas fighting one's worldly desires was the greater *jihad*.[30]

Kartosuwirjo's views seemed to change dramatically after Indonesia became independent, however. From 1947, he led Hizbullah forces from Garut in battles against the Dutch. He was also prepared to use terror if necessary. In 1948, he ordered his troops to 'kidnap and murder all traitors against religion, the state and the nation.'

In March 1948, his followers carried out these actions under the auspices of a group called Darul Islam Heroes (PADI or Pahlawan Darul Islam). One of the organisation's reports explained its actions:

> Since the issuance of that order, PADI has started to take action against the traitors that have become its prey in all locations throughout Priangan and western Java. After the special forces of PADI targeted these vermin, their bodies in no small numbers were sprawled dead in the middle of the road or floated as corpses down the rivers.[31]

The founding of Darul Islam

In December 1949 the conflict with the Dutch came to an end when the Netherlands formally recognised Indonesian independence. Kartosuwirjo had, however, already shifted the focus of his struggle. His dissatisfaction with the Indonesian government had been growing. He accused it of being controlled by Socialists and Communists, and of accepting agreements with the Dutch that harmed Indonesia. It was one such accord – the 1948 Renville Agreement which ceded West Java to the Dutch – that prompted Kartosuwirjo to launch his own rebellion. In May 1948, Kartosuwirjo proclaimed himself the Imam (leader) of a new state, which he called Darul Islam – which also became the name of his movement – in the first regional rebellion to follow Indonesia's declaration of independence.[32] He followed this on 7 August 1949 with a proclamation of Negara Islam Indonesia (NII), the Islamic State of Indonesia, in Cisampak, West Java.

At the core of this state was the implementation of Islamic law. The specifics were set out in the NII Criminal Code (KUUHPNII – Kitab Undang-Undang Hukum Pidana Negara Islam Indonesia). In its initial articles this code established four categories of enemy: *bughot*, or those who did not abide by the laws of the NII government, and would either be exiled or executed; *munafik* (hypocrites) – those who had been educated about NII and said they supported NII but actually supported the Republic of Indonesia, and were therefore to be sentenced to death; *fasik* (unrighteous) people, who understood Islamic law but did not carry it out, who would be ordered to repent; and finally, those who aided the enemy, who would also be sentenced to death.[33] The code assigned punishments to a catalogue of crimes including murder, adultery, consuming alcohol, theft and robbery, as well as apostasy and abandoning prayer. The punishments were often severe. For example, for theft:

> Whosoever steals a quarter dinar from its proper storage place, in the first instance shall have their right hand and wrist cut off. If they steal for a second time their left foot is to be cut off. If they steal a third time their left hand is to be cut off. If they steal a fourth time their right foot is to be cut off, and if they steal again they are to be exiled to a location a minimum of 1 *qashar* (16 posts) distant.[34]

To implement the code, Darul Islam divided Indonesian territory into three zones. The first zone, Area I, were those parts of Indonesia where Islamic law was in force. In this area, the NII Criminal Code was implemented in its entirety. The area also served as a base for Darul Islam's *jihad*. Males aged between 16 and 24 years old were required to take part in military training as 'national service'. Upon completion they were sent back to their villages to become the Darul Islam vanguard. Residents were also required to organise a weekly patrol and to give over 2.5 per cent of their income to NII. The second zone, Area II, comprised regions partially under the control of NII and partially under the control of the Indonesian government. Darul Islam cadres in this area were required to rebel, to transform the territory into Area I. The third zone comprised regions controlled by the enemy. The task for the Darul Islam cadres in these areas was to gain the sympathy of all local residents to convert this area into Area II.[35]

This division into regions appears to have been inspired by the Islamic idea of dividing the world into realms of Darul Islam and of

Darul Harb – literally, 'abode of war' – the region of the unbelievers where Islamic law cannot be upheld. This division became problematic when applied to Indonesia, however, because the majority of Indonesia's population were Muslims. Darul Harb, in its traditional definition, described territory occupied by unbelievers against whom it was permissible to wage war. This raised the question of what the status of Muslims living in the second and third zones was. Were they to be considered unbelievers too?

In this matter, Kartosuwirjo drew upon the idea of *takfir* – the declaration of a Muslim as apostate. This *takfiri* stance is evident in the NII Criminal Code, where an apostate is defined as anyone who rejects the laws of the Islamic state, even if they were born a Muslim from Muslim parents.[36] Consciously or otherwise, Kartosuwirjo's philosophy appears to have reflected the war-like conditions he faced, which demanded a black and white stance so that one could differentiate between friend and foe.

One example of Kartosuwirjo's *takfiri* philosophy was his conflict with Yusuf Taudjiri, owner of the Cipari Islamic boarding school. Taudjiri had been Kartosuwirjo's religious teacher. They had known each other for nearly twenty years and had struggled together in PSI and Hizbullah. Wiwiek, Kartosuwirjo's wife, was a close friend of Taudjiri's daughter. Their dispute arose when Kartosuwirjo proclaimed himself the leader of Darul Islam and rebelled against the Indonesian Republic. Taudjiri did not agree with these political moves, angering Kartosuwirjo, who declared his former teacher an apostate against whom war must be waged. From 1949 to 1958, Darul Islam forces attacked the Cipari boarding school 47 times. The most serious attack took place on the night of 17 April 1952. Around 3000 Darul Islam troops attacked the boarding school for around eight hours. Taudjiri and his students resisted with just six old firearms, pistols and grenades. The attackers succeeded in destroying the school buildings, but failed to kill Taudjiri. On the boarding school's side, 11 people were killed; more than ten Darul Islam soldiers also perished.[37]

Kartosuwirjo also formulated steps to achieve a Darul Islam in Indonesia, through studying the annals of Muhammad's struggle. As mentioned previously, he deemed one of the keys to victory to be *hijrah*. *Hijrah* referred to the Prophet Muhammad's flight from Mecca – where his teachings had initially been rejected – to Madina. He found acceptance among the tribes in Madina, and established a secure base there before returning to conquer Mecca. Kartosuwirjo argued that '*hijrah* was a deed of the greatest importance on the part of the Prophet, because after the *hijrah* Muslims were in a new era, an era of clear weather, because a divine light shone on Madina.'[38] *Hijrah* alone was insufficient to achieve victory, however. According to Kartosuwirjo, *hijrah* had be paired with *jihad*.[39] In his view, a '*hijrah* that does not employ *jihad* is negative in the sense of rejecting vice (*nahi munkar*) without embracing virtue (*amar ma'ruf*).'[40]

Whist Kartosuwirjo's ideas about *takfir* and *jihad* would later be echoed in the ideas of Salafi Jihadism, one aspect of his philosophy would certainly not have found favour – his attachment to Sufi mysticism. Kartosuwirjo used mystical practices in support of Darul Islam's objectives. For example, every night in Area I, 41 religious scholars and holy men were tasked with praying and chanting praise of Allah (*zikir*). One of their objectives was to gather 'supernatural signs observed from day to day and inform the local leadership, both civilian and military, to be conveyed to central level as necessary.'[41] Kartosuwirjo also collected sacred objects.

Kartosuwirjo was convinced that these mystical practices would strengthen the belief and loyalty of Darul Islam followers in his leadership. He cultivated an image of himself as a holy man with supernatural powers, including the ability to vanish, and of being invulnerable to bullets.

A story also spread that Kartosuwirjo had received the 'Divine Inspiration from Cakraningrat' (the divine summons to lead) when he was resting on Galunggung mountain, and that a light had emerged and had come close to him, suddenly forming into the Islamic confessional sentence on his brow. He then ordered his followers to paint the confessional sentence as calligraphy and distributed these images as amulets to be revered.[42] These stories increased Kartosuwirjo's standing and the loyalty of his followers. Many Darul Islam members were afraid to leave because they believed they would incur disaster and curses from their mystical Imam. Reports that people who left Darul Islam had died strengthened these beliefs. In fact, in cases where people had died after leaving it had usually been because they had been executed by Darul Islam members.[43]

Darul Islam in wartime[44]

By the beginning of the 1950s, the West Java–centred Darul Islam rebellion spread to several parts of Indonesia. On 20 January 1952, Kahar Muzakar and his forces in South Sulawesi joined the rebellion. A year later, on 20 September 1953, it was the turn of Aceh to be claimed as NII territory, when the Acehnese leader Daud Beureueh joined Darul Islam with his followers. In South Kalimantan a rebellion under the leadership of Ibnu Hajar also joined.[45]

These local leaders did not join for religious reasons, however. They rebelled against the Republic of Indonesia because they were disappointed with the Jakarta government's policies towards their region or group. In the case of Aceh, one of the reasons Beureueh rebelled was because Sukarno revoked Aceh's autonomous status and made it a part of North Sumatra province. In South Sulawesi, Muzakar revolted because his forces, which had been part of the South Sulawesi Guerrilla Unit (KGSS – Kesatuan Gerilya Sulawesi Selatan), were not granted a place in the Republic's newly formed armed forces. While religion was not the main trigger for these rebellions, Islam became a unifying factor for their leaders.[46]

The addition of these regions raised the morale of the Darul Islam forces in West Java, which had seen many of their leaders killed and captured. In 1951, the military killed Oni Kital, who had been NII's defence minister, and captured Gozali Tusi, the justice minister.[47] A shift in Indonesian government policy under the leadership of new Prime Minister Muhammad Natsir also helped lift morale. Natsir wanted to resolve the Darul Islam problem at the negotiating table.[48] Financial and material losses from the revolt had grown. According to the Army Chief of Staff, General Abdul Haris Nasution, the war against Darul Islam was just as intense as the guerrilla war against the Dutch had been.[49]

Although Darul Islam forces achieved many victories, it was almost inevitable that the revolt would fail. From the outset, the movement lacked significant financial resources. Their main source of income was the various fees levied on communities in territory they controlled, as well as armed robberies. Darul Islam forces would enter villages at night to collect money from the population. If anyone was unwilling to pay, Darul Islam troops would normally enter his or her house directly and seize all available possessions. Darul Islam forces would also frequently enter towns in West Java and occupy them for several hours, usually looting what they could. They destroyed houses and public facilities, killing in the process. In September 1956, for example, fighters carried out attacks for seventeen days in the Tasikmalaya area of East Priangan and burned 254 houses, two mosques and a school. At the end of the year, the terror campaign escalated further. In November, a Darul Islam force of 320 men attacked Terayu and burned 100 houses, while in East Priangan fighters murdered 20 civilians and burned 373 houses in the space of a week. In total, in 1956 they killed 224 people and burned 2044 houses.[50]

These activities sowed the seeds of the movement's destruction by generating community anger. In 1958 the Indonesian government started trying to isolate the rebels and gain the sympathy of the community, with the army providing food, accommodation and health aid. The army also carried out development work in areas damaged by war. By 1962 this strategy had turned the tide against the rebels. One by one, Darul Islam leaders began to surrender. In May 1962, Darul Islam in Aceh ended its rebellion. Also in May, Kahar Muzakar in Sulawesi broke with the other Darul Islam movements and declared the establishment of the United Islamic Republic of Indonesia (RPII – Republik Persatuan Islam Indonesia), a federation that would include West Java and Aceh, but with himself as 'Caliph'.[51] Only a few Darul Islam leaders were prepared to continue with the rebellion, including Kartosuwirjo and Agus Abdullah, DI's regional commander for Java and Madura.[52]

Kartosuwirjo's last days[53]

At this point Kartosuwirjo knew that the war that he had fought for thirteen years would end in defeat. On 15 May 1962, he received a report that the Darul Islam forces spread over the Cakrabuana, Guntur and Galunggung mountains in West Java were in disarray. He also heard that the troops were in increasingly weak physical condition. His own condition was little different. Kartosuwirjo was ill, suffering diabetes and malnutrition. Government forces were closing in on his 46-person strong headquarters. Kartosuwirjo's son, Muhammad Darda, known as Dodo, the headquarters commander and Aceng Kurnia, Kartosuwirjo's aide, were determined to fight to the death when the enemy arrived. 'If the enemy comes, we will shoot. Surrender is a sin. We must be ready to kill or be killed (*yuqtal au yaqlib*),' insisted Darda. Hearing his son say this, Kartosuwirjo was silent for a moment before saying that current conditions no longer fulfilled the conditions for '*yuqtal au yaqlib*'.

On 4 June 1962, Kartosuwirjo's group reached a valley between the Sangkar and Geber mountains, in the vicinity of South Bandung. That morning, driving rain and strong winds buffeted the area. The Darul Islam forces chose to shelter in emergency tents. Gunshots suddenly rang out at the foot of the mountains. Three platoons had surrounded Kartosuwirjo's group. All of his guards prepared their weapons, intending to fight to the death. Aceng and Dodo took position, ready to shoot. As the Indonesian army approached Kartosuwirjo's tent, he suddenly said 'Don't shoot – if we do as Dodo wishes, all the *mujahideen* will die'. Hearing this order, Aceng and Dodo laid down their weapons, and came out with their hands raised. An Indonesian officer, Second Lieutenant Suhanda, met them outside with two of his soldiers, Amir and Suhara.

Suhanda greeted them and asked, 'Where is the Imam?' 'That's him,' said Dodo, pointing to the tent. Suhanda entered and saw Kartosuwirjo lying on the floor of the hut in a serious condition, wearing a military jacket and a sarong. Although he was 55 years old when he was captured, he looked much older.[54] Without saying much, Suhanda ordered his soldiers to make a litter. Aceng and Dodo then helped Kartosuwirjo into the litter. Kartosuwirjo suddenly whispered, 'This is our *Hudaibiyah*' – a reference to the cease-fire agreement between the Prophet Muhammad's followers and the rival Quraish tribe. He is reputed to have said this three times, once while looking at Aceng, once to Dodo, a third time as if for emphasis.[55]

Kartosuwirjo's capture signalled the end of thirteen years of political upheaval that had greatly damaged the development of West Java. Its agricultural production had fallen sharply, displacement had occurred on a massive scale, and infrastructure in the interior regions had been destroyed. Twenty-two thousand eight hundred and ninety-five civilians had been killed, injured or kidnapped. The state suffered losses of Rp. 650 million.[56]

Two days after his capture, Kartosuwirjo ordered Dodo to issue an appeal for Darul Islam forces to come down from the mountains and lay down their weapons. Dodo did not obey at first, because he felt he did not have the authority to issue an order. Eventually he gave it. Some forces in the mountains believed in its authenticity and surrendered, but others did not. The order raised many questions in Darul Islam circles. Was it an acknowledgement of defeat and surrender? Did the order truly come from the Imam? Even if it had, some Darul Islam fighters maintained they could not follow it, because the Imam could not issue an order while in enemy custody.

Nevertheless, the morale of Darul Islam fighters collapsed. Many of those who did not come down from the mountains were captured by the military. Darul Islam forces in Central Java under the leadership of Ismail Pranoto (known as Hispran) were among the last to give up, and only surrendered in 1967.

Almost all of the Darul Islam troops received an amnesty. On 1 August 1962, rebel leaders were required to make what became known as the Joint Pledge (Ikrar Bersama) of loyalty to the Republic of Indonesia, emphasising that Darul Islam was a misguided movement that had deviated from the teachings of Islam. The pledge was signed by thirty-two of Darul Islam's key figures, including Adah Djaelani, Danu Muhammad Hasan, Tahmid Rahmat Basuki, Dodo Muhammad Darda, Ateng Djaelani and Djaja Sudjadi.

Kartosuwirjo received treatment for two months. In August 1962 his condition began to improve. That same month, he came before the Java and Madura Wartime Army Court, and was charged with attempting to overthrow the Indonesian government, rebellion against the legitimate authorities, and planning to assassinate President Sukarno. In its third session, the court found Kartosuwirjo guilty and sentenced him to death. On 20 August 1962, he filed for clemency, stating his utmost regret for his past actions. Sukarno rejected the plea.[57]

Kartosuwirjo wrote his will at the beginning of September 1962. It included two messages for his followers, two for his family. To his followers, he emphasised that to the last second he had continued to act as Imam and Supreme Commander of Darul Islam's forces. He argued that in everything he had done he had referred to the Qu'ran and the *Sunnah* of the Prophet. He was convinced, he said, that his aspirations for an Islamic state would be realised at some point in the future. He also sought to correct the Joint Pledge, which had stated that the Darul Islam struggle had been misguided. On 4 September 1962, Kartosuwirjo said his goodbyes to his family. The next day at dawn on 5 September 1962, a firing squad took him to an island in the Thousand Islands off the coast of Jakarta. At precisely 5.50 am he was executed and his body was buried on a beach on the island.[58]

Kartosuwirjo's aspiration for an Islamic state in Indonesia did not die with him. Several months after his execution, new efforts were already being made to revive the movement. Ahmad Sobari, former Darul Islam district head of East Priangan Timur, established Negara Islam Tejamaya (NIT – Tejamaya Islamic State), named after a village in Tasikmalaya, West Java that served as a base for the group.[59] He criticised Darul Islam fighters who had surrendered, and considered all who had come down from the mountains to have forsaken the struggle. Sobari's group considered anyone outside their circle to be not true Muslims, as evident in their refusal to eat the meat of animals slaughtered by non-group members. The group never truly seriously challenged the Indonesian government, and its influence was limited to the area around Tasikmalaya and Cianjur.[60]

A more serious effort to revive Darul Islam began in the 1970s, when former members began to regroup. Their movement became known as Komando Jihad.[61]

2
Komando Jihad

After Kartosuwirjo's execution, Darul Islam members formed a new organisational structure and in 1973 chose the Acehnese Islamic leader Daud Beureueh as their new Imam. They also revived Kartosuwirjo's teachings of violent *jihad* against the Indonesian government.

In his final message Kartosuwirjo had likened Darul Islam's defeat to the *Hudaibiyah* treaty that brought about a ceasefire between the Prophet Muhammad and his adversaries. While this idea continued to inspire his remaining followers it was not the only motivation for former Darul Islam members trying to revive their struggle. In Aceh, Beureueh had grown concerned by what he saw as moral decadence caused by the growing industrialisation of the province. He felt that the only way to redress it was to uphold Islamic law. Under President Suharto there was no possibility of striving for Islamic law through formal political channels, so Beureueh felt he had no choice but to rejoin Darul Islam and revive *jihad*.

Beureueh and his associates formed an organisational structure based on Communiqué No. 11, which had been issued by Kartosuwirjo in 7 August 1959 with the goal of creating an Islamic army.

They recruited former Darul Islam members and tried to seek funds and weapons from Libya. But in 1977, the security forces got wind of their efforts and carried out large-scale arrests of Darul Islam members.

In response to this new round of repression, Darul Islam leaders began to develop a clandestine organisation (*tanzim siri*), based on a cell structure. It was the first clandestine Islamic organisation in Indonesia and would serve as a model for a variety of Islamic movements in later years. This new iteration of Darul Islam also came to rely heavily on armed robberies to fund its activities, which were justified by the movement in Islamic terms as *fa'i* – robbing unbelievers to fund *jihad*. But security forces were never far behind, and in 1981 the remaining Darul Islam leaders were captured.

• • •

Darul Islam's *Hudaibiyah*

Many of Kartosuwirjo's remaining followers benefitted from a general amnesty after his death in 1962. The government began a transmigration and rehabilitation program, moving many key Darul Islam leaders from the areas in which they had fought. Battalion commanders and above were required to undergo re-education by the Siliwangi military command in West Java. They received jobs and capital to start businesses. For example, one commander, Ules Sujai, became a staff member at Siliwangi, administering the rehabilitation program. Two other senior cadres, Ateng Djaelani and Adah Djaelani, became kerosene distributors in Bandung and Jakarta.

In September 1965, political turmoil shook Indonesia. A number of left-leaning soldiers kidnapped and murdered six generals and a lieutenant. The soldiers said they had acted to prevent a planned coup against President Sukarno by American-supported generals. They established a Revolutionary Council in Jakarta to implement Sukarno's policies and to neutralise counter-revolutionary forces. The Revolutionary Council was to be short-lived. Within days, army troops under the leadership of Major General Suharto defeated it. These events triggered further political chaos. The Indonesian Communist Party (PKI) was accused of having been behind the murders. School and university students, as well as members of Muslim organisations, took to the streets with military support to demand that the PKI be disbanded. President Sukarno was urged to step down from his position because of his perceived closeness to the PKI. The military arrested key PKI figures, and many Communist activists and suspected sympathisers were hunted down and murdered throughout Indonesia.[1]

In Java, this military-led assault on the PKI involved former Darul Islam soldiers under the coordination of Siliwangi military command personnel including H.R. Dharsono and Aang Kunaefi, as well as key members of the National Intelligence Coordination Agency (BAKIN) like Yoga Sugama and Ali Moertopo. They had sought the assistance of former Darul Islam leaders like Ateng Djaelani, Adah Djaelani, Danu Muhammad Hasan and Dodo Muhammad Darda to mobilise the former Darul Islam members in West Java and Central Java.[2] These leaders agreed to help, as they had strong anti-Communist views. According to Adah Djaelani, Darul Islam members contributed their own funds to these operations, while the military lent them weapons.[3]

After the upheaval of 1965, relations between several Darul Islam leaders and the Indonesian military grew even closer. The army provided Darul Islam members with various payments for their services, including by providing business concessions. Ateng Djaelani, for example, became the Bandung municipality chairperson of the Association of Oil and Gas Companies (Gapermigas) in 1968, with support from the Siliwangi military command. Ali Moertopo also recruited Danu Muhammad Hasan to work for BAKIN, providing him with an official car and residence and a monthly salary.[4] For those Darul Islam members now benefitting from the military's largesse, aspirations for an Islamic state became moot. 'At the time we had no thoughts at all of reviving the Darul Islam movement,' said Adah Djaelani.[5]

Aceng Kurnia and Djaja Sudjadi

This sentiment did not last, however. Inspired by two key figures – Aceng Kurnia, Kartosuwirjo's former aide, and Djaja Sudjadi, Darul Islam's former finance minister – the movement began to revive in the late 1970s. Aceng and Sudjadi had studied Kartosuwirjo's final message and, in particular, its reference to how the Darul Islam struggle was entering a *Hudaibiyah* period. They re-evaluated their view of their political defeat in 1962 and recast it as a transitional stage on the path to ultimate victory.

The two also studied the status of *jihad* during the Prophet Muhammad's *Hudaibiyah* period. They concluded that *jihad* had changed from *qital fisabilillah* – war in the name of Allah – to *jihad fillah*, a spiritual *jihad* without force of arms. Whereas *jihad fisabilillah* meant to fight vice physically and openly, *jihad fillah* meant the rejection of vice in one's heart. But the *jihad fillah* was also only temporary. Once the Islamic community was strong enough, it could wage *jihad fisabilillah*. That would be the sign that the *Hudaibiyah* period had come to an end, and the commencement of what was termed Darul Islam's 'period of victory'. This was referred to as the *'Futtoh Mecca'* period (literally, 'Mecca victory'), which was seen as analogous to the Prophet's conquest of Mecca after the end of the *Hudaibiyah* peace.[6]

At the end of 1968, Djaja Sudjadi began to meet with former Darul Islam fighters in West Java, particularly in Garut, to popularise the concepts of *Hudaibiyah* and *jihad fillah*. Aceng Kurnia meanwhile began to educate the children of Darul Islam members in his house in the Cibuntu area of Bandung. Aceng saw recruitment and caderisation as vitally important. He noted that the Prophet Muhammad had greatly increased his supporters during the *Hudaibiyah* period through preaching and the dissemination of Islamic teachings. Historical records showed the size of the Prophet Muhammad's army to have increased from just 1400 troops when he signed the *Hudaibiyah* peace treaty to a 10000-strong force when the *Hudaibiyah* period ended.[7]

Aceng commenced the caderisation process with eleven people, including Tahmid Rahmat Basuki (Kartosuwirjo's son), Ridwan and Mamin Masyur.[8] Once they had been educated, they were given the task of recruiting and educating new Darul Islam members. Later, Aceng's students were incorporated into an organisation called Pergerakan Rumah Tangga Islam (the Islamic Households Movement – PRTI). PRTI was just an alias; the organisation's real name was Persiapan Tentara Islam Indonesia (Preparations for an Indonesian Islamic Army – PTII). Its members were the first cadres for what Aceng anticipated would be Darul Islam's *'Futtoh Mecca'*.[9]

In 1969, Aceng had given his students in PRTI the task of re-enlisting former Darul Islam military cadres. These efforts did not succeed. A PRTI member complained:

> The difficulty was, if we approached a squad commander, he would say he had not received an order from his platoon commander. If we approached a platoon commander, he would say he had no order from his company commander. Then the company commander would say he had no order from his regiment commander and so on. In the end, we and Aceng Kurnia came to the view that to mobilise former Darul Islam soldiers, we would need to lobby the regional commanders.[10]

Ironically, Aceng's decision to approach former commanders appears to have been inspired by the Indonesian military's use of former Darul Islam fighters to battle the Communists.

In 1970, Aceng approached Adah Djaelani, Ateng Djaelani and Danu Muhammad Hasan. He reminded the former commanders of Kartosuwirjo's bequest regarding *Hudaibiyah*, explaining that this final message from Darul Islam's Imam reinforced the validity of Darul Islam's struggle. He tried to convince them that Darul Islam's experience was faithfully repeating the history of the Prophet Muhammad's struggle. Despite their close collaboration with the Indonesian military in the fight against the Communists, the successful businesses they had established and the professional lives they were now leading, Aceng succeeded in convincing the former Darul Islam military leaders to return to the struggle. They agreed to contact their former soldiers and see if they were willing to do the same.

The Situaksan meeting and BAKIN

Although the Darul Islam leaders had decided to revive the movement, they knew it would not be an easy task. They needed both time and money, but they would be assisted in their goal by the political situation in Indonesia in the early 1970s.

The first election of the New Order era under former General and now President Suharto was to be held in June 1971. For a year prior to the election, BAKIN and the Siliwangi military command had been approaching Darul Islam members to encourage them to channel their political aspirations through the new regime's electoral vehicle, the Golkar party. At the end of 1970, several Darul Islam leaders such as Danu Muhammad Hasan and Ateng Djaelani issued a Joint Pledge on behalf of former members, affirming their loyalty to Indonesia and stating that they would not support any political party. Privately, Darul Islam members pledged their support for Golkar, which could be justified by the fiction that it was not a political party.[11]

Following this joint declaration, Danu had the idea of asking for funds from BAKIN to organise a Darul Islam reunion that would be used as a public show of support for Golkar. Aceng agreed to the idea and asked PRTI members to become the reunion committee. BAKIN also agreed to the event and provided Rp. 250 000 to fund it.[12] The reunion was held in Bandung on 21 April 1971. This event became known as the Situaksan meeting, after the name of the Bandung suburb where Danu Muhammad lived and where the meeting was held. This three-day event was very important because for the first time many former Darul Islam members were able to gather together – around 3000 people, according to one participant, although his estimate may be high.[13] Colonel Pitut Suharto, a BAKIN official (no relation to President Suharto), was among the speakers, and he invited those present to support Golkar. But behind the official speeches, the attendees were conducting internal consultations on how to revive the Darul Islam struggle.

Darul Islam was able to arrange continuing financial support from BAKIN. The key to this odd arrangement was Danu's personal relationship with BAKIN deputy Ali Moertopo. They had known each other since they were active together in the Hizbullah militia during the revolution. Danu greatly trusted Moertopo because he believed that he had once saved Darul Islam from extinction. In 1965–1966, according to one account, Suharto had intended to annihilate all of his political enemies, including Darul Islam. Moertopo had lobbied Suharto, however, and convinced him that the anti-Communist Darul Islam members could be exploited to attack the PKI. Darul Islam members like Danu even trusted Ali Moertopo's commitment to Islam. They were convinced that he shared their goal of establishing an Islamic state.[14]

The relationship between BAKIN and Darul Islam did not sit well with all Darul Islam leaders, however. This included Djaja Sudjadi, the former Darul Islam finance minister, who held firm to Kartosuwirjo's uncompromising politics. Djaja was also motivated by his ambition to lead Darul Islam. Rumours emerged after the Situaksan meeting that Adah Djaelani was to be appointed Darul Islam's new Imam. Djaja considered that as a former Member of the Supreme Command, a ministerial-level position, he was better suited.[15] He was also disappointed that Aceng had invited people like Adah and Danu back into the movement. Many members believed that Aceng, a blacksmith who made hoes, had become financially dependent on Adah, a successful businessman who frequently gave him money.

In the end, Djaja chose to strike out on his own. In 1971, he approached Daud Beureueh in Aceh and, in a meeting with him, criticised the Darul Islam figures who had issued the Joint Pledge in 1970. He also complained about the increasing prevalence of vice, such as gambling and prostitution, particularly in Bandung. He invited Beureueh to rejoin the Darul Islam struggle. Beureueh was unwilling to do so but said that he would not forbid Darul Islam members in West Java to revive the movement if they wished.[16] Djaja's efforts to mobilise former fighters more broadly did not succeed because, despite his seniority, he had not been part of the chain of command for the movement's military cadres. Moreover, the concept of *jihad fillah* that he advocated was a very abstract one. In the end he only succeeded in recruiting people who had been close to him in the past, such as Haji Yusuf Kamal, Djaja's former secretary, and Otas and Oneng, former Darul Islam financial staff.[17] Nevertheless, in 1975 Djaja formally proclaimed the establishment of a *jihad fillah* group in Limbangan, Garut.

Despite this conflict with Djaja, Aceng Kurnia and his associates continued their efforts to revive Darul Islam. Throughout 1972 they held a number of meetings with key Darul Islam leaders. The most important took place in October 1972 at Aceng's house in the Cibuntu area of Bandung. This meeting agreed that the platform for their efforts to revive the movement would be 'the implementation of Islamic Law in Indonesia'.[18] The meeting also discussed the importance of expanding cooperation with other former Darul Islam members, particularly in Sulawesi and Aceh. By chance, Aceng himself had family and personal ties that could be used to link the different Darul Islam movements. Aceng's son-in-law Muhammad Jabir was a former Darul Islam Sulawesi member. Aceng also knew Gaos Taufik, a Darul Islam member who lived in Medan, whom Daud Beureueh trusted. In the end, it was agreed that Dodo Muhammad Darda would meet with a delegate from Sulawesi who was coming to Jakarta in early 1973, whereas Aceng himself would meet with Beureueh.[19]

Around November 1972, Aceng left for Aceh. With the assistance of Gaos Taufik, he was able to meet with Beureueh and explain the plans of Darul Islam in Java to work toward the application of Islamic law in Indonesia. Beureueh said that he shared that goal and that his followers in Aceh remained united and continued to listen to his advice.[20] Aceng considered the meeting to be a positive signal that Darul Islam in Aceh was prepared to cooperate.

At the beginning of 1973, Darda met with a delegate of RPII, the movement of former Darul Islam members in Sulawesi, at the house of Aceng Kurnia's son-in-law in Kalibaru, Tanjung Priok, the port area of Jakarta. The RPII figure, Ali Achmad Tholib (also known as Ali AT), revealed in the meeting that armed fighters remained in the mountains conducting guerrilla activities, under the leadership of Sanusi Daris, Kahar Muzakar's 'defense minister'. RPII also had a leader living in Malaysia, Kaso Gani, whose role was to seek donations of weapons from the Middle East. By the end of the meeting, the West Java and Sulawesi wings of the movement had agreed to cooperate.[21]

Efforts to revive Darul Islam were accelerating. In September 1973 a historic meeting took place on Mahoni Street in Tanjung Priok at the house of Ramli Yakob, a former Darul Islam Sulawesi figure. The Mahoni meeting, as it became known, was the first time that senior Darul Islam figures from the three regions came together, with Daud Beureueh from Aceh, Gaos Taufik from Medan, Ali Achmad Tholib from Sulawesi, and Aceng Kurnia, Adah Djaelani and Dodo Muhammad Darda from Java.[22] Ironically, Beureueh had come to Jakarta to take up an invitation to meet President Suharto. Aceng and his associates had taken advantage of his visit to organise the meeting.[23]

Aceng opened it, urging the need to wage *jihad fisabilillah* to uphold Islamic law in Indonesia. Adah Djaelani argued a similar point. The participants also discussed organisational matters, as a revived movement would need a leader. Adah stated his intention to hand over the leadership to Beureueh, arguing that 'Of our ex-officers, none is more senior than Daud Beureueh [especially since] Agus Abdullah [a West Javanese leader] and Abdul Qahar [Kahar Muzakar] have died.'

Initially, Beureueh rejected the nomination, saying he felt there were other more suitable figures. He finally agreed, however, saying: 'If we mean to educate the community and I can unite the *mujahideen*, then I do not object. But don't choose me next time.' Beureueh's attitude to his new responsibilities was similarly cautious. Responding to Aceng on the issue of *jihad fisabilillah*, Beureueh said that under the present circumstances they needed to be patient. They had no resources and had made no preparations. Nor should they move too speedily against the Indonesian government. They should take advantage of the government's good will, and give advice. If the government did not heed this advice, they would again rebel.

The Mahoni meeting produced an agreement among the three regions to work together. In addition to Beureueh's appointment as Imam, Djaelani was chosen as the representative of former Darul Islam members in Java and Madura, and Ali Achmad Tholib was appointed as Sulawesi representative. The brevity of the Mahoni meeting – it lasted just 90 minutes – meant that no agreement was reached regarding a joint program of work. Nor did the participants want such an agreement, as each region faced different circumstances. It was left to each regional representative to determine his own activities and program.[24]

There was also no agreement on how Darul Islam would be reorganised. After the meeting, several key participants including Djaelani, Aceng and Gaos Taufik began discussion of a new structure based on Kartosuwirjo's Indonesian Islamic State War Forces (APNII) Communiqué No. 11, issued on 1 September 1959. The communiqué, issued as part of the mobilisation of Darul Islam forces to wage war throughout Indonesia, divided Indonesia into seven levels of war regions or *sapta palagan*. The first, covering all of Indonesia, was called the All Indonesia War Command (KPSI). KPSI was to be led by a senior Darul Islam figure who would also be the APNII High Commander. The second was called the Greater Regional War Command (KPWB) and was further divided into three regions, each led by a KPWB War Commander. The first of these regions, KPWB I, consisted of Java and Madura. The second, KPWB II, comprised all of eastern Indonesia, including Sulawesi. The third, KPWB III, covered Sumatra. Each KPWB consisted of several Regional War Commands (KPW), each led by a KPW War

Commander. Beneath these three levels, there were still four more, each smaller than the one above it, namely the residency, district, subdistrict and village level war regions.[25]

Reviving *jihad*

At the end of 1974 Daud Beureueh met in Sigli, in Aceh, with other senior Darul Islam leaders, including Rifa'i Ahmad (Lampung), Bardan Kindarto (Palembang), Gaos Taufik (Medan), Aceng Kurnia (West Java) and Ali Achmad Tholib (Sulawesi).[26] The meeting was to reflect a dramatic shift in Beureueh's thinking about the movement's activities. At the meeting, Beureueh urged all Darul Islam cadres in the various areas to make preparations to wage *jihad* to uphold Islamic law in Indonesia. Beureueh planned to request funds and weapons from Libya. Under Colonel Gaddafi's leadership, Libya had previously helped Muslim rebels in Mindanao to wage war against the Philippine government. Beureueh also ordered Gaos Taufik to take up residence in Jakarta to facilitate coordination between Darul Islam cadres in Sumatra, Java and Sulawesi.[27]

At the Mahoni meeting in 1973, Beureueh had asked Darul Islam to be patient, and had argued that their efforts should focus on advising Suharto and his government. Now he was suddenly urging *jihad*. The situation in Aceh may have triggered his change of heart – in particular, the social consequences resulting from the discovery of the Arun gas field in Lhokseumawe, in North Aceh. The rapid industrialisation of this region spurred the growth of prostitution, discotheques and pubs across Aceh, as well as the influx of western companies. In Beureueh's eyes this moral decadence and sidelining of religious values in the province could only be addressed by a return to *jihad*.[28]

Following the Sigli meeting, Gaos Taufik prepared his cadres to undertake military training in Jakarta. Nine participants were sent from Sumatra, including Timsar Zubil, Asli Pohan and Syarif Hidayat from Lampung. Part of their training was in bomb-making.[29] Their trainer was Saleh Amin, an ethnic Bugis who worked as a fisherman in Jakarta.[30] He was a student of Muhammad Jabir, Aceng Kurnia's son-in-law, who was himself a former member of Darul Islam South Sulawesi. The bomb-making course was held at Jabir's house in Tanjung Priok.[31]

Meanwhile, Gaos Taufik and his associates prepared plans to request weapons and funds from Libya. Taufik estimated they would need some 300 000 weapons, ranging from semi-automatic to automatic firearms. They would also need various types of grenades and bombs, as well as military equipment including uniforms, telecommunications equipment and medicines, and approximately US$12 billion in funding. Taufik asked Rifa'i Ahmad to travel to Malaysia to meet with representatives of the Libyan government.[32] In July 1975, Taufik drafted a letter to the Libyan embassy in Jakarta. Jalaluddin Muthalib, a lecturer who had graduated from a Libyan university, translated the letter into Arabic. The letter was then taken to Aceh for Daud Beureueh to sign.[33] Beureueh also organised for two trusted people in Malaysia, Hasan Tiro and another individual, to lobby the Libyan Embassy in Kuala Lumpur.

In September 1975, Rifa'i Ahmad went to Malaysia, where he met with one of Beureueh's Malaysian associates. This individual told Rifa'i that the Libyans would only provide financial and military support if there was violent turmoil in Indonesia. He suggested sabotaging the offices or oil pipelines of Pertamina, the state-owned oil and gas company. He also explained that the Libyan government had offered to take a number of Darul Islam cadres to Libya for military training. Several days later Beureueh himself went to Malaysia to meet with the Libyan Embassy in Kuala Lumpur. The Libyan government, however, continued to reject Darul Islam's requests for assistance.[34]

Preparations for *jihad* in Java

Preparations for *jihad* developed differently in Java. Following the Sigli meeting, Danu Muhammad Hasan and his associates took the initiative to undertake what they called the 'conditioning' of the Islamic community in Indonesia.[35] This included propaganda activities, in the hope that the Islamic community would welcome *jihad fisabilillah*. They produced and distributed clandestine leaflets to the community and to Islamic figures.[36] For Danu, such 'conditioning' operations were nothing new. He had worked for BAKIN, which had conducted similar actions. He also took part in the Army Special Operations team that had been responsible for an incident known as Malari (Malapetaka Lima Belas Januari – the 15 January tragedy) in 1974, in which *agents provocateurs* instigated riots during a student protest against the visit of the Japanese Prime Minister.[37] The riots became an anti-Japanese and anti-Chinese pogrom that resulted in the deaths of eleven protestors and the destruction of hundreds of cars and buildings.

Danu and his associates raised several issues in the leaflets. One described efforts to 'Christianise' Indonesia. They also claimed that dozens of Communist cadres from China had infiltrated Indonesia to prepare for a revolution in 1980. Another leaflet argued that Suharto and his henchmen had to be deposed and even specified who would replace them. The former Siliwangi military commander Ibrahim Adjie, was to be the president. The vice-president was to be General Soemitro, the Deputy Chief of the Armed Forces who was forced to resign after the Malari incident.[38]

At the end of 1975, Adah Djaelani and his associates received a visit from Gaos Taufik. He came to Bandung carrying a written order from Beureueh, who had just returned from Malaysia, for local members to organise in accordance with Communiqué No. 11. Following on from Beureueh's order, Adah and his associates promptly drew up a new structure and began filling key positions. A recruitment campaign in Java followed, which sought to fill the district-level regional command posts, many of which were vacant. These focused on Central Java and East Java, where Hispran, with assistance from Dodo Muhammad Darda and Tahmid Rahmat Basuki, was given the task of recruitment. Central Java was not a difficult area to work, as Darul Islam had enjoyed a reasonable base of support there in the past.

The recruitment process appears to have been quite successful. By 1976, almost all vacant positions in the new Darul Islam structure were filled. It is not actually clear how many people joined the organisation, although it seems that large numbers did. One Darul Islam leader from the era said that almost 90 per cent of positions in the Darul Islam structure in Java were filled, from the central level down to the villages.[39] Working from the structure set out in NII Communiqué No. 11, we can thus estimate that more than 1000 people were recruited.[40]

The influx of large numbers of new members encouraged Darul Islam leaders to consider commencing their *jihad* against the Indonesian government. At the beginning of 1976, Gaos Taufik discussed this matter with Danu Muhammad Hasan. Danu said that their people were ready, but they did not have weapons or funds. He said that he had requested weapons from BAKIN to arm an anti-Communist Pancasila front militia comprised of former Darul Islam members, but BAKIN had refused. The failure to obtain weapons and funds domestically led the leaders to again think of seeking assistance from Libya. Gaos reminded his colleague that Libya would only help if there was political upheaval in Indonesia. Danu suggested that Darul Islam members carry out sabotage and terrorism operations.[41]

Gaos acted on this discussion straight away. In March 1976, his associates formed a *jihad* organisation led by Agus Sulaiman, aided by several assistants including Timsar Zubil and Mafahid Harahap.[42] They planned various acts of terror, including hijacking a plane, detonating explosives in various locations and seizing weapons. To raise funds they planned armed robberies. The first targeted a rubber plantation in Marbu Selatan, North Sumatra in June 1976. The group seized around Rp. 250 000 (around US$600) in funds. They continued to pillage the Batang Sereh Belawan area, seizing gold and jewellery. Timsar and his associates also started making bombs, using explosives obtained in Lampung.[43] The first target was the Immanuel Hospital, a Christian facility in Bukittinggi.[44] In Medan they exploded bombs at the Methodist church and at the Budi Murni college, another Christian school.[45] In Padang, they detonated a bomb at the Nurul Iman mosque and lobbed a grenade during a Qur'an reading competition.[46] They also bombed entertainment venues including the Riang cinema and Apollo bar in Medan.[47]

The group's acts of terror were well prepared. They carefully chose each target and the time at which to detonate the bomb. After these attacks, Timsar produced a clandestine leaflet in the name of the Indonesian Christian Youth Movement (Angkatan Muda Kristen Indonesia) claiming responsibility. He and his associates hoped that the West Sumatra bombs would provoke Muslim–Christian religious conflict, thereby causing the instability and unrest in Indonesia that they were seeking.

Their calculations were also evident in the bombing of the entertainment venues. The Apollo bar bombing, for example, aimed to make people afraid to go to what the Darul Islam activists considered places of vice. Timsar chose the Riang cinema because he was aggrieved that it had shown an Egyptian film that he thought denigrated Islamic teachings. The Medan group had actually planned a larger operation to bomb all entertainment places in Medan simultaneously, but it was cancelled for lack of funds.[48]

Darul Islam leaders believed that the Sumatra attacks would improve their lobbying efforts with the Libyan government. Around October 1976, Gaos Taufik met with Darul Islam leaders in Sumatra, bringing the news that his followers would commence an armed action, starting in Aceh from March 1977. He also said that efforts to lobby Libya for weapons had succeeded. To check if this were true, Adah Djaelani ordered Ules Sujai to go to Aceh to meet Daud Beureueh. Ules was happy to take on this task, not least because he 'wanted to experience catching a plane'. Once he met with Beureueh, Ules was convinced that Taufik's news had been correct. Beureueh said that Hasan Tiro had successfully lobbied the

Libyan government, and that two warehouses full of weapons could be dropped in Aceh at seven hours' notice.[49]

In West Java, within his 7th Regional Command, Aceng Kurnia formed a *jihad* force of sorts called the Pasukan Berani Mati (Willing to Die Force), comprised of former Darul Islam soldiers and led by a student of Aceng Kurnia's, Syaiful Malik (also known as Kyai Alit and Ajengan Cilik).[50] Meanwhile, Hispran ordered his personnel in East Java, specifically in Kediri, Nganjuk, Tulungagung and Blitar to form 'sabotage special forces'. These were to be tasked with destroying telephone and electricity cables, but also to destroy train lines, to stop the military from sending reinforcements from East Java to West Java. He ordered his people to undertake a reconnaissance of the south coast beaches of East Java to identify suitable sites for weapons drops. All Darul Islam forces were placed on readiness for an order to go to war. The command would use the code phrase '*Takbir* Command Order' (Perintah Komando Takbir). The plan was for the war command in Bandung to issue it at the beginning of February 1977.[51]

But the order never came. Daud Beureueh and Hasan Tiro fell out in Aceh. Beureueh was determined to establish an Indonesian state based on Islamic law, whereas Tiro wanted to establish an independent Acehnese state. Their conflict culminated in the declaration of the Gerakan Aceh Merdeka (Free Aceh Movement – GAM) on 4 December 1976. In interviews with the author in 2004, Darul Islam members claimed that Tiro had taken full control of the Libyan weapons; it remains unclear whether there ever were any.

A series of arrests in Sumatra and Java also shook the movement. The authorities captured Timsar Zubil on 17 January 1977 and then his associates in Medan, Palembang and Lampung. They arrested Hispran in Java the same month, and this was followed by the arrest of Darul Islam members in West Java, Central Java and East Java. Danu Muhammad Hasan, Dodo Muhammad Darda, Ateng Djaelani, Zainal Abidin, Mahmud Ghozin and Kadar Fa'isal were among those arrested. Gaos Taufik was taken into custody in June 1977. The government subsequently labelled the Sumatra- and Java-based Darul Islam groups involved in the planned uprising as 'Komando Jihad'.

One key question that emerges from this period is about the level of knowledge held by Indonesia's national intelligence service about the planning for these attacks, given the close relationship between key figures in BAKIN and Darul Islam. It is difficult to verify the exact circumstances because many of the individuals involved have passed away. Nevertheless, it does appear that BAKIN allowed Adah Djaelani and his associates to revive Darul Islam, and waited for them to start committing terrorist acts before rounding them up. From the outset Ali Moertopo knew that the former Darul Islam members would perpetrate various subversive acts. After the Situaksan meeting in 1971, he received routine reports from his close contact in the movement, Danu Muhammad Hasan.[52] Moertopo appears to have decided that as long as Darul Islam's plans remained incomplete, he would leave its members alone. For example, after the arrest of two important Darul Islam figures, Abdul Fatah Wiranagapati and Syamsudin Marzuki, in East Java in October 1975, the security forces took no further steps to arrest other Darul Islam figures.[53] The same occurred in 1976. Ateng Djaelani, a Darul Islam figure with close relations with the Siliwangi military command, also admitted to having passed information to the command on the group that Adah Djaelani and his associates were creating. But the security forces did not act.[54]

Large-scale arrests began only in 1977, when Darul Islam members began openly carrying out acts of terror ahead of the general election in May. While it is not surprising that the authorities would move against the movement when its actions became more violent, it also appears that the move was designed to discredit the United Development Party (Partai Persatuan Pembangunan – PPP), a government-created coalition of Islamic parties that seemed to be gathering strength as a channel for opposition to the Suharto government. The authorities knew that PPP members had made repeated approaches to Adah Djaelani and Danu Muhammad Hasan to seek the support of former Darul Islam members. They used this information against the PPP in an effort to bolster support for the ruling Golkar party, which won the election with more than 60 per cent of the vote.

Hijrah

Several Darul Islam leaders and members were able to escape arrest in 1977. Even as the security forces pursued them, the leaders worked to regroup. In May 1977, several central Darul Islam figures who had been scattered by the security sweep met up at Adah Djaelani's hideout in the Pasar Sindang area of Tanjung Priok. In this meeting, which was attended by Aceng Kurnia, Tahmid Rahmat Basuki, Ules Sujai and Toha Mahfud, Adah issued an order for all Darul Islam members to flee their homes and their families and continue with recruitment.[55] The attendees promptly conveyed this order to those members they were still able to contact. Aceng

Kurnia and Tahmid fled to Banten. Ules, Toha and Adah hid in Jakarta. In another meeting at Pasar Sindang in Jakarta at the end of 1977, Aceng Kurnia, Toha Mahfud, Tahmid and Ules Sujai agreed that henceforth Darul Islam would adopt an underground struggle.

In 1978, Darul Islam also began to reorganise its leadership. The position of Imam was left vacant because Daud Beureueh had been placed under house arrest in Jakarta. In his absence the movement was effectively led by two 'elders' – Adah Djaelani and Aceng Kurnia. This arrangement confused some members as they did not know who to take orders from. In the end, Adah Djaelani took the initiative to arrange for the election of a new Imam. This took place on 1 July 1979 at the residence of Haji Syukri in Tangerang. There were eleven invitees in attendance: Opa Mustopa, Jarul Alam, Toha Mahfud, Ules Sujai, Tahmid Rahmat Basuki, Aceng Kurnia, Syaiful Imam, Ahmad Husein, Adah Djaelani, Basyar and Heru Raidin. Each participant was given a piece of paper on which to write the name of one of the candidates, after which the papers were folded and collected. The result: ten voted for Adah Djaelani and only one voted for Aceng Kurnia.[56]

To finance the movement, at the end of 1978 Adah ordered members to seek funds by means of *fa'i* or armed robbery, but only with the permission of their respective regional commanders.[57] As leader, Djaelani received 4 per cent of the overall proceeds of *fa'i* operations.[58] He ordered Ules Sujai to use the Sumatra fugitives for these operations. Their leader was Warman, a senior figure from Garut, West Java, renowned in Darul Islam circles at the time as the '*fa'i* king'. Warman's real name was Warsa.[59] He began using the alias when he joined the movement and had been a Darul Islam subdistrict head in Gunung Haruman. Warman also went by the name 'the Tiger of Haruman' (*Macan Haruman*) – a reference to his frequent killing of Indonesian soldiers as well as villagers whom he deemed to be traitors.

When Darul Islam had lost the war in 1962, Warman also surrendered. He then joined the transmigration program to Lampung, where he became a farmer. At the beginning of the 1970s he rejoined the movement and invited people he knew to join up. When Gaos Taufik and his associates conducted their attacks in Medan, Bukittinggi and Padang in 1976, Warman and his associates also began a series of actions, mostly robberies. He stopped operations in 1977, after the security forces arrested around 300 Darul Islam members in Lampung. Many Lampung members fled to Java, including two of Warman's close associates, Syarif Hidayat and Gustam Efendi, who ended up in Jakarta with Farid Ghozali, another Darul Islam member from Lampung. Warman himself initially held out in Lampung by moving from house to house. As time passed, it became more difficult for him to hide, and Farid Ghozali and his friends eventually decided to bring Warman to Java. In mid-1978, Warman joined Syarif Hidayat, Gustam Efendi and Farid Ghozali in Jakarta.

The security forces were soon on their trail, however. On 19 August 1978 they raided Farid Ghozali's house in Kelapa Gading. A shootout resulted, and in the chaos, Farid escaped, and shot dead two personnel from the Greater Jakarta military command. He fled with Warman, Syarif Hidayat and Gustam Efendi to Tasikmalaya. They came out of hiding only after Adah Djaelani issued an order to conduct *fa'i* robberies. Warman and his associates joined several Darul Islam members from the 1st and 7th regional commands, including Iyus (Garut), Jafar (Garut), Sofyan (Majalengka), Empon Daspon (Rajapolah, Tasikmalaya) and Lukman, alias Banban (Cianjur). Together they formed a *fa'i* group under Warman's leadership.[60]

The Warman *fa'i* team operated in West Java and Central Java. Its first action was in the Bandung area in late 1978, when a group led by Syarif Hidayat robbed a government official in Cicalengka and took off with Rp. 1 million (US$1600). As 1979 began, they became increasingly active. Their targets varied: they stole money from the Islamic university, and robbed gold traders in the market. The security forces shot Farid dead in January 1979; Warman was arrested two months later in March 1979 after a robbery in Malang. His capture exposed Darul Islam's network in Yogyakarta.[61] These arrests did not slow down Syarif Hidayat and his group, however. They continued to carry out various robberies, taking in more than Rp. 30 million (US$48 000) in all.[62]

Warman and his team also formed a hit squad to murder those considered to have betrayed Darul Islam. One case was the murder in February 1979 of Hasan Bauw, a student at the Yogyakarta State Islamic Institute, whom Warman believed had informed on a Darul Islam member, leading to his death. Another was the murder of Bahrowi and Rusli, two Tasikmalaya members considered traitors for having left the movement in July 1979. Within Darul Islam circles, however, the most contentious case was the murder of Djaja Sudjadi, who together with Aceng Kurnia had helped revive Darul Islam in the late 1960s. Djaja was rumoured to have helped the security forces arrest Darul Islam members, but there was also a rivalry between him and Adah Djaelani over the leadership of the movement after Kartosuwirjo's death.[63]

Toha Mahfud was assigned the task of carrying out the murder. In February 1979, Mahfud, Syarif Hidayat and Empon Daspon left

Rajapolah for Malangbong in Garut. They arrived after prayers at sunset, then walked towards Djaja's house, and saw from outside that he was sitting in his guest room. Without waiting, Hidayat and Daspon entered the yard, each carrying a pistol. Toha did not join them but hid a few metres from the house. Soon after, several gunshots rang out. The three took off and returned to Rajapolah, where they reported to Ules Sujai that they had completed their task. The next day, news of the murder appeared in the media, reporting that Djaja Sudjadi and one of his sons had been killed. The reports suggested the murder might have been politically motivated, as nothing had been taken from his house.[64]

Fa'i brings misfortune

Fa'i robberies gave rise to disputes among Darul Islam leaders, who squabbled about whether the money was being shared equally. The robberies also increased the chances of the Darul Islam network being uncovered, as had happened in Central Java. But they were difficult to stop. *Fa'i* had become Darul Islam's largest source of funds, and the money was also financing the personal lives of Darul Islam leaders, paying for everything from rent and rice to the purchase, in one case, of a colour television. In February 1980, the *fa'i* team was incorporated into Darul Islam's organisational structure and given the name of Darul Islam special forces.[65] Syarif Hidayat was appointed commander. In the first half of 1980, the group gained an extra member when Warman escaped from prison after breaking through the ceiling of his cell, after which he fled to Tasikmalaya.[66]

The special forces carried out their largest action in May 1980. Syarif Hidayat, along with Gustam Efendi, Empon Daspon, Iyus,

Sofyan and Jafar, robbed the Banjarsari subdistrict Education and Culture office in Ciamis, carrying off almost Rp. 20 million (about US$32 000) in salaries. This proved to be a disaster for Darul Islam in West Java, however. After a three-month investigation, security forces uncovered the special forces network. In August 1980, police captured Sofyan, one of the robbers. They learned from him that several robbers were hiding in a house in Kampung Jati, Tasikmalaya. On 22 August 1980, ten police raided the house, which belonged to Syarif Hidayat's father-in-law, and found Gustam Efendi and Iyus. The two fugitives and the police exchanged fire and when it was over, two police officers were dead and the Darul Islam men had escaped.[67] Gustam and Iyus hid in rice fields in Kampung Jati, where Opa Mustopa picked them up that night; Syarif Hidayat, Empon Daspon and several others arrived soon after. They then fled to the Ciawi area of Tasikmalaya.[68]

The death of the two police angered the security forces and they formed a special unit to hunt the robbers. Within days they arrested dozens of Darul Islam members in Rajapolah and Ciawi. On 9 October 1980, they raided a house in the Bayongbong area of Garut. Another shootout ensued. This time Iyus could not escape, and was shot dead. The police also killed Mang Aslah, a student of Aceng Kurnia's, in the shootout. This chain of arrests and killings was the heaviest blow for Darul Islam since Komando Jihad.

Tanzim siri

Anticipating the arrests, Darul Islam leaders fled to Jakarta. In November 1980, Adah Djaelani and others regrouped in the Tangerang area. They decided to change Darul Islam's structure from a military command to one that more resembled a corporation, hoping thereby to disguise the organisation and protect it from the security forces. Under the new system, the Imam was to be called the director. The chief of staff became the coordinator. They also formed teams for propagation, education, and logistics and finance.

This structure included cells at the directorial and branch level that would incorporate five to ten members. Each cell was to be led by a chairperson assisted by a secretary and treasurer. The chain of command for each cell depended on its position in the structure. A directorial cell was responsible to Tahmid Rahmat Basuki as co-ordinator. A branch-level cell was responsible to the branch head, or, in the old terminology, a regional commander. Only the cell leader would have contact with the director or branch head. The cell system was extended from branch level down to local levels. The remaining special forces members were also incorporated into a cell equivalent to the branch level. It was headed by Syarif Hidayat and directly responsible to Toha Mahfud.

This clandestine organisation, or in Arabic *tanzim siri*, harked back to the Prophet Muhammad's struggle. When he first began to spread Islam in Mecca, Muhammad was forced to preach in secret, only coming into the open when the Islamic community was strong. In Indonesia, Darul Islam was the first Islamic movement to adopt the principle of a clandestine organisation. Subsequently, all Islamic movements in Indonesia in the New Order did so, including the Tarbiyah movement (the forerunner of the Prosperous Justice Party or Partai Keadilan Sejahtera – PKS), Hizbut Tahrir and Jema'ah Islamiyah.

Efforts to apply the cell system started at the beginning of 1981. But it came too late for the movement. In the early hours of 23 July

1981, the security forces, still in vigorous pursuit of those behind the Banjarsari robbery, quietly surrounded a small hut in Soreang Kolot village, outside Bandung. It was Ramadan at the time. The occupants had just awoken for the pre-fast meal and were not aware that they were surrounded. Seeing them awake, the security forces shouted for them to come out and surrender. The occupants answered with gunshots from inside the house. The security forces then threw a smoke grenade into the hut. One of the occupants burst through the side bamboo wall, spraying bullets from the FN .45 pistol he was holding. He tried to run towards a cassava field but was struck by several bullets fired by the security forces. In the corner of the field near a coconut tree, the man fell down dead. It was Warman.[69]

The raid on Warman stemmed from the police's earlier arrest of Asmui Dalimunte, a Darul Islam figure from the West Priangan region. Dalimunte's arrest led the police not only to Warman, but also to other key Darul Islam leaders, including Adah Djaelani, Aceng Kurnia, Ules Sujai, Tahmid Rahmat Basuki, Edi Raidin, Jarul Alam, Opa Mustopa, Syaiful Imam and Ahmad Husein. The entire leadership was arrested, down to village level. In effect, the old Darul Islam generation that had struggled alongside Kartosuwirjo was now in custody. But a new generation of leaders would soon take over the movement.

3
New ideology and new recruits

In its efforts to regroup, it was as important for Darul Islam to revisit its ideology as it was to reform its organisation. Aceng Kurnia, Kartosuwirjo's former aide, made the greatest contribution to this effort. He studied the history of the Prophet Muhammad's struggle, but he was also strongly influenced by the books of Islamist thinkers Sayyid Qutb from Egypt and Abul Ala Maududi from Pakistan, whose works were published in Indonesia in the 1970s. To these ideas Aceng Kurnia contributed his own thoughts – although many did not know it at the time.

Darul Islam's ideology was central to its efforts to recruit new members, particularly in the modernist community in Indonesia. Darul Islam's success in recruiting from among these organisations was, however, also linked to New Order policies that marginalised modernist political activists and led them to seek new vehicles and arenas for their ideas.

Among the new recruits to Darul Islam were two men who would go on to play a critical role in Indonesian jihadist circles in years to come – Abdullah Sungkar and Abu Bakar Ba'asyir. This chapter will explore their growing influence inside the movement, particularly among the Darul Islam community in Yogyakarta and Solo. Indeed, their emergence marked a geographic shift in the movement, from West Java to Central Java, and with it, a new generation of leaders who had no experience of fighting under Kartosuwirjo.

Abdullah Sungkar and Abu Bakar Ba'asyir also reinforced the rise of Salafi ideas in Darul Islam. But Salafism was not the only ideology to influence the thinking of Darul Islam members in Solo and Yogyakarta. They were also deeply influenced by the ideas of the Muslim Brotherhood, particularly with respect to ideological training.

• • •

Ideological reformulation

From the end of the 1960s, Aceng Kurnia had been training the children of Darul Islam families and organising them into Pergerakan Rumah Tangga Islam (PRTI – the Islamic Households Movement). By the mid-1970s Darul Islam leaders had also embarked on a major recruitment drive outside the movement. Most of these recruits were drawn from youths and student activists. To recruit and train new members, Aceng Kurnia reformulated Darul Islam's ideology with a heavy emphasis on *tauhid*.[1] *Tauhid* literally refers to the idea of Allah's oneness and expresses the monotheistic nature of the Islamic faith. While it is one of the fundamental beliefs of Islam, the details and nature of this belief have been the subject of debate by theologians, thinkers and Islamic activists for centuries.

Tauhid has been interpreted in mystical, philosophical and theological ways, but it has also been interpreted politically. Aceng Kurnia's own interpretation focused on the political side, emphasising the implementation of Allah's law and His rule.

Aceng saw a heavy emphasis on *tauhid* as key to the future success of Darul Islam. He noted that the Prophet Muhammad had taken thirteen years in Mecca just to teach his followers this concept.[2] Their strong belief in *tauhid* subsequently led them to sacrifice their possessions and lives in Medina to wage *jihad* until the Islamic community eventually attained victory. The problem for Aceng was that Darul Islam did not possess a comprehensive doctrine on the subject. Kartosuwirjo had provided a relatively complete explanation in several of his books on the concepts of *hijrah* and *jihad*, but he had only made a passing reference to *tauhid*.[3]

As a result Aceng relied on explanations of *tauhid* provided in translations of works by Islamic thinkers from the Middle East and South Asia. Many of these had been published in Indonesia in the 1970s by Dewan Dakwah Islamiyah Indonesia (DDII – the Indonesian Islamic Propagation Council) under the leadership of Muhammad Natsir, the former head of Masyumi, the old Islamist party from the anti-colonial era. After the New Order government banned Natsir from active involvement in the political world, he turned to religious outreach, forming DDII in 1967. DDII worked extensively with international proselytisation organisations like the Saudi-based Rabitah al-Alam al-Islamy (Muslim World League) and the International Islamic Federation of Student Organizations (IIFSO), essentially a university student wing of Rabitah. It obtained funds through IIFSO to translate and print the works of religious scholars, including from the Egyptian Muslim Brother-hood and the Pakistani Jamiat al-Islamy.

Of these works, Sayyid Qutb's *Signposts* (translated into Indo-nesian as *Jalan Yang Lurus*) had a strong impact on Aceng Kurnia's thinking. Qutb wrote that for thirteen years of the Islamic struggle in Mecca, the Prophet Muhammad preached solely on the confes-sional sentence, *la illaha illa llah* ('There is no god but God'). As one of Aceng Kurnia's students noted, the importance of Qutb's inter-pretation of *tauhid* was that it 'went beyond matters of the name and characteristics of Allah, widely taught in the traditions of *ilmu kalam* (the study of theological principles through debate and argu-ment), to include matters pertaining to political power.'[4] According to Qutb, to acknowledge the oneness of Allah is to acknowledge His 'supreme power' – including His political power. Qutb referred to this as *hakimiyah* – the idea that there is no other valid political or legal authority other than Allah and any form of earthly gover-nance would be judged solely by the criteria of whether it applied Allah's laws.

Although Qutb's book provided Aceng with a new understand-ing of *tauhid* as it pertained to *hakimiyah*, Qutb did not explain the doctrine of *tauhid* in detail. For this, Aceng turned to the ideas of the Pakistani Abul Ala Maududi, using his *Islamic Political Theory (Teori Politik Islam)* and *Four Terms in the Qu'ran (Empat Istilah Dalam Al Quran)* as references. In Darul Islam, Aceng's formulation based on these writings came to be known as *Tauhid RMU*.[5] This was a reference to the three components of the doctrine: *tauhid rububi-yah*, based on the Qu'ranic term *rabb*, which refers to Allah as the 'sustainer and master', and which was interpreted by Aceng to mean that absolute authority to make laws rests only in Allah's hands;

tauhid mulkiyah, which means recognition of Allah as *Malik* or King who must be obeyed, manifest in the establishment of Allah's kingdom on earth, which uses His laws to regulate state life; and *tauhid uluhiyah*, the willingness to follow Allah's laws. It should be noted that although Aceng was greatly influenced by Maududi's books, the concept of *tauhid mulkiyah* was relatively original.[6]

The strength of the *Tauhid RMU* doctrine as a recruitment tool lay in its practicality. Previously in Indonesia *tauhid* had frequently been taught with reference to the abstract tradition of *ilmu kalam*, which was difficult to apply in daily life. But because *Tauhid RMU* established acceptance of Allah's laws as a sole indicator of faith it became an easy gauge of the strength of any person's religious commitment. In effect, to reject Allah's laws was to be an unbeliever. Waging *jihad* against the Indonesian government, therefore, which rejected Islamic law, was an expression of faith fighting against unbelief.

Aside from giving Darul Islam a more political focus, *Tauhid RMU* gave rise to a strong *takfiri* strand in Darul Islam thinking. *Takfir* (literally to declare a Muslim an unbeliever) is the practice adopted by some militant Islamist groups whereby fellow Muslims are declared to be apostate, and therefore lawful to kill, if they do not accept the movement's ideas and beliefs. In this view, virtually any Muslim who refused to join Darul Islam was considered apostate.[7] This *takfiri* stance was reflected in *fa'i* robberies that targeted Muslims whom the movement considered to be outside the faith – or at least the faith as they interpreted it.[8] This radical view contradicted Sunni teachings which deem anyone born of Muslim parents, or committed to joining the faith by saying the confessional sentence, to be a Muslim. While Muslims can be considered no longer believers if they abandon fundamental Islamic principles, stringent evidence is required to prove their misdeeds and is usually only decreed by a senior Islamic scholar.

Recruiting the modernists

This new emphasis on *tauhid* brought Darul Islam into closer ideological proximity with modernists. *Tauhid* was a key preoccupation in modernist thinking. But there were other reasons why modernists became attracted to Darul Islam as a movement and why movements such as Muhammadiyah became the major source of new recruits for Darul Islam. Many modernists shared Darul Islam's goal of implementing Islamic law in Indonesia. Others shared the movement's concern at the Communist threat to religion in Indonesia. But an even more important reason was the obstruction of formal political channels of activism for modernist Muslims by the New Order regime.

The New Order government and the army understood that political Islam's influence would rise after the destruction of the Indonesian Communist Party (PKI) in 1965–67. It attempted to deny Islam any opportunity to become a new political force in the country. This was evident in the government's refusal to rehabilitate the Masyumi party. The government banned former Masyumi figures like Muhammad Natsir and Muhammad Roem from participating in formal politics, including from becoming office bearers in Parmusi (Partai Muslimin Indonesia – the Indonesian Muslim Party), a new modernist Islamic party established in 1968.[9]

Following the crushing win of the ruling Golkar party in the 1971 elections, the Suharto government forced all other political parties to amalgamate into just two opposition parties. In January 1973, the United Development Party (PPP – Partai Persatuan Pembangunan) was established as a merger of four Islamic parties including Nahdlatul Ulama and Parmusi. Five nationalist and Christian parties were merged to become the Indonesian Democracy Party (PDI – Partai Demokrasi Indonesia). Except during election campaign periods, these two parties were not permitted to have branches below district level. The ban did not apply to Golkar, which the regime maintained was not actually a political party. From that time onwards, political parties no longer posed a serious challenge to the government.[10]

The government also became increasingly bold in issuing policies that were seen in the Muslim community to be anti-Islamic. For instance the 1973 People's Consultative Assembly (Majelis Permusyawaratan Rakyat – MPR) session removed religion as a foundation for development in the Broad Outlines of State Policy and proposed recognising traditional spiritual movements in Indonesia as religions, placing them on an equal footing with Islam.[11] The same year the government proposed a draft marriage law that placed limits on polygamy and permitted Muslim women to marry non-Muslims.[12]

These actions spawned an ideological backlash among sections of the Muslim community and offered Darul Islam a new opportunity for recruitment. As one internal Darul Islam document noted:

> The Suharto regime's tyranny against the Islamic
> community in reality has been to the advantage of
> progressive Islamic leaders, religious scholars, youths and
> the community, whose holy ambitions remain strong: to

uphold the word of Allah in this homeland of ours. We
have established good cooperation with these groups,
bringing tangible results for the Islamic Revolution in
which we are now leading the way. The people, particularly
the Islamic community, are now truly against the Suharto
regime. This is very different from the Sukarno–Hatta
regime (1950s) which had the full support of the Islamic
community, meaning [many Muslims] automatically
doubted us. As a result at present we do not have too
difficult a task to attract [new members].[13]

Abdullah Sungkar

Most of the Islamic activists that Darul Islam recruited in this period
thus came from modernist Islamic organisations, such as Muhammadiyah, or mass organisations close to DDII, such as Pelajar Islam
Indonesia (PII – Indonesian Islamic Students) and Gerakan Pemuda
Islam (GPI – Islamic Youth Movement). Among those recruited into
the movement were two men who would go onto play a central role
in Darul Islam, and in later years, in jihadist circles in Indonesia:
Abdullah Sungkar and Abu Bakar Ba'asyir. Like other modernists,
Sungkar appears to have been drawn to Darul Islam by the lack
of opportunities to participate in the formal political system. He
once described the ban imposed on former Masyumi members like
Muhammad Natsir as a 'very disturbing and disappointing' New
Order policy.[14]

Sungkar was born in Solo in 1937. He received his religious
education from his father, Ahmad bin Ali Sungkar, an immigrant
from Yemen. As a child Sungkar studied at the al-Irsyad Primary

School in Solo. In 1951 he continued his education at the Modern Islamic School, also in Solo. He was active in Islamic organisations in junior high school, where he joined the al-Irsyad scouts. He also joined the Solo branch of Gerakan Pemuda Islam Indonesia (GPII – the Indonesian Islamic Youth Movement). At a very young age, he had become a sympathiser of the Masyumi Party, led at the time by Muhammad Natsir. Sungkar admired Natsir, whom he often called 'a straightforward and clean politician'.[15]

In 1957, Sungkar graduated from high school. He was unable to continue on to university because his family was unable to finance further study. To help his parents, he traded in *batik*. Sometimes he took his goods as far as his mother's hometown of Jombang in East Java. There he became acquainted with the Ba'asyir family, also of Yemeni descent, and often bought *batik* from them. They had a son the same age as Sungkar, named Abu Bakar Ba'asyir, who would become Sungkar's close friend and comrade.[16]

Although they had known each other for a long time, Sungkar and Ba'asyir only became close friends in 1965 at the time of the pogrom against the Indonesian Communist Party (PKI) that eventually led to the overthrow of the Sukarno regime. At the time Sungkar and Ba'asyir were involved in the al-Irsyad youth movement. Ba'asyir was the general secretary of al-Irsyad Solo, whereas Sungkar was a board member in the movement's religious outreach section. He also forged relationships with Islamic youth figures and politicians in Jakarta including Muhammad Natsir.[17]

In 1967, Sungkar established a radio station in Solo with Ba'asyir and another friend, Hasan Basri, called the al-Irsyad Broadcasting Commission Islamic Proselytization Radio (Radio Dakwah Islam ABC). Other members of al-Irsyad in Solo were not fond of the trio because they considered their preaching to be too hard line. Eventually the three agreed to leave the radio station, but established a new station called Radis (Radio Dakwah Islamiyah Surakarta – Surakarta Islamic Proselytization Radio).[18] They worked together with Abdullah Latif, the owner of the Al Mukmin Islamic Education and Shelter for Orphans and the Poor Foundation (Yayasan Pendidikan Islam dan Asuhan Yatim/Miskin – YPIA) in the Gading Kidul area of Solo. One of the station's policies was its refusal to play Western music. The station proved quite popular and Sungkar and his associates were able to keep it going with donations from a listeners' group that they formed. They also formed a religious study forum at the Solo Grand Mosque that became known as the *dzuhur* (noon) lecture group, because it was usually held after the noon prayer.

In 1970 Muhammad Natsir appointed Sungkar as the head of the Solo branch of DDII and suggested that he establish an Islamic boarding school (*pesantren*). Sungkar welcomed the idea and asked Abdullah Latif to build the school. On 10 March 1972, the Al Mukmin Islamic boarding school was established in Gading Kidul 72A, the same site as their radio station, Radis.[19] After the school had been operating there for several years, Sungkar received financial assistance from Ustadz Asad, a rich supporter in Solo, to buy land in the hamlet of Ngruki, some 13 kilometres north of Sukoharjo town, and moved the school there. After the move the Al Mukmin *pesantren* also became known as the Ngruki Islamic boarding school or Pondok Ngruki.[20]

In his lectures Sungkar repeatedly stressed the importance of upholding Islamic law and of rejecting man-made laws. The Indonesian security forces saw these lectures as a challenge to the state's authority. In 1975 Radis was banned by military authorities in

Central Java, but this did not deter Sungkar. In a lecture at the Solo Grand Mosque, he explicitly invited people to leave the ballot paper blank in the 1977 election as he said there were no leaders fit to vote for.[21]

In 1976, Sungkar decided to form a community (*jama'ah*) that would work toward the establishment of an Islamic state. The idea emerged after he and Ba'asyir had studied the *hadith* of the Prophet. Sungkar felt that the Islamic struggle in Indonesia had paid insufficient attention to Islamic teachings. The struggle had been undertaken through Islamic mass organisations and parties, whereas the Prophet's instructions were clear that the only legitimate struggle was via a community. Sungkar discussed the idea with twelve religious scholars in Solo who were not affiliated to political parties, including Abdullah Tufa'il Saputra and Abdullah Marzuki. They met several times, but when Sungkar and Ba'asyir proposed a community as a vehicle of struggle, the twelve rejected the idea. Sungkar and Ba'asyir decided to go ahead anyway, and planned to call their community Jema'ah Islamiyah.[22]

At this point, however, for reasons that are not clear, Sungkar and Ba'asyir abandoned their plans, deciding to join Darul Islam instead. Sungkar had already forged relations with Darul Islam figures like Hispran, Tahmid Rahmad Basuki and Basyar. In 1976, Hispran and others had been recruiting in Central and East Java and invited Sungkar to join the movement, with its goal of upholding Islamic law in Indonesia. Their aims matched Sungkar's and he and Ba'asyir joined in December 1976. After he had taken the membership oath, Sungkar was appointed as head of Darul Islam in the Solo area and made Ba'asyir his deputy. News of this development reached Muhammad Natsir, who asked Sungkar to choose between the movement and DDII; he could not be a member of both. Sungkar chose Darul Islam.[23] He immediately began recruiting new members in Solo and approached several of his close friends. One was Hasan Basri, one of the founders of Radis radio. In January 1977, Sungkar swore Basri in[24] and gave him authority to recruit others. Sungkar's religious study group students also joined.

In January 1977, Hispran was arrested in a security sweep of Darul Islam members in Java and Sumatra. A senior leader in Central Java who escaped arrest, Ahmad Husein, met Sungkar in Solo and appointed him as Second Commander of Darul Islam's Central Java 2nd Region. Husein also ordered Sungkar to intensify recruitment of new members at the subdistrict level.[25]

On 12 March 1977, eight members of the Indonesian army's Surakarta District Military Command picked up Abdullah Sungkar at his house. They promised to free him after he met with their commander. In fact, Sungkar was held for 48 days at the office of Suharto's internal security administration in Semarang, accused of urging people not to vote in the 1977 election.[26] This short stint in prison did not appear to deter him, and after his release he returned to active preaching and recruitment. He frequently spoke in private at the houses of Darul Islam members in Solo, but also gave public lectures. Usually there would be two sessions for his public talks: a general lecture for the broader public, then a special lecture afterwards that focused on potential recruits for Darul Islam.[27]

Sungkar's entry into Darul Islam marked the growing influence of Salafi ideas inside the movement in Solo and subsequently in Yogyakarta. Sungkar himself was steeped in this approach to Islam. At the Ngruki school, Sungkar relied heavily on the works of Muhammad bin Abdul Wahhab, the 18th-century Islamic scholar whose ideas formed the basis of the Saudi Wahhabi movement.[28] Abdul Wahhab deemed anyone who worshipped or obeyed anything apart from Allah, including laws that did not accord with Islam, to be *thogut* (literally, 'idolator', but it has also taken on the meaning of 'tyrant' or 'oppressor'). Abdul Wahhab's influence was very clearly evident in Sungkar's lectures. Sungkar often criticised the compulsory flag ceremony held at schools every Monday and the playing of the national anthem, considering both idolatrous. As he argued:

> ... it's strange, at 4:30 am when a Muslim is performing the dawn prayer they are still saying *inna shalati wa nusuki wa mahyaya wa mamati lillahi rabbi al alamin* (truly I surrender my prayer, my worship, my life and death to Allah). By 7:00 am that has already changed. 'To you, my country we promise, to you my country we pay homage, for you my country we serve, for you my country, our body and soul.' Just imagine. This is taught at Al Irsyad schools, at Muhammadiyah schools too. It's clearly a church-style song, a Christian composer wrote the song. Then the lyrics are pure idolatry. Just ask, what is idolatry then if this is not? For a Muslim it is clear, we promise to You Allah, we pay homage to You Allah, we serve You Allah, for You Allah our body and soul.[29]

Sungkar and Ba'asyir forbade flag ceremonies at the Ngruki Islamic boarding school, but their concerns went much further. Sungkar argued that the state's use of Pancasila as the source of all law in Indonesia was akin to idolatry because it gave Pancasila the same status as the Qur'an and Islamic *hadith*, which Sungkar believed to be the source of all law for all Muslims.[30] The influence of the Salafi ideas was also evident in the religious practices of Darul Islam members in Solo. Darul Islam cadres strongly rejected traditional Indonesian Islamic practices such as *tahlilan* (chanting at ceremonies for the dead) which they considered to be *bid'ah* (innovation) – one of the main targets of Salafi preaching.

Solo and Yogyakarta

By 1978 Sungkar's hard line views and public lectures began to attract even more attention from state authorities. In a lecture at the Ngadiliwulih Islamic boarding school in Matesih, Karanganyar, Solo on 20 January 1978, Sungkar said Pancasila was the work of humans and meaningless compared to the Qur'an, which was a divine vision. He also charged that two key government officials were Indonesian Communist Party (PKI) members.[31] As a result of the speech, the Surakarta District Military Command again summoned Sungkar for questioning. Knowing what was in store, Sungkar fled and hid in Jombang in East Java.

This did not weaken the movement in Solo, however. Sungkar's friends Abu Bakar Ba'asyir and Hasan Basri took over his duties. A Darul Islam activist from Lampung, Abdul Kadir Baraja, also came to Ngruki from Jakarta to hide from the security forces. While in Jakarta, he finished his manuscript, '*Hijrah* and *Jihad*', which was to become a reference book for Darul Islam in Central Java. Baraja was a friend of Ba'asyir's from their days as high school students at the Gontor Islamic boarding school. The two were also related by marriage.[32] Ba'asyir welcomed Baraja's arrival and used him to replace Sungkar as a teacher at Ngruki.

At the time, Darul Islam had started to spread to Yogyakarta. One of the first to join was Tolkah Mansyur, a university student at the Sunan Kalijaga State Islamic Institute, and he then began to recruit others. In March 1978, he invited a classmate, Yusuf Latief, to visit the Ngruki school. There the two of them met Abdul Kadir Baraja who convinced Yusuf to join Darul Islam. Yusuf then met Abu Bakar Ba'asyir, who gave him the task of recruiting members in Yogyakarta.[33]

Tolkah and Yusuf performed their task well. Within a month, they were able to encourage their friends to come to Ngruki to be sworn in as new members. Among them were Fihirudin (now known as Abu Jibril) and Hasan Bauw, a State Islamic Institute student from Papua, whom Hasan Basri inducted with Abu Bakar Ba'asyir as witness. The two Ngruki teachers then ordered the students to form a command structure in Yogyakarta and conduct a Darul Islam recruitment and training program. They were also granted permission to swear in new members.[34]

In early May 1978, the Darul Islam structure in Yogyakarta was formed. At a meeting at the Sudirman Mosque in Yogyakarta, Hasan Bauw was chosen as the leader of Darul Islam Yogyakarta. Yusuf Latief and Mulyono were chosen as deputies.[35] They began to recruit through public religious study sessions, attracting both university students and members of the general public. They monitored the participants and approached the most enthusiastic, inviting them to private discussions where they talked about the obligation to uphold Islamic law and about *jihad* as the way to do this.

In May 1978, Darul Islam Solo gained a new leader. Abdullah Umar, a Darul Islam member from Medan accused of involvement in Komando Jihad, came to Ngruki. Like Baraja, Umar came to

Solo to hide from the security forces. Ba'asyir welcomed Umar as another alumnus of the Gontor Islamic boarding school and gave him the dual task of teaching at Ngruki and training Darul Islam members in Yogyakarta.[36]

In 1978, a coordination meeting was held between the Darul Islam structures in Solo and Yogyakarta. The meeting was held in Abdullah Sungkar's hiding place in Jombang. Hasan Bauw and Yusuf Latief were among those present from Yogyakarta. Abu Bakar Ba'asyir, Abdul Kadir Baraja and Abdullah Umar represented Solo. The Yogyakarta delegation argued that now was the time to commence an armed struggle. Sungkar disagreed and said religious training had to be the immediate priority.[37] After the meeting, the Darul Islam Yogyakarta members increased their special religious study sessions to once a week.

Another coordination meeting between Solo and Yogyakarta was held in August 1978 in Yogyakarta, with Sungkar in attendance. Abu Bakar Ba'asyir, Hasan Basri and Abdullah Umar represented Solo. Hasan Bauw and Yusuf Latief were among around nine members who represented Yogyakarta. The meeting discussed the idea of recruiting all Ngruki students into Darul Islam.[38] It was felt, however, that it would be difficult for all the students, particularly the younger ones, to keep their membership secret, so the idea was rejected. Participants also agreed to a plan to invite Islamic figures in Yogyakarta to join Darul Islam and set out to lobby, among others, Syahirul Alim, a lecturer at Gadjah Mada University; Basyir Wahid, a lecturer at the same university; A.R. Fahrudin, the chair of Muhammadiyah's Central Board; and Syafi'i Maarif, a lecture at the Yogyakarta Teacher Training Institute. None responded positively.[39]

In November 1978 a Darul Islam coordination meeting was held for all of Central Java. Delegates came to Kudus from across Central Java, including Solo, Yogyakarta, Boyolali, Semarang, Magelang, Sragen, Brebes, Kebumen, Purwokerto and Pati. Nuri Suharsono attended the meeting, representing Yogyakarta. Ahmad Husein, the Central Java 2nd Region Commander, led the meeting. The meeting agreed to establish Central Java as a *hijrah* area for Darul Islam activists from outside Java whom the security forces were pursuing, including Warman and Farid Ghozali.

The idea that Central Java could serve as a safe haven proved to be mistaken, however. On 10 November 1978 the security forces traced Sungkar and apprehended him in Keplaksari village, Peterongan, Jombang. A week later Hasan Basri and Abu Bakar Ba'asyir were also arrested, together with several other of Sungkar's followers, including Sunarto and Fihirudin.

The arrests of Sungkar and Ba'asyir angered their followers, in particular the university students in Yogyakarta, who were determined to take revenge. Their target was Parmanto, a lecturer at the Sebelas Maret University in Solo who was accused of leaking information to the security forces. In January 1979, Hasan Bauw, Warman, Farid Ghozali and Abdullah Umar murdered Parmanto at his house. Soon after, however, the security forces detected the presence of Warman and his associates in Yogyakarta. They captured Abdul Kadir Baraja and shot Farid Ghozali dead. The capture gave rise to suspicion that there was treachery within Darul Islam ranks. Warman and his associates suspected Hasan Bauw had 'sold' Ghozali and Baraja to the security forces. They reported this to Ahmad Husein in Kudus. Husein then ordered Warman to execute Hasan Bauw, which he did in January 1979.[40] Not long after,

Warman was captured by security forces. Abdullah Umar, Yusuf Latief, Nuri Suharsono and others were also among those arrested and sent to Mlaten prison in Semarang, where they joined Sungkar and Ba'asyir.

Although their leaders were now detained, Darul Islam cadres in Solo and Yogyakarta continued with their struggle, led by some of the new recruits. Two figures in Yogyakarta played a particularly important role. They were Muchliansyah and Irfan Awwas Suryahardy. Muchliansyah came from Kalimantan and studied at the Indonesian Islamic University (UII) in Yogyakarta. Irfan Awwas was Fihirudin's younger brother, a student at the Sunan Kalijaga State Islamic Institute. To avoid capture, Muchliansyah and Irfan, along with the Darul Islam cadres who had eluded the security forces, joined the Yogyakarta Mosque Youth Coordination Board (BKPM – Badan Koordinasi Pemuda Muslim) as an organisational cover. They were also active in the Sudirman Mosque's youth association (Himamumes – Himpunan Angkatan Muda Mesjid).

This strategy proved quite effective. Muchliansyah and Irfan were able to re-organise the remaining Darul Islam members in Yogyakarta and Solo. Meanwhile, several Darul Islam cadres who had been arrested were released in early 1981, Sunarto and Fihirudin among them.[41] After their release, the movement began to show signs of life again, in particular by applying organisational ideas from a new source – the Muslim Brotherhood.

Influence of the Muslim Brotherhood

While Salafi ideas continued to permeate its ideology, the Darul Islam movement adopted the Egyptian Muslim Brotherhood's teaching and training method, called *usroh* (or, in Arabic, *nizam al-usar*). An *usroh* is a small religious study group with around ten to fifteen members led by a *naqib*, who is responsible for providing religious instruction to the members once a week. It is not just an ordinary study group, however. *Usroh* in Arabic means family, and *usroh* groups were as close as families, bound not by blood but by religion. Emotional and personal ties among members were firmly established. This closeness resulted from three firmly applied concepts: *ta'aruf*, or mutual familiarity among *usroh* members; *tafaahun*, or mutual understanding; and *takaful*, mutual help.[42]

Muslim Brotherhood influence on Darul Islam arose in part from the translation of the writings of Muslim Brotherhood scholars, many of which were published in Indonesia in the 1970s and 1980s. Darul Islam activists also met with several Brotherhood figures who came to Indonesia in connection with the Arabic Language Education Institute (Lembaga Pendidikan Bahasa Arab – LPBA), which was established in Jakarta in 1980.[43] Founded by the Imam Muhammad bin Saud Islamic University in Riyadh, Saudi Arabia, LPBA cooperated extensively with the Muhammad Natsir–led DDII. Apart from providing Arabic language instruction, it also had a program to provide guest lecturers to *pesantren*.

On DDII's recommendation, LPBA sent lecturers. some of whom were Muslim Brotherhood activists, to teach at Ba'asyir and Sungkar's Ngruki school. They included Khalim Khamada, a Brotherhood member originally from Iraq. The visitors also brought books by Brotherhood religious scholars that had not yet been translated into Indonesian.[44] These included the works of Sayyid Qutb, Syrian Muslim Brotherhood intellectual Sayyid Hawa, and Brotherhood founder, Hassan al-Banna. These books were copied and taken to the Darul Islam inmates in Semarang prison. There, Sungkar, Abu Bakar Ba'asyir, Abdullah Umar and others studied them and agreed that they would be added to Darul Islam training materials in Solo and Yogyakarta.

The books were attractive in part because their arguments were similar to those used in Darul Islam's doctrine of *Tauhid RMU* (*rububiyah, mulkiyah* and *uluhiyah*). Darul Islam cadres in Solo and Yogyakarta used Sayyid Qutb's *In the Shade of the Qur'an* (*Fi Zilal al-Qur'an*) to interpret the Qur'an. Some of its contents were translated and serialised in a bulletin that Muchliansyah edited. The influence of these Brotherhood ideas was clearly illustrated by Sungkar's use of Sayyid Hawa's *al-Islam* in his defence plea when he finally came to trial in 1982, after being held since his arrest in 1979. He used the book to criticise the idea that Pancasila was the source of all law in Indonesia, arguing that this was idolatry, an unforgivable sin for which the perpetrator could be eternally tortured in hell.

Syahirul Alim

In addition to building the *usroh* system, activists in Yogyakarta and Solo also sought to convince local Islamic figures to join Darul Islam. As noted above, one of the figures approached was Syahirul Alim, a chemistry lecturer at the Gadjah Mada University Faculty of Mathematics and Science. He was also a preacher and DDII Yogyakarta activist. Among student activists in Yogyakarta, Alim was a popular speaker and *tauhid* was one of his favourite themes. In lectures he often discussed the importance of purifying *tauhid* by rejecting all forms of idolatry. In his view, anything that was praised, worshipped or revered to a greater degree than Allah was an idol; it could be an object, a law or a conviction or belief.[45]

In early 1982, Fihirudin was given the task of approaching Syahirul Alim because among Yogyakarta cadres he was considered the most senior, with the broadest religious knowledge. Fihirudin introduced himself as a mosque activist. He said he wished other mosque youth in Yogyakarta would be more militant in their preaching. According to Fihirudin, the entire Muslim community in Indonesia aspired to a country blessed by Allah, which could only happen if the community fully implemented Islamic law. Alim was impressed with Fihirudin at their first meeting, particularly by his fiery and fluent speaking style. 'I was pleased to see there was an Islamic youth with such enthusiasm,' said Alim.[46] Fihirudin did not touch upon Darul Islam and its goal of an Indonesian Islamic State in his first three meetings with Syahirul, but rather kept the discussion to religious issues and ways of upholding Islamic law.[47]

As Syahirul recalled, 'It was only in about the fourth meeting that he said that the aim was an Islamic state called Negara Islam Indonesia, not a Pancasila State', because the content of Pancasila was unclear and could easily be idolatrous.[48] Fihirudin's statement startled the professor and he tried to refute it, saying that although Indonesia was a Pancasila state, it guaranteed freedom of worship. Fihirudin rejected this argument. He said that although Muslims were free to worship, Islamic law did not apply in full in Indonesia and many officials were non-Muslims. Many other officials said they were Muslims, but actually followed traditional spiritual beliefs. Syahirul answered that Islamic law could not be applied when the majority of Muslims had minimal religious knowledge; they needed a long period of instruction first. Fihirudin responded that the instruction process would not be effective if not conducted by the state.[49]

The meeting ended when Syahirul cut off what he considered to be a dangerous discussion, but Fihirudin was not discouraged and he continued to come to visit. 'In the ensuing meetings Fihirudin and I just went back and forth debating whether or not there was a need for NII,' said Syahirul. In these meetings, Fihirudin became angry when the professor said that religion could not be forced, and that if it were Allah's will then Islamic law would be in force in Indonesia. According to Syahirul, Fihirudin retorted:

> Don't take cover behind fate. It's obligatory for us to work
> to establish Negara Islam Indonesia in accordance with the
> message from the Imam, Daud Beureueh, and the scholars
> who preceded him like Kartosuwirjo and Tjokroaminoto, and
> also following the example of the Islamic community in other
> countries like Pakistan, Iran, Saudi Arabia, Jordan and others.[50]

Syahirul argued back, saying that the best reference was the Qur'an, where the term 'Islamic state' does not appear. But Fihirudin countered that Islamic law could not be upheld without state institutions.[51]

After some twelve meetings, Fihirudin invited Syahirul to join Darul Islam. The professor was still hesitant and asked Fihirudin to name other Darul Islam members in Yogyakarta and Central Java. Fihirudin mentioned one name that Syahirul Alim knew, namely Abdullah Sungkar; he would not name any others. He said that if Syahirul wanted to get to know other members, he was welcome to come to the next meeting at the Sudirman Mosque. Syahirul agreed.[52] A week later, around March 1982, Alim met some ten Darul Islam members from Yogyakarta and Solo, including Adung, Irfan Awwas, Najib Mabruri and Muchliansyah. Fihirudin announced Syahirul as a new member and the professor, who had been hesitant a week earlier, did not contradict him.[53]

A new leader and new revolutionary plans

In April 1982, Darul Islam members in Yogyakarta began to establish contacts with some of the fugitives in Jakarta and West Java who were still in hiding. One man they approached was senior Darul Islam figure Muhammad Jabir, the son-in-law of Aceng Kurnia and a member of the movement in South Sulawesi. Through Jabir they also established relations with Ageng Sutisna and Nuriman, two of Aceng Kurnia's students. Their aim was to reconsolidate the movement.

In August 1982 the first meeting between the Yogyakarta and West Java branches of the movement was held in Yogyakarta. Ageng Sutisna, representing West Java, met with Fihirudin and Muchliansyah. At the meeting Fihirudin passed on the information that Syahirul Alim had officially become a Darul Islam member and suggested that he be invited to the meeting scheduled for that night. Sutisna agreed. After evening prayers, Sutisna, Fihirudin, Muchliansyah and Syahirul discussed how to rebuild the Darul Islam movement. Ageng pointed to the disarray and conflict in the movement since Adah Djaelani's arrest. All agreed that the question of Darul Islam's leadership had to be immediately resolved. The idea emerged to appoint Syahirul Alim as Darul Islam leader in Central Java.

Meanwhile, at the end of 1982, Abdullah Sungkar and Abu Bakar Ba'asyir were released after standing trial at Sukoharjo District Court in Surakarta. The prosecutor sought a sentence of 15 years, and the judge sentenced them to nine. The pair appealed to the Central Java High Court, which reduced their sentence to four years. The prosecutor then appealed to the Supreme Court, but that appeal stalled. Because the High Court's reduction of their sentence matched time served, the two were released.[54]

Shortly thereafter, Darul Islam activists from Jakarta, West Java and Central Java gathered in Solo. They included Muhammad Jabir (Jakarta), Abdullah Sungkar (Solo), Abu Bakar Ba'asyir (Solo), Mursalin Dahlan (Jakarta/Bandung), Muchliansyah (Yogyakarta), Fihirudin (Yogyakarta), Irfan Awwas (Yogyakarta), Syahirul Alim (Yogyakarta), Ageng Sutisna (Bandung) and Thoriqudin (Kudus). Sungkar opened the meeting and said that its purpose was to appoint a new Imam. Sutisna suggested Sungkar, but Sungkar refused, saying conditions did not allow it, for although he had just been released, he could be detained again if the Supreme Court granted the prosecutor's appeal.

He nominated Syahirul Alim.[55] The other participants agreed. Initially the professor was hesitant. He said he was a civil servant, besides which his wife did not wear a headscarf, but the forum responded that these were not obstacles. Sungkar also explained that the position was temporary in nature and that Daud Beureueh, who was sick and under house arrest, still formally held the position of all-Indonesia Imam of Negara Islam Indonesia. In the end, Syahirul agreed.[56]

The selection of Syahirul Alim as Imam marked a shift in the movement's leadership from West to Central Java. Moreover, for the first time the movement came under the leadership of an individual with no experience of waging war under Kartosuwirjo. Some members of Darul Islam's Jakarta 9th Regional Command, led by Abi Karim, alias Solihin, rejected the appointment, dismissing it as unconstitutional. They decided at the meeting to split with Sungkar.

Despite the new Imam's initial reluctance to become a member, Darul Islam would be no less militant under Syahirul Alim. In a meeting in Solo in 1983, he suggested that the movement engage in armed resistance, including using a bomb to assassinate President Suharto at the inauguration of the renovated Borobudur temple in late February 1983. The assassination would be part of a plan to overthrow the New Order. The inspiration for such a lofty aim had come from the Islamic revolution in Iran in 1979 – which was ironic, given the antipathy most Salafis feel toward Shia Muslims. Unlike Iran, however, the Islamic revolution in Indonesia would fail.

4
Revolution

Many Darul Islam members thought that Indonesia was as ripe for revolution as Iran. At the beginning of the 1980s the opposition to the Suharto regime was strengthening and it was not confined to Islamic groups. Against this background Darul Islam members planned a popular uprising, carrying out acts of terrorism and trying to foment revolution in cooperation with other like-minded groups outside the Darul Islam movement. But the revolution they proclaimed in early 1983 ended in failure. In the aftermath, Darul Islam members left politics behind and returned to a focus on training and preaching. The Salafi nature of the movement also became increasingly pronounced.

• • •

The Iranian Revolution

The selection of Syahirul Alim in January 1983 as Darul Islam's new Imam marked a new era for the movement. The domination of the older generation leadership had ended. It was also a time of growing anger toward the Suharto regime. Darul Islam increasingly saw the New Order government not just as an opponent of Islamic law but as a threat to the survival of Indonesia's Muslim community. They considered the New Order government to be worse than the Dutch colonial regime. As one member argued:

> In hundreds of years of colonising this country the Dutch only concentrated on the economy, and did not heed matters of belief. By contrast the current regime uses nationalism under the guise of unity with the aim of wiping out Islam in this country, even trying to extract Islam from the minds of its adherents. In politics, they have introduced spiritual beliefs in the Broad Outlines of State Policy (GBHN – Garis-garis Besar Haluan Negara) as a rival religion, even though the majority of the nation does not agree. In education too, they have poisoned the students' faith with PMP (Pancasila Moral Education) lessons. The next step will be to relentlessly isolate and terrorise students who wear the headscarf as part of their Muslim identity, and if needed for the Minister of Education and Culture to forbid people who wear the headscarf from studying at state schools. The reality is that many already have moved to private schools.[1]

This concern for the fate of their fellow Indonesian Muslims marked a shift in Darul Islam's thinking. In the 1970s, Darul Islam cared little for the problems Muslims faced in Indonesia. It was silent when other Islamic organisations protested government decisions which were seen as hostile to Muslims. Darul Islam leaders saw any Muslim who was not a member of their movement as be living in a state of ignorance akin to the pre-Islamic period that preceded the Prophet's establishment of the first Muslim community.[2] This stance toward other Muslims began to change, however, as Darul Islam cadres from Solo and Yogyakarta took over the leadership. One reason was a revision in the movement's radical *takfiri* stance which saw virtually anyone outside the movement labeled as an unbeliever. This revision took place in the early 1980s and was partly the result of discussions between Darul Islam leaders and Muslim Brotherhood activists who were teaching at the Arabic Language Education Institute (LPBA). From this point on, Darul Islam members in Yogyakarta and Solo confined their *takfiri* stance to the government and its agents.[3] This correction gave rise to a new view of the wider Muslim community in Indonesia. They now saw their fellow Muslims not as pagans and unbelievers but as victims of an apostate anti-Islamic government.[4]

Darul Islam began to express its anger towards the Suharto government openly. Its magazine, *al-Ikhwan*, criticised government policies and called the New Order regime 'the most infidel, cruelest and most oppressive tyrant!'[5] The decision to be open in its political opposition was also a break from the more secretive tactics of the past. In part it reflected the nature of Darul Islam's membership at the time. In Yogyakarta, the majority of Darul Islam members were university students, a group that in Indonesia has long played a key role in sociopolitical protest. Another reason for this more confrontational stance was Abdullah Sungkar, who never shied away from openly challenging the state. His willingness to do so was evident during his 1982 court trial. He turned his defence plea into an attack on human rights violations, corruption, electoral misdeeds, Pancasila and violence by the military against the Muslim community.[6]

There was, however, a third factor that drove Darul Islam's new willingness to openly confront the state – the Iranian revolution. Ayatollah Khomeini became a respected figure among Darul Islam activists. Abu Bakar Ba'asyir said that after the Iranian Revolution, many posters of Khomeini were put up in the Ngruki school. This would be unimaginable today, because the Ngruki school is strongly anti-Shi'ite, in line with Salafi ideology. At the time, however, people were not too concerned with the differences between Sunnis and Shi'ites and were impressed by Khomeini's success in bringing down a regime considered to be anti-Islamic.

After the revolution the Iranian Embassy in Jakarta began a major propaganda effort in Indonesia. One part of this effort was a magazine called *Yaum al-Quds*, published by the Iranian Embassy Information and Press Section in Jakarta and distributed for free. It contained stories about the revolution and provocative speeches made by Khomeini inviting the Muslim community to oppose all anti-Islamic regimes. Translations of books by Iranian intellectuals and religious scholars also provided a new, more revolutionary viewpoint on Islam.[7] Indeed, the Iranian success convinced Islamic activists in Indonesia, in particular Darul Islam members, that they could carry out a similar revolution at home.[8]

The idea of seizing power through popular revolution was a novelty for Darul Islam. Darul Islam had always thought that armed action was the one and only path to defeat the Indonesian government. For young Darul Islam activists like Syahirul Alim, Muchliansyah, Fihirudin and their associates, however, armed *jihad* was not an option because they did not have the military capabilities or weapons. A people's revolution was more plausible. Moreover, they saw a political opportunity to mobilise the Muslim community and other groups, given the growing opposition to Suharto.

One trigger for this opposition among Muslim activists had been rumours of a document called Masterplan for the Nation's Development (*Master Plan Pembangunan Bangsa*) published by Indonesia's Centre for Strategic and International Studies (CSIS). The study reportedly argued that Islam was the greatest obstacle to development in Indonesia, meaning a path must be sought to erode the values of Islamic teachings among the Indonesian Islamic community. It was rumoured that this line was quoted by General M. Panggabean, Armed Forces Commander and Defence Minister, in an armed forces leadership meeting in January 1978. He was reported to have said that the Muslim community was the most dangerous enemy of the government.[9] No one ever produced a copy of the alleged document, and it is not clear that it ever existed, but some Muslim leaders believed the statements to be true.

Belief in such a master plan increased after the government issued policies perceived as anti-Islamic. This included the state's recognition of traditional Javanese mysticism as a religion. This was seen as an effort to undermine the Muslim community. Abdul Qadir Djaelani, a leader of Gerakan Pemuda Islam Indonesia (GPII – Indonesian Islamic Youth Movement), argued at the time:

> the first aim of the recognition of Javanese mysticism
> is to destroy the majority of the Islamic community in
> Indonesia, with the hope that the millions of Muslims in
> Java referred to as *abangan* [those who incorporate Javanese
> cultural traditions into their religious practice] can be

103

classed as members of mystic groups and leave behind their Islamic identity. If these efforts succeed, the Islamic community will lose 40 to 50 million members, a very large number.[10]

Another concern was government efforts to deepen the indoctrination of school students, university students and civil servants in Pancasila, which was viewed as anti-Islamic. Opposition was not just limited to radical activists. In November 1977 the Indonesian Council of Islamic Scholars (Majelis Ulama Indonesia – MUI), a body created by Suharto, firmly rejected the effort to raise the status of Javanese mysticism and to deepen Pancasila indoctrination.[11]

The government's moves prompted protests on the street and in the parliament. A number of Islamic youth groups formed an Action Front that held street protests during the March 1978 session of the People's Consultative Assembly (MPR). They also planned to surround the CSIS office in Tanah Abang to seize the alleged Development Master Plan. Their protests ended in violence and a car was burned near the Hotel Indonesia roundabout. The orchestrator of the Action Front, Abdul Qadir Djaelani, was arrested by security forces.[12] Within the parliament the Islamic United Development Party (PPP) rejected the Pancasila indoctrination program and the decision to recognise Javanese mysticism, and walked out of the MPR General Session in protest.

Islamic groups were not the only source of opposition to the government, however. Before the 1977 election, students from the country's premier universities – the University of Indonesia, Bandung Institute of Technology, Bandung Agricultural Institute, Gadjah Mada University and others – actively campaigned for voters to leave their ballot forms blank in response to the violations and intimidation that had marked the election campaign. In early 1978, the student movement aimed its protest directly at the centre of power. They criticised President Suharto's leadership and called for him to step down. They outlined their criticism in the 'White Book of the Student Struggle' (*Buku Putih Perjuangan Mahasiswa*), which pointed to the errors that had been made in Indonesia's development. The book criticised the government for pervasive corruption and repressive actions against community members who expressed dissenting views.[13] The government responded to these criticisms with an iron fist. In mid-January 1978, the army was ordered to occupy campuses. Some 34 student leaders were arrested, and the government froze the student councils and banned the student press on a number of campuses. A new decree was issued entitled 'Normalising Campus Life' which proscribed political activity on campus and limited student activities to areas like sport, the arts and religion.[14]

The Suharto regime also faced opposition from among retired military personnel, particularly former members of the Siliwangi, Diponegoro and Brawijaya divisions – the main Java-based divisions – of the army. From the mid-1970s, former members joined together in the Brawijaya–Siliwangi–Diponegoro (Brasildi) Forum, where they discussed national political developments and the role of the armed forces. In April 1978, the Army Chief of Staff, General Widodo, formally incorporated this discussion group into what was called the Communication Forum for Army Retired Senior Officers (Fosko-AD). Although General Widodo financed their activities, Fosko-AD continued to criticise government policies. It called, for example, for the sociopolitical role of the armed forces to be reappraised. It also argued that the military should adopt a neutral political stance and abandon active support for the ruling Golkar party. These criticisms enraged the government and in 1979, General Widodo replaced Fosko-AD with a Retired Soldier Study and Communication Forum. None of the new forum's studies or activities were to be communicated externally, but it did not end military criticism of the regime.[15] The government was particularly concerned because it appeared a number of active duty officers supported the criticisms advanced by their retired colleagues.

In the face of this opposition, Suharto went on the offensive. At an armed forces leadership meeting in Pekanbaru, Riau on 27 March 1980, Suharto attacked all rival ideologies to the Pancasila, from Marxism to Islam. He reminded the armed forces of their commitment to defend Pancasila and the 1945 Constitution. He argued that this meant that the military needed to be close to the one political force that had shown its commitment to both – namely, Golkar. A month later Suharto repeated these same ideas at a speech marking the anniversary of the Indonesian army special forces, Kopassus. He also took the opportunity to refute rumours that he had a mistress, and rejected accusations of corruption surrounding his family.[16]

The president's speech drew an immediate response from his critics. The Armed Forces Commander, Mohammad Jusuf, stated that the president's speech did not represent the military's views. Not long afterwards, the Retired Soldier Study and Communication Forum invited various opposition groups to a meeting to discuss the president's two speeches. They formulated a 'Statement of Concern' signed by 50 prominent Indonesians including former prime ministers, former senior army officers and other political figures. This became known as the 'Petition of 50' (Petisi 50). It accused Suharto of using Pancasila as a tool to attack his political opponents and of misusing the Armed Forces by demanding it take sides in political matters. The petition rapidly circulated on the streets, even though the government had forbidden the media from publishing statements by the group's members.[17] Suharto also took economic revenge on the signatories, for example by denying them credit at banks, although their international reputation afforded them a degree of protection; they could not easily be arrested.[18] Petisi 50 became the most important opposition group during the 1980s and its act of opposition continued to resonate for years.

Revolution *à la* Iran

It was against this background that a number of Darul Islam activists, together with two individuals, Mursalin Dahlan and H.M. Sanusi, plotted a popular revolution. Mursalin was a Darul Islam member but also an activist in Badan Pembangunan Muslimin Indonesia (BPMI – Indonesian Muslim Development Agency); Sanusi was a member of Petisi 50. They had very different ambitions for this uprising. While Mursalin wanted to form an Islamic state, Sanusi's aim was a secular democracy. What united them was their desire to overthrow the Suharto regime.

In Sanusi's view, Suharto should be replaced by a coalition of opposition groups that he dubbed Nasabri, an acronym for the Indonesian words for 'nationalist', 'religious' and 'armed forces'. The Nasabri coalition would implement democratic reforms which would see the creation of a number of political parties, including Islamic parties. Darul Islam members like Muchliansyah, Fihirudin and Dahlan strongly believed that because the majority of Indonesians were Muslims, Islamic parties would dominate. When the Islamic parties won the election, they would eventually establish an Islamic government.

Sanusi offered a concept for overthrowing the Suharto regime which he called 'Strategy for the Phases of Revolution'. This strategy imitated the stages of the revolution in Iran.[19] In the first phase of the Iranian revolution, the Shah was forced to flee the country. In Indonesia Suharto's rule had to be ended by either forced exile or assassination. The second phase would be a brief transitional period, as it had been in Iran, with the vice-president becoming president in accordance with the Constitution, to maintain stability. In the third phase the transitional arrangement would be swept away; in Iran Ayatollah Khomeini became the new head of state, and in Indonesia the Nasabri coalition would assume power. In the fourth phase, popular demonstrations in support of the new leadership would be organised, as they had been in Iran. In the fifth phase, the state apparatus would be purged. The sixth phase would see a new democratic political system established. Whereas in Iran in the seventh phase, an Islamic state was proclaimed, Indonesia would return to the Jakarta Charter and implement a system of Islam *kaffah* – comprehensive Islam.

Mursalin, Fihirudin and the others enthusiastically welcomed Sanusi's strategy of phased revolution. Fihirudin, representing Darul Islam Yogyakarta members, suggested that the takeover of power in phase one could be achieved through mass demonstrations in Jakarta. The demonstrations would be packaged as a Grand Rally which would begin at the huge Istiqlal Mosque in Jakarta. Fihirudin and his associates asked that Syahirul Alim, Darul Islam's Imam, sit on the Nasabri coalition as a representative of the movement. The plan was to begin the revolution in 1983, in the lead-up to that year's MPR General Session.

To prepare the first steps, Sanusi asked Mursalin to train militant cadres who could strengthen the popular bases of the revolution. Mursalin did so through BPMI, which had a program in Bandung called Pesantren Express, a short immersion course in Islamic values. Participants were usually young activists from various Muslim community organisations. Student groups from universities and high schools were particularly prominent, with the organisations Ikatan Mahasiswa Muhammadiyah (IMM – Muhammadiyah Students Association) and Pelajar Islam Indonesia (PII – Indonesian Islamic Students) well represented, as well as the network of high school Islamic study clubs called ROHIS.

The training was not too different from that of Darul Islam's *usroh* groups in Solo and Yogyakarta. In addition to religious training, the goal of Pesantren Express was to establish a sense of community. Participants worshipped, slept and ate together. The program culminated on the final morning, approaching dawn, when the instructor made each participant swear an oath of allegiance that included a promise to struggle to uphold Islamic law and to avoid committing great sins. After the oath-taking, there was another ritual to close the event. The participants were given new *hijrah* names that were more Islamic than their original ones. The aim was not to hide participants' identities, but to remind them that they had now fled from unbelief to Islam.[20]

All of the Pesantren Express graduates were put in groups called *fiah qolilah*, which resembled the *usroh* groups, led by a *naqib*. They met once a week, usually on Saturday night. The meeting commenced with a reading of the Qur'an and a test of each participant's memorisation of a passage. After that, the *naqib* would normally lecture on religion, and this was followed by discussion. Usually the meeting ended there, but sometimes they would then sleep, wake for early morning prayer and then engage in morning sporting activities together.

Together with the Darul Islam cadres from Yogyakarta and Solo the members of the *fiah qolilah* constituted the core strength of the revolutionary movement that Mursalin and Sanusi were building. In 1982, Mursalin organised a consolidation meeting in Bandung that agreed that all BPMI networks and Pesantren Express programs in West Java and East Java would be put under the auspices of a new body called Pesantren Express Development and Education Institute (Lembaga Pendidikan dan Pengembangan Pesantren Kilat – LP3K). The focus of LP3K activities would be to organise more training activities and *fiah qolilah*, with the aim of producing revolutionary cadres.[21]

The plan to assassinate Suharto

On 4 May 1982, Indonesia held a general election, and Golkar won 62.11 per cent of the vote – slightly more than it received in 1977. Suharto felt empowered by the victory. On 19 July 1982, in front of the leadership of the Indonesian National Youth Committee, he declared his intention to make the Pancasila the sole ideological basis for the Indonesian state. Implicitly, he was saying that any organisation or party that had an ideology other than the Pancasila had no right to exist in Indonesia. The president's speech incensed Darul Islam members. For them, Suharto's words were an act of apostasy and an attack on Islam. In August 1982, the would-be revolutionaries organised a large meeting in Jakarta. Muhammad Achwan came representing Surabaya and Malang. Enceng Syarif represented Bandung. Syahirul Alim, Muchliansyah and Fihirudin represented Yogyakarta and Solo. Jakarta's representative was Hasanudin Hajad, an Acehnese who claimed that Daud Beureueh had appointed him as commander of Darul Islam's army. In the meeting, Sanusi demanded that the Muslim community as the majority in Indonesia save the country from Suharto's dictatorship.

The first step was to assassinate Suharto, prior to launching a popular action in the form of a Grand Rally for Muslim Unity. Even before the August coordination meeting Sanusi was already preparing a special team to carry out the assassination. Its members were Nuriman and Ageng Sutisna, two of Mursalin's old colleagues. The plan was to bomb the presidential motorcade on one of central Jakarta's main streets, Jalan Cut Mutia.[22]

Meanwhile, the planning for the Grand Rally continued, with Syahirul Alim bringing two close friends, Marwan Ashuri and Sudjatmono, into the plot. Both were former GPII Central Java activists and, according to Syahirul, experts in mobilising crowds. In September 1982, Sanusi asked them to work with Mursalin, BPMI activist Nunung Nurul and Hasanudin Hajad on the rally. The conspirators discussed how to accommodate protestors from various provinces in Indonesia in Jakarta without attracting the suspicion of the security forces. They agreed to use mosques. Plans were even made for Hasanudin Hajad to prepare 1000 fully armed men to become a revolutionary guard to safeguard the new cabinet that would be formed.[23]

Towards the end of 1982 Mursalin, Muchliansyah and Fihirudin began to prepare their cadres to depart for Jakarta. Sanusi meanwhile finalised his strategy for his seven-stage revolution and established contact with activists in a number of Islamic mass organisations. He presented his strategy at a meeting in Yogyakarta in the second week of December 1982 at Sudirman Mosque, attended by, among others, Dahlan, Fihirudin, Irfan Awwas, Syahirul Alim and Muhammad Achwan. They reviewed the plan. First, the small team led by Mursalin would assassinate Suharto 'before the first rooster crowed in 1983'.[24] Second, they would hold a massive rally to support the new government and cabinet. Sanusi claimed he already had the support of a number of Islamic groups including BKPMI (Badan Koordinasi Pemuda Masjid Indonesia – the Indonesian Mosque Youth Coordination Board), Perguruan Tinggi Dakwah Islam (PTDI – Islamic Propagation Institutes), Gerakan Pemuda Islam (GPI – Islamic Youth Movement) and Lembaga Studi Islam (LSI – Islamic Study Institute).[25]

A revolutionary organisation under Sanusi's leadership would also be established consisting of six sections – Finance and Logistics, Mass Mobilisation, Coalition Building, Freeing Political Prisoners, Intelligence and Security, and Sabotage and Kidnapping.[26] To safeguard the revolution, they discussed the kidnapping and assassination of the men of Suharto's inner circle, whom they considered anti-Islamic. They included Daud Yusuf, Minister of Education and Culture; Ali Moertopo, now Minister of Information; Amir Machmud, Home Affairs Minister; Amir Murtono, head of Golkar; and L.B. 'Benny' Murdani, commander of the armed forces. Syahirul Alim asked Sanusi at the meeting whether he had consulted with, or gained the approval of, Muslim community figures such as

Muhammad Natsir for the plan. Sanusi answered that clearly Natsir would not agree, but if the revolution were to succeed Natsir would 'smile and be happy'. He also said that Natsir would be included in the new government.[27]

The plan remained a plan, however. By the end of 1982 Suharto was still very much alive. In December, Nuriman reported to Sanusi that their tests of the remote control bomb had failed. He suggested using a rocket-propelled grenade instead, and was sent to Malaysia to buy one. Sanusi gave him Rp. 4 million for the purchase.[28] It turned out no rockets were available, but Syahirul Alim had a back-up plan: killing the President at the opening of the newly restored Borobudur Temple, which was to be held on 23 February 1983.[29] Sanusi agreed, and Alim, Marwan Ashuri, Muchliansyah and Ageng Sutisna sought assistance from Muhammad Jabir, Aceng Kurnia's son-in-law.

On the morning of 8 February, Ashur and Sudjatmono met with Abdul Syukur, chairman of BKPMI, whose support for the rally they had earlier obtained. At the meeting they agreed to hold the event on Friday 25 February, and to issue invitations in the name of the Majelis Ulama Indonesia.[30] They gave Rp. 400 000 to Jabir to buy explosives, which he did.[31] He then asked Saleh Amin, one of his team, to make a bomb.[32] By mid-February, the bomb was ready, but there was a new problem – they had no one to carry out the attack. Two of Jabir's people who had previously agreed to do so withdrew, so a new team had to be put together.

Ashur and Syukur began to print invitations to the rally using the name of Majelis Ulama Indonesia. They forged the letterhead, stamp and signature of Syukri Ghozali, the MUI chair. They called the event 'Grand Rally for the Declaration of Islamic Unity' (Apel

Akbar Ikrar Wahdatul Islam). Dated 19 February 1983, the invitation letter read:

> Recalling that Pancasila is to be proclaimed as the sole
> ideology, a kind of religion that will bring salvation in
> the afterlife (Speech of President Suharto, Cendana, 19
> June 1982, in front of the Central KNPI), this is clearly
> an effort to convert the entire Islamic community to
> apostasy. To date the Islamic community has been tolerant
> in all areas, but this time our faith has been attacked. It is
> thus time for the Majelis Ulama Indonesia together with
> the entire Islamic community to hold a Grand Rally for
> the Declaration of Islamic Unity of the Indonesian and
> specifically the Jakarta Islamic Community.[33]

As the day of the rally approached, participants from outside Jakarta began arriving in the capital. LP3K cadres from Bandung and Tasikmalaya stayed at a mosque in the Mampang area, as well as a mosque behind the Sarinah department store. Rally participants from the Yogyakarta *usroh* group were accommodated at Muchliansyah's house in Kebon Pala, Halim, East Jakarta. The plan was for the crowd to reach maximum strength the day after the assassination of Suharto.[34] On Wednesday, 23 February 1983, Suharto inaugurated the newly renovated Borobudur Temple. Alim, Ashur and Sudjatmono gathered at the Grand Rally guard post at Sanusi's house. They listened to the radio broadcast of the Borobudur event with beating hearts. But the broadcast ended without incident. Sanusi asked Syahirul what happened. He replied: 'Clearly it was not yet fated to happen; humans make plans but certainty rests solely in Allah's hands. Perhaps the perpetrators were afraid or the equipment froze or the perpetrator did not find a safe path to place the bomb in a strategic location.'[35]

Aware that the plan had failed, Syahirul decided to pack up and return to Yogyakarta. Ashur and Sudjatmono remained in Jakarta. They were unwilling to proceed with the rally because the risk was too great. They immediately cancelled the plan to bring in crowds from outside Jakarta. But it was too late – the invitation had already been distributed all over the capital. MUI board members who received it were shocked to see it issued in the MUI's name. On Thursday, 24 February 1983 Syukri Ghozali, the MUI General Chair, reported the invitation to the internal security agency Kopkamtib, National Police Headquarters and the State Intelligence Agency (BAKIN). He then issued a statement to the press saying that it was a fraud.[36]

On Friday, 25 February 1983, the number of worshippers at the Istiqlal Mosque in Jakarta was far higher than usual. Seeing the overflowing crowd, a board member at the mosque read out the statement that MUI had never organised any Islamic unity rally. The statement was repeated at the conclusion of Friday prayers. Eventually the worshippers went home.

The failure of the rally and the plan to assassinate Suharto did not cause Sanusi and Darul Islam allies to give up entirely. In April 1983, the MPR General Session issued Resolution No. II/ MPR/1983 on the Pancasila as the sole ideological foundation for the state and all political parties. This was rejected by a wide range of Islamic parties and mass organisations. Sanusi and Mursalin sought to exploit the issue. They organised a *tabligh akbar* – a large public religious gathering – in August 1983, attended by a number of Islamic figures, including Syahirul and a young preacher named Toni Ardie. Ardie, a member of Korps Mubaligh Indonesia (KMI – Indonesian Preacher Corps) was the star of the show. He gave a red-hot speech that fired up the crowd, inviting the Muslim community to follow the example of Moses fighting the Pharaoh – a clear reference to Suharto. The audience for Ardie's lecture filled the al-Azhar mosque.[37]

The success of the event resulted in a plan to repeat it outside Jakarta, but the military took Toni Ardie into custody and accused him of incitement. Security forces also raided the offices of the Sudirman Mosque's Mosque Youth Coordination Board (BKPM) in Yogyakarta, which also served as the local Darul Islam headquarters, arresting several people. At the beginning of 1984, Irfan Awwas, Fihirudin's younger brother, was also apprehended.

The arrests drove a wedge between Darul Islam in Yogyakarta and Solo and LP3K. Darul Islam members suspected that the intelligence services had penetrated the Pesantren Express group through Hasanudin Hajad, an Acehnese trusted by Mursalin who claimed to be Darul Islam's military commander but who was also very close to LP3K. Their suspicions grew after Fihirudin sought information about Hajad from a Darul Islam Aceh figure called Fauzi Hasby. Hasby said that Hajad was not Daud Beureueh's right-hand man as he claimed, but had merely been a courier, although Hasby himself was also later shown to have links to intelligence.[38]

Relations between Sanusi and Mursalin also worsened. Sanusi felt that Mursalin was all talk. He broke away from the Darul Islam leader and returned to the group of 'Petition of 50' activists and Gerakan Pemuda Kabah (GPK – Kabah Youth Movement) activists, the youth wing of PPP – until his arrest in 1984.

Jakarta *usroh*

Meanwhile, the arrest of Irfan Awwas left the *usroh* movement in Yogyakarta in disarray. Syahirul became less active out of fear of arrest and several activists left Yogyakarta. Fihirudin fled to Kalimantan, but many of the activists ended up in Jakarta. There they connected with Muchliansyah, who had established an *usroh* movement in the capital as part of the preparations for the Grand Rally. He used his mother-in-law's house in Halim, East Jakarta as the headquarters for his *usroh* group, as well as a place to stay for Yogyakarta and Solo activists seeking refuge. Several *usroh* cadres from Yogyakarta helped Muchliansyah set up the network, including Agus Harisun and Ahmad Furzon (alias Broto).

Muchliansyah also worked with Muhammad Jabir, who was based in the Kalibaru area in Tanjung Priok, North Jakarta. Jabir introduced Muchliansyah to individuals who would go on to play an important role in the Jakarta *usroh* network. They included two teachers: Aos Firdaus, a Darul Islam member who had graduated from the Miftahul Huda *pesantren* in Tasikmalaya,[39] and Wahyudin (also known as Ustadz Bahri), a teacher at the Rahmatul Ummah *pesantren* in Rengasdengklok, Karawang.[40] Jabir also introduced Muchliansyah to donors, including Dody Ahmad Busubul, owner of the Genteng Abadi company that made roof tiles, and Hasnul Ahmad, a contractor. Ahmad's house in Jalan Wijaya, South Jakarta, became the centre of the *usroh* movement in South Jakarta.[41]

The at-Toyibah mosque in Condet became the headquarters for the *usroh* movement in east Jakarta. The East Jakarta network was developed after two *usroh* members from Tanjung Priok, Husein Ilham and Adnan, moved to a house near the mosque, which had long been a centre of student and youth activism. They introduced local activists to Muchliansyah and his associates, who recruited several for the *usroh* training program.

At a meeting in March 1984 to form a new *usroh* board for the capital, Muchliansyah became head and Muhammad Jabir, coordinator, with Ustadz Wahyudin and Aos Firdaus head of *dakwah* and training respectively. The meeting decided to change the name of the movement from Darul Islam to Ahlus Sunnah Wal Jama'ah.[42] The new name was a reference to one of the *hadith* of the Prophet, which said that at the end of time the Islamic community would split into 73 groups. Those who were to be saved would be called Ahlus Sunnah Wal Jama'ah, which means a group that follows the Prophet's *Sunnah* and lives as a community.[43] Indeed, Muchliansyah and the others followed Salafi practice in adopting what they understood to be the Prophet's lifestyle, eating and sleeping as the Prophet had, growing beards and wearing their trousers above the ankles. The aim was to apply Islamic law in their personal lives.[44]

The name Ahlus Sunnah Wal Jama'ah itself signalled the increasingly pronounced Salafi slant of the *usroh* group, thanks in large part to Abdullah Anshori (alias Ibnu Thoyib) – a student at the Arabic Language Education Institute (LPBA) and a protégé of Abdullah Sungkar's – who had joined the Jakarta group.

Anti-Christian and anti-Western

Whereas Darul Islam was more focused on recruitment, training and perfecting its teachings, LP3K – the Pesantren Express movement established by Mursalin Dahlan – took a different path. In 1984, its leaders continued their efforts to overthrow the government. They allied themselves with a Shi'ite group in Malang under the leadership of Habib Husein bin Abu Bakar al-Habsyi, head of the Yayasan Pendidikan Islam (YPI) Islamic boarding school in Bangil. In 1983, al-Habsyi organised a religious study group in his house every Thursday night, attended by youths and university students. He gave fiery lectures declaring, for example, that a civil servant's salary was *haram* (illicit), because the government obtained revenue from taxes on vices such as gambling, prostitution and alcohol.

Apart from al-Habsyi, Ibrahim Jawad often led these religious study sessions. He was a preacher from Lawang, Malang, who had just returned from Iran. His real name was Krisna Triwibowo, and he had been an English-language major at Jember University. He was obsessed with the Iranian Revolution and in 1982 decided to go to Qom to study religion. At the beginning of 1984 he returned to Indonesia and became active in al-Habsyi's religious study sessions. Jawad discussed the importance of maintaining the spirit of *jihad* and of using one's life and property to uphold Islamic law.[45] He also repeated rumours about the corruption and misdeeds of the Suharto family, including a conspiracy theory that in 1970 the World Council of Churches Congress in Rome had chosen Suharto to lead the Christianisation of Indonesia. He often referred to the threat of Zionism and American imperialism against the Islamic world.

LP3K members came to know these two Shi'ite teachers through Muhammad Achwan, a Pesantren Express activist who lived in Malang. The two groups got on straight away because they had similar aims. Together they formed a new group called the Ikhwanul Muslimin – Muslim Brotherhood – although there was no connection with the Egyptian Muslim Brotherhood.[46] This new organisation had two goals: to produce new cadres and to inspire revolution in Indonesia. To achieve these aims, Ikhwanul Muslimin formed a revolutionary organisational structure, which it called the Command Coordinator, based on Sanusi's earlier concept.[47]

Their plan for armed revolution was accelerated in September 1984 after a bloody incident in which more than a thousand Muslim residents of Tanjung Priok clashed with security forces.[48] The armed forces commander at the time, General Benny Murdani, stated that nine people were killed and fifty-three wounded in the incident.[49] Survivors claimed, however, that over a hundred people had been killed, although the actual death toll remains unclear. The military's efforts to cover up the truth stoked more anger toward the government among Islamic activists. The fact that Murdani was a Christian contributed to perceptions of an anti-Muslim conspiracy. Several weeks after the Tanjung Priok riot, three bombs exploded in Jakarta's ethnic Chinese–dominated business district, damaging two branches of Bank Central Asia owned by Liem Sioe Liong, one of Suharto's richest and most trusted business allies. The security forces subsequently uncovered that the bombers were GPK activists close to Sanusi. Sanusi was arrested and accused of financing the bombings.

Ikhwanul Muslimin activists were also angry and decided to take revenge. They obtained explosives from Lampung with help from Abdul Kadir Baraja, the Darul Islam Lampung activist and Ngruki teacher who had been arrested on accusations of involvement in Komando Jihad. In October 1984, Muhammad Achwan, Husein al-Habsyi and Ibrahim Jawad organised a major meeting of Ikhwanul Muslimin at a sugar plantation in Dringu village, Probolinggo, East Java.[50] Those in attendance included Simpuang Abdul Malik, an LP3K activist from Surabaya, and Lutfi Ali, a Shi'ite figure from Probolinggo, as well representatives from Jakarta and Bandung.[51]

Al-Habsyi and Jawad opened the meeting by saying that Islam in Indonesia would not achieve victory through democratic institutions but only by means of the sword. Lutfi Ali pointed to the example of the Iranian revolution. LP3K activists from Jakarta and Bandung suggested that they abduct and assassinate President Suharto, his wife Tien and General Murdani. Alongside this effort to create a leadership vacuum they would launch a wave of popular protest through a new dare-to-die organisation they called the Prepared for Martyrdom Forces (Pasukan Siap Syahid – PASISA). Al-Habsyi even suggested that Ayatollah Khomeini should be Indonesia's new Imam. He urged his fellow conspirators to take revenge for the Tanjung Priok killings through bombings – or what he called 'a melody of tom-toms'. Participants agreed that PASISA should be formed immediately in Malang and Surabaya.

A follow-up meeting was held in early October 1984 in Surabaya, led by Simpuang Abdul Malik. Those present agreed to conduct a propaganda campaign by distributing flyers discrediting the government. Suggested titles included 'General Murdani is the Brains behind the Slaughter of the Islamic Community' (Jenderal Murdani Otak Pembantaian Umat Islam), 'Bring Murdani to Justice to Take Responsibility for the Bloody Tanjung Priok Incident' (Seret Murdani ke Pengadilan Mempertanggungjawabkan Peristiwa Berdarah Tanjung Priok), 'The Christian Army Has Murdered the Islamic Community' (Tentara Kristen Telah Membunuh Umat Islam), 'O Army of Islam, Rise up and Fight Against the Christian Army' (Wahai Tentara Islam Bangkit Melawan Tentara Kristen) and 'Signing a Golkar Card Means Signing a Contract to Go to Hell' (Menandatangani Kartu Golkar Berarti Teken Kontrak ke Neraka).

The plan was to print some 100 000 copies of the flyers and stick them up on houses, on the streets and at mosques. This propaganda campaign would be accompanied by bombings, abductions and assassinations. Targets included provincial parliament buildings, churches and Chinese-owned shops. Those slated for abduction and assassination included Golkar figures, regional parliament members, government officials and ethnic Chinese in Surabaya.[52]

In November 1984 Jawad started to make a bomb from the explosives purchased in Lampung, with the chosen target the mausoleum built for the Suharto family in Yogyakarta.[53] He apparently learned to make bombs while he was in Iran, where he received military training alongside his religious education. Abdul Kadir al-Habsyi, al-Habsyi's relative, and Achmad Muladawilah, his student, were to carry out the bombing. Approaching Christmas 1984 the bombs were ready but the target had changed to churches. They called the planned attack a 'Christmas Party', as revenge for what they saw as the Christian-led army slaughtering Muslims at Tanjung Priok. In the middle of the night they bombed the Southeast Asia Bible Seminary complex and the Catholic Pastoral Church complex in Malang.[54] The police quickly arrested a number of suspects, although none were the real perpetrators of the bombings.

In January 1985, al-Habsyi and Jawad turned to a bigger target – Borobudur. The preparations were conducted in great secrecy. In mid-January, Jawad invited Muladawilah and Abdul Kadir al-Habsyi to go camping. Both enthusiastically agreed. Only when they arrived in Yogyakarta did Jawad inform them that they were going to bomb the temple at Borobudur. The two were startled and angry that they had been lied to, and also afraid. Nevertheless, for several days they surveyed the temple complex. Jawad had prepared fourteen bombs for the project, although one was discovered to be inoperable before it was placed. They agreed that they would detonate the bombs on the night of 21 January 1985.[55] At it turned out, only nine of the bombs exploded, destroying or damaging several stupas.[56] The attack shocked Indonesia and the international community, especially as a UNESCO-financed restoration had only been completed a year earlier.

Jawad and al-Habsyi were determined to strike again. In February 1985 they chose a new target. This time it was not a church or a temple, but Bali, the perceived den of iniquity that catered to foreign tourists.[57] The choice reflected the strong anti-Western views that al-Habsyi and Jawad had formed, in part under the influence of Ayatollah Khomeini's rhetoric. It was the first time since the colonial era that foreigners had been made a target of terror in Indonesia.

For the Bali bombing project, they used the code words 'studying Arabic language'. At the end of February 1985, Husein al-Habsyi ordered Abdul Kadir al-Habsyi and Sadik Musawa, Abdul Kadir Baraja's nephew, to survey tourist locations in Bali.[58] At the end of February, Jawad gave Muladawilah a course in bomb-making and eventually handed the explosives over to him, including ready-to-explode bombs that had been placed in plastic pipes. The survey team had determined that they would attack the Nusa Dua Hotel, one of the most famous on the island, among others.[59]

Al-Habsyi prepared a small team to carry out the attack. Muladawilah got cold feet and dropped out as a bomber, although he continued to help with bomb construction. The new team consisted of Abdul Kadir al-Habsyi, and three students of Hussein al-Habsyi's, all trained by Jawad, namely Abdul Hakim, Hamzah (alias Supriyono) and Imam (alias Gozali Hasan). On 7 March 1985, Jawad left for Iran with his wife and two children. On 15 March, Muladawilah and friends finished the bombs to take to Bali.

That same night, the bombing team led by Abdul Hakim left for Bali on the Malang–Bali Pemudi Express bus, which carried twenty-nine passengers in total. The trip was relatively smooth, and the bus stopped briefly so the passengers could have dinner.[60] It then resumed its journey towards the port in Banyuwangi, to take the ferry crossing to Bali. The bus had reached a speed of about 90 kilometres per hour and some of the passengers were fast asleep. As it entered the hamlet of Curah Puser in Sumber Kencono village, Banyuwangi, there was an explosion and the bus filled with white smoke. Part of the bus was destroyed and seven passengers lay dead, including several members of the bombing team. Abdul Kadir al-Habsyi survived, with a wound to his ear, and was able to get out of the bus and flee, although the police arrested him later that night.[61]

Husein al-Habsyi found out about the explosion on the Pemudi Express on the Indonesian broadcast of ABC Australia radio. In the morning he fled to Bangil, where he got in touch with a friend and asked to be taken to Juanda Airport in Surabaya. From there he flew to Kalimantan.[62] But after the arrest of Abdul Kadir, his followers were arrested one by one, including Muladawilah. The two masterminds of the bombing, Husein al-Habsyi and Ibrahim Jawad, disappeared. In 1990, several years after the bombers had stood trial, Husein al-Habsyi was arrested in Garut. Ibrahim Jawad was never captured.

The fall-out from the attempted bombing in Bali was not limited to those immediately involved. In the subsequent crackdown, several key Darul Islam members were also caught, most notably Mursalin Dahlan, Muhammad Achwan, Sanusi and Syahirul Alim. Around the same time, the long-delayed decision of the Supreme Court appeal in the case of Abdullah Sungkar and Abu Bakar Ba'asyir led to an order for their re-arrest, and so saw them decide to flee to Malaysia. These developments threw Darul Islam into disarray once again. But it would also mark the beginning of a dramatic new chapter in the history of Indonesian jihadism that would take a new generation of activists to training camps in Afghanistan.

5
Hijrah and *jihad*

After their failed attempt at revolution, Darul Islam turned inward, focusing on training and preaching. But this did not mean that the movement's ambitions were diminished. In 1985, forced to flee to Malaysia to avoid capture by the security forces, Abdullah Sungkar and his followers continued to plan for armed *jihad* in Indonesia. With the Soviet Union's invasion of Aghanistan, a new opportunity arose for military training, and from 1985 to 1994 more than 200 Darul Islam cadres departed for the Pakistan–Afghanistan border. Their aim was not to assist the Afghan *mujahideen* in waging war against the Soviet army, but to build the capacity to fight the New Order government in Indonesia.

• • •

Hijrah

In February 1985, the Indonesian parliament passed Law No. 3/1985, on the obligation of political parties to adopt the Pancasila as their sole ideological basis.[1] To enforce the new law, the government began to target a number of Islamic groups, including Darul Islam.

Abdullah Sungkar and Abu Bakar Ba'asyir were at that point still not out of legal trouble. Their case was still open because prosecutors had lodged an appeal to the Supreme Court against the High Court's decision to reduce their sentence to four years. In March, as the Supreme Court was finally due to hand down ruling, the judgement was leaked to Sungkar and Ba'shir: the original sentences of nine years were reinstated, which would mean a return to prison. The two discussed the news with Khalim Khamada, the Muslim Brotherhood activist from Iraq, who at the time was a lecturer at the Arabic Language Education Institute (LPBA) in Jakarta. Khamada suggested that they flee.[2]

Initially Sungkar and Ba'asyir fled to Jakarta, accompanied by Sunarto (alias Adung), Sungkar's driver and right-hand man.[3] With the help of the *usroh* network, they rented a house and monitored developments in Solo. They heard that the security forces had turned the Ngruki *pesantren* upside down looking for them, and that their wives had been arrested. When they were not found, the security forces focused their search efforts on Surabaya, where the pair had frequently led religious study sessions.[4] Jakarta, for the moment, seemed safe.

In April 1985 Sungkar received an important message from Muhammad Natsir, recommending that he and Ba'asyir flee to Saudi Arabia, but the two felt this was too far from home. In the end they settled on Malaysia, from where it would be easier to communicate with Darul Islam cadres and closely supervise the political situation in Indonesia. Natsir agreed.[5] He then prepared a path for them to flee to Malaysia via Medan. Darul Islam's leader in Jakarta,

Muchliansyah, ordered Muzahar Muchtar and Fajar Sodik, two *usroh* cadres from Yogyakarta who had also fled to Jakarta, to go to North Sumatra to check the route. There they met with two GPI activists whom Natsir had also sent and who knew how to enter Malaysia illegally. Muchtar told Muchliansyah that the route was safe.[6]

In April 1985, Sungkar, Ba'asyir, Adung and several Ngruki students arrived in Tanjung Balai, Asahan, outside Medan, where they met Muchtar, Sodik and the two GPI members who were to take them to Malaysia. Fihirudin and other Darul Islam cadres were also there, ready to join the *hijrah* (flight) to Malaysia. In total, there were twenty-three people in the group. They first arrived at Ketam, an island in Malaysian waters, close to Kelang port. There they were divided into four groups and entered the mainland via Kelang. From there they went to the Bandar Baru Bangi area of Kuala Lumpur.[7]

Natsir had also already arranged for someone to take care of them in Malaysia. While waiting for a rental house, Sungkar, Ba'asyir and Adung stayed with one of Natsir's contacts in a National University of Malaysia (UKM) lecturers' housing complex. For one month, members of the group were forbidden to leave the house, because they did not have identity cards. Eventually their host was able to help the group obtain the necessary documents for a payment of 350 ringgit each.[8]

Soon after they arrived, Sungkar and other members of the group went for Friday prayer to a mosque in the Kuala Pilah area of Kuala Lumpur. The mosque was managed by a Salafi school, Madrasah Itiba As-Sunnah, led by one Ustadz Hasyim Abdul Gani. Sungkar immediately expressed his intention to rent a house nearby so that he could be close to a community with a similar religious outlook. Others in the group continued to live in Bandar

Baru Bangi. Both places became temporary headquarters for Darul Islam's exiled leaders in Malaysia.[9]

In mid-1985, another Darul Islam group arrived from Jakarta, including Muchliansyah, Aos Firdaus, Ibnu Thoyib, Safki and Ahmad Hikmat (alias Sahroni). They had fled to Malaysia after a botched *fa'i* attempt in which a taxi driver had been murdered. Muchliansyah, as head of Darul Islam Jakarta, had approved the *fa'i* actions because the movement was short of funds – the group had earlier attempted to falsify cheques and print fake money. Muchliansyah formed a *fa'i* team under Ibnu Thoyib's leadership, but in the attack on the taxi driver, whom they wrongly believed to be Christian, the perpetrators had acted recklessly. They had seized the car and murdered the driver in front of the house of Dody Ahmad Busubul, one of Darul Islam's major patrons, and had taken the corpse to the house after the robbery.[10]

At about the same time, Sungkar had hosted a visit by Abdul Wahid Kadungga. Kadungga, then living in the Netherlands, had been the personal secretary of Muhammad Natsir. He had stopped in Malaysia and met the Darul Islam exiles on his way home to Indonesia. He told them about a recent visit to Afghanistan where he had met with *jihadi* figures like Abdullah Azzam and Abdul Rasul Sayyaf. He mentioned that Azzam had opened Maktab al-Khidamat, an office to facilitate the arrival of *mujahideen* from outside Afghanistan. He also mentioned that Sayyaf, working with Azzam, had opened a military training program (*tadrib askary*) for foreign *mujahideen*. Sungkar immediately thought of sending Darul Islam members to Afghanistan.[11]

After Kadungga's visit, Sungkar and Ba'asyir – according to the account of one of their group, who recorded the story on tape while in prison in Jakarta almost two decades later – received an invitation to meet a leading Malaysian Muslim leader. In the meeting, the leader explained that he had received a letter from Natsir asking him to help the two of them go to Saudi Arabia. Sungkar also asked the leader about the attitude of the Malaysian Prime Minister, Dr Mahatir Mohamad, to their presence in the country. The leader claimed that the Prime Minister was aware of their presence, but had closed his eyes to it.[12]

After the meeting, Sungkar and Ba'asyir met with Muchliansyah, Fihirudin, Adung and several others and disclosed their plan to go to Saudi Arabia to seek funds for their activities. They also decided to stop in Afghanistan on the way back, to explore the possibility of sending Darul Islam cadres there. They believed that they needed to strengthen communication between the membership in Indonesia and the leadership in Malaysia, and so appointed Muzahar Muchtar as a go-between. His job would be to pass messages from the exiled leaders to the movement, particularly in Jakarta and Solo. Muchtar was also given the task of accompanying Darul Islam members and their families when they travelled to Malaysia.[13]

Several days after the meeting, Muchtar returned to Indonesia. He met Ustadz Bahri in Ciputat, and passed on a letter from Muchliansyah instructing Bahri, who had replaced Muchliansyah as leader of Darul Islam Jakarta, to reactivate the group. Aos Firdaus and Ibnu Thoyib, who returned from Malaysia with Muchtar, would assist him. In Solo, Muchtar met with Wiyono Muhammad Sidiq and passed on a similar message for Wiyono: that he should reactivate the *usroh* groups and the religious study sessions there.[14]

Soon after, Sungkar and Ba'asyir left for Saudi Arabia on forged passports. Natsir had lobbied the Saudi embassy in Malaysia to issue them visas, while his contact in the Malaysian government provided funds for airfare and living expenses in Saudi Arabia.[15] At Natsir's recommendation Sungkar and Ba'aysir flew to Dhahran. They were met by Muhammad Nadzar and Wahid Alwi, DDII board members in Saudi Arabia who had been asked to assist Sungkar and Ba'asyir for the duration of their stay. From Dhahran they travelled by car to Riyadh.[16] While in Saudi Arabia, Sungkar and Ba'asyir called on a number of Saudi religious scholars, including Abdul Aziz bin Baz, the Head of the Saudi Council of Religious Scholars, and one of the world's foremost Salafi scholars. In their meeting with Bin Baz, Sungkar recounted the ups and downs of the Darul Islam struggle in Indonesia. Bin Baz advised them to keep on with the struggle and not to let their spirits sag. He told them that what Sungkar and fellow exiles were experiencing was akin to what the Prophet Muhammad's followers had gone through. Suffering and pressure, he said, were a mandatory part of a struggle.[17]

After several weeks in Saudi Arabia, Sungkar and Ba'asyir travelled to Pakistan. They arrived in Peshawar and met with Abdul Rasul Sayyaf, with whom they discussed the possibility of cooperation between Darul Islam and Sayyaf's organisation, al-Ittihad al-Islamy. Sayyaf offered Sungkar a program of military training for Darul Islam cadres, including assistance with travel and accommodation costs.[18] This was exactly what Sungkar had been hoping for.

Upon return to Malaysia, Sungkar and Ba'asyir began to prepare the training program. Ibnu Thoyib was given the task of recruitment in Indonesia. The first group of five men left in 1985, but in 1986 the arrest of several key members of the Jakarta *usroh* network, including Ibnu Thoyib, disrupted the program. Aos Firdaus, Muzahar Muchtar and Hasnul Ahmad were captured; Ustad Bahri fled Malaysia.[19] Ahmad Furzon, known as Broto, took over the leadership of the Jakarta *usroh* group, assisted by Ahmad Harisun, Yoyo (alias Asep Danu) and Ade Buchori. They also took over Ibnu Thoyib's task of selecting Darul Islam cadres to send to Afghanistan.[20]

Harby Pohantum

The Darul Islam cadres were not the first, nor the only, Indonesians to go to Afghanistan. Several Salafi activists studying in Saudi Arabia or Pakistan had gone there as early as 1984 and joined a group called Jamaat ad-Da'wah, led by Afghan *mujahideen* leader Jamilul Rahman, headquartered in Kunar province. The Kunar Salafis strictly applied the principles of Wahhabism. As well as waging war on the Soviets, they also waged war on idolatry in Afghan society. They were very exclusivist and refused to join the main umbrella organisation of the *mujahideen*. The Indonesians who fought with Jamaat ad-Da'awah went on to become important figures in Salafi circles in Indonesia, including Chamsaha Sofyan, better known as Abu Nida, a key figure in Yayasan At Turots, a Salafi foundation in Yogyakarta, and Jafar Umar Thalib, the former commander of Laskar Jihad, a paramilitary group that participated in civil conflicts in Maluku and Poso, eventually disbanding in 2002.[21]

In total, ten batches of Darul Islam recruits went to Afghanistan between 1985 and 1991. The number in each batch varied. The second had fifty-nine, the sixth in 1988 only ten.[22] One member of the fourth batch would become infamous: born Enjang Nurjaman in West Java, he became better known by his alias, Hambali.[23]

He had been a student of Mamin Mansyur, a Darul Islam member from Bandung who fled to Malaysia in the 1980s.[24]

There were three main sources of recruits. The majority came from the *usroh* network, including Ngruki students, teachers and alumni. In 1987, Sungkar also started sending Darul Islam cadres from outside that network, including those recruited in Malaysia. The third source of recruits was the network of Darul Islam families. For example, Thoriqudin, who later became known as Abu Rusdan, went to Afghanistan in the second class in 1986. He was the son of Haji Faleh, a Darul Islam figure from Kudus in Central Java. Another recruit was Taufik, son of Ahmad Husein, the leading Darul Islam figure in Central Java who had helped recruit Sungkar and Ba'asyir in 1976.[25]

Recruitment also took place through personal contacts. Non–Darul Islam members could take part on the recommendation of close associates of Abdullah Sungkar, although they still had to join Darul Islam before they went to Afghanistan. One example was Nasir Abbas, a young Malaysian who later became the most senior JI leader to switch sides and help the Indonesian police. He went to Afghanistan on the recommendation of Hasyim Gani, the schoolmaster who helped Sungkar in exile and became his close friend. Abbas was inducted into Darul Islam shortly before he departed.[26] The same thing happened in the case of Ali Imron, who would go on to be one of 2002 Bali bombers. Originally from Lamongan, he was able to go to Afghanistan on the recommendation of his older brother, Ali Ghufron. Like Nasir Abbas, he had never been a member of Darul Islam previously.[27]

Before leaving for the camp on the Pakistan–Afghan border, all Darul Islam cadres went first to Malaysia to receive instruction from Sungkar. Sungkar explained to them that they were not being sent to Afghanistan to wage war on the Soviet Union, but instead for military training. In the future, they would use the training that they obtained to wage *jihad* in Indonesia. He also explained the regulations that would apply while they were in training. Every student was required to have an alias. The participants were forbidden to reveal their Indonesian nationality or speak Indonesian; usually they were told to say they were from the Philippines. They were also required to take an oath which read, *Ba'yatuka 'alas sam'i wat thoah fil usri wal yusri* – meaning 'I swear to listen and obey in happy and difficult times.'[28] The aim was to bind them to the organisation and reinforce their commitment to the Darul Islam struggle.

From Malaysia, the Darul Islam cadres went first to Karachi, Pakistan then to Peshawar, near the Afghan border. Darul Islam had an office of sorts in Peshawar, managed by alumni of the first and second batches. They included Aris Sumarsono, known as Zulkarnaen, from the 1985 class and Achmad Roihan, also known as Saad, from the class of 1986. Their tasks included preparing accommodation for the participants, helping arrange visas, and setting up their program on the border. From there, the participants were taken to Harby Pohantum Mujahidin Afghanistan al-Ittihad al-Islamy – the military academy of Sayyaf's al-Ittihad al-Islamy. Initially, the military academy was located near the town of Pabbi, Pakistan, but in 1987 it was moved to Saada, just across the border from Afghanistan. Darul Islam cadres studied at the academy for six semesters. The curriculum was based on the Indian military training system. Most of the instructors had been commanders in the Afghan army who had deserted but who had undertaken military studies in India.[29]

The school had five faculties: Infantry, Engineering, Logistics, Cavalry and Communications. Because they had no previous military experience, the Indonesian students were given a special program that taught all military subjects, including basic infantry tactics, map reading and navigation, weapons training, infield engineering, and how to make bombs, explosives and detonators.[30]

Taking part in the military academy program required prime physical and mental strength. The first semester was typically the most difficult. Indonesian students were unused to such strict disciplinary regulations, let alone such rigorous physical activity. Several dropped out in the first semester. Suheri was one such student. 'There is no *i'dad* [training] in Islam that leaves you bleeding, bruised and battered,' he said later.[31]

Initially the Indonesians studied with Afghan instructors who taught in English. This caused considerable difficulty for the Indonesians, who lacked the necessary language skills. In 1987, instructors from Indonesia, recruited from the first and second classes, replaced the Afghans. They included Zulkarnaen and Imam Baihaqi, later known as Musthopa and as Abu Tholut, Adi Suryana, alias Muhammad Qital, and Thoriqudin. The training materials were also translated into Indonesian.[32]

The training became more effective, but there were still problems. The Indonesian instructors were typically junior Darul Islam cadres. For example, Adi Suryana had only joined the *usroh* network in 1986. Often they found themselves instructing more senior members of the movement. For example, Fihirudin and Muchliansyah, who took part in the fourth military academy class in 1987, were forced to take orders from instructors who had been their former students. They were quick to take offence, and argued with their instructors over the most trivial matters. In the end, the instructors successfully lobbied Sungkar to send both home before they had graduated.[33]

All students who graduated from the sixth semester were required to undergo *tathbiqot* – a practical exam where each student had to shoot, make a mine, build a bomb and put infantry techniques into practice in a war setting. Usually the test was held in the northern part of Khowst province in Afghanistan. The students also got the opportunity to use artillery, firing heavy weapons into enemy areas. A final exam determined whether they graduated. Abdul Rasul Sayyaf, the leader of Ittihad al-Islamy, always attended the graduation ceremony.[34] The Darul Islam board members in Peshawar would appoint the best graduates as instructors, with some selected for further training in weapons and explosives. The rest were sent home to Malaysia or Indonesia.[35]

The Jaji battle and Osama bin Laden

To put their training into practice, the Indonesian students were given the opportunity to take part in battles with the Afghan *mujahideen*. Typically they joined al-Ittihad al-Islamy troops led by Sayyaf. However, the Indonesian students were not permitted to take part on the front line and typically fought with the artillery in the rear. Sayyaf argued that Indonesians needed to be spared so that they could fight when they returned to Indonesia.[36] Being in the rear did not, however, guarantee the safety of the Darul Islam fighters. Two were killed: Sofyan (class 7/1989), who died in a bomb explosion, and Jamaluddin (class 5/1987), who stepped on a mine.[37]

Several Indonesians did, however, fight in what became a legendary battle among foreign *mujahideen* – the battle of Jaji. It was also a battle that would make the reputation of a young Saudi volunteer in Afghanistan – Osama bin Laden. Jaji was the name of a mountainous area in Paktia province, South Afghanistan. Located 10 kilometres from Jalalabad, the area was the main entry point for deliveries of supplies, ammunition and weapons from Pakistan to Afghanistan. Bin Laden, the pious son of one of Saudi Arabia's wealthiest businessmen, had gone to Afghanistan and thrown his wealth and connections into the struggle against the Soviets. He built the al-Ansar camp at Jaji specifically for Arab *mujahideen* who volunteered to go to Afghanistan to join the struggle.[38] In May 1987, the camp was attacked by Soviet troops. The Jaji battle pitted hundreds of Soviet soldiers equipped with tanks and warplanes against a small number of Arabs, including bin Laden. Al-Ittihad al-Islamy troops fought in support of the Arab *mujahideen* and included in their ranks several Indonesian students from the first and second classes, including Achmad Roihan, Thoriqudin and Ali Ghufron. After three weeks of fighting, and despite being outnumbered, the *mujahideen* successfully defended their position and the Soviets were pushed back. Mukhlas described his involvement at Jaji as a 'sweet experience'.[39]

The Indonesians who met Osama bin Laden in Afghanistan were greatly impressed. Mukhlas recounted his feelings after meeting with the Saudi:

> … At that moment I was convinced that Allah had
> blessed my life by bringing me together with a servant
> of Allah who had qualities that were not given to others.

Seeing him it was as if I had been brought together with
a companion of the Prophet, such as Othman bin Affan
or Abdurrahman bin Auf because the companions had
a similar characteristic, namely going to war with their
property and their souls. Sheikh Osama bin Ladin is not
just a millionaire but a billionaire or more than that, but he
does not use his riches in the way that rich people usually
do, instead he goes to war with his property and soul and
is prepared to live a spartan life on the battlefield like the
other mujahideen. Thus at the time my heart whispered
that a person like this is not just any man and that there is
no man like him in a million, and to this day I have not met
a person who comes close.[40]

The experience on the battlefield in Afghanistan left a deep
impression on the Indonesians. Mukhlas would later write:

In my experience, I have not set foot on one piece of the
earth that made me happier or was as invigorating as the
field of war. If I were to describe it, although it is in fact
very difficult to imagine ... [it would be as] ... a pleasure
unknowable except to those who have felt it.[41]

Another Afghanistan alumnus noted:

What Mukhlas said is true, that the pleasure of the field of
war is difficult to express in words. We became addicted.
I cried in great sadness when I was not chosen to go to the
battlefield. We are so close to the door to heaven there.

And the one and only way to enter heaven is by *syahadah*
(death in battle). I was very jealous when a friend from
Ngruki died as a martyr when a mine killed him. I always
prayed for it to be my turn for martyrdom.[42]

1989: a year of joy and sorrow

In February 1989, the Soviet Union withdrew from Afghanistan.
This victory gave great confidence to the foreign *mujahideen*,
including the Indonesian students. As one later noted:

This victory strengthened our conviction that *jihad*
was the one and only form of worship to defeat the
enemies of Islam. We were able to defeat even the Soviet
Union superpower, [so we would be] all the more so
able to defeat the New Order *thogut* government [in
Indonesia].[43]

That new confidence did not stop divisions from opening up
among both the Afghan and foreign fighters. Among the foreigners there was disagreement over the next step in their *jihad* against
Islam's enemies. One side took the view that the *jihad* should continue
in Muslim lands that were occupied by unbelievers such as Palestine, Kashmir and the Philippines. Abdullah Azzam, the legendary *mujahid* who had brought many foreign fighters to Afghanistan,
was in this camp. The other side, led by Ayman al-Zawahiri, from
the radical Egyptian movement Islamic Jihad, held that the foreign
mujahideen should return to their countries of origin and wage *jihad*
on apostate governments at home.

According to several Indonesian veterans of Afghanistan, there was no real difference between these two views. *Jihad* to free occupied Muslim lands and to fight against governments in Muslim countries that did not apply Islamic law were both *fard al-ain* – an obligation on all Muslims. The difference was only one of strategy and priority. The experience of the different proponents also clearly played a role in their views. Al-Zawahiri had long worked to overthrow the secular Egyptian government, while Azzam, who was born Palestinian, was more naturally focused on occupation. Additionally, Azzam still hoped to obtain financial assistance from Arab governments to wage *jihad* in Palestine in the future, and was therefore reluctant to get involved in any campaign to overthrow them.[44]

The dispute confused the Darul Islam members in Afghanistan. Emotionally they were closer to Abdullah Azzam, whom they greatly admired and who had helped them come to Afghanistan. But al-Zawahiri's viewpoint was closer to their priorities. They had, after all, primarily come to Afghanistan get the skills necessary to overthrow the New Order regime at home. Darul Islam members chose, therefore, not to take sides.[45] In the end the dispute was never resolved. In November 1989 Abdullah Azzam was murdered in Peshawar along with two of his children when a bomb blew up his car moments after they had left for Friday prayers.

After the death of Azzam, many foreign *mujahideen* returned home. Others chose to stay in Afghanistan, because the situation in their home countries made it difficult for them to return. This included a number of Darul Islam members who wanted to continue the military academy program. In 1990, Darul Islam members in Afghanistan began to cooperate with a radical Egyptian Islamic group, al-Gama'ah al-Islamiyah (GI), and participated in training at a GI camp in the north of Khowst province. This included commando training, weapons and ammunition maintenance, marksmanship training, and instruction in electronics, chemicals and explosives. Several alumni of the fifth batch took part in this program. GI even asked Darul Islam cadres to become military instructors at the camp. In early 1990, three alumni of that batch, Nasir Abbas, Mughiroh and Zuhroni, assisted by Syawal Yasin from the first batch, gave military training to 100 Kashmiris.[46] In 1990, Sayyaf provided financial assistance to Darul Islam to construct its own military training camp in the Torkham area of Nangahar province. A few alumni of the Saada academy managed the camp and helped train *mujahideen* from various countries.[47]

By the early 1990s events in the region and in Afghanistan were sharpening Darul Islam's hostility towards the West, and the United States in particular. In August 1990 Iraq invaded Kuwait, triggering the arrival of American forces in the region to protect the Gulf states. Despite the fact that US forces were invited by regional rulers, the presence of the American military in Saudi Arabia, a country that contained Islam's holiest cities, sparked great controversy in Islamic circles. Many saw it as an affront to Islam, and even as part of an American conspiracy to control the Arabian peninsula.[48] In mid-1992, Abdul Rasul Sayyaf, Darul Islam's great patron, was targeted in an assassination attempt. A convoy in which he was travelling was ambushed and fired upon. Sayyaf escaped, but a trusted aide was killed. At the funeral for his aide, Sayyaf blamed the attack on the United States. One Indonesian present noted:

> When we buried the body, Abdul Rasul Sayyaf gave
> opening remarks, which indicated that America and its

> lackeys had masterminded the ambush. Investigations
> showed that America and its lackeys were also behind
> the murder of Abdullah Azzam ... This was the basis for
> making America the main enemy against whom war must
> be waged after the collapse of the Soviet Union. Thus we
> always waited for the opportunity to wage war against the
> American army and to oppose and wage war on America by
> whatever method available.[49]

By 1992, the outbreak of the Afghan civil war made it impossible for the military academy program to continue. By this time more than 200 Darul Islam cadres had taken part either in the military academy program, or the shorter *takhasus* training program. A number of these alumni would go on to play major roles in jihadist movements in Indonesia, including eventually in Jema'ah Islamiyah (JI), including Hambali; Bali bombers Mukhlas, Dulmatin and Umar Patek; and commander-turned-police assistant Nasir Abbas.

Changes in ideology

Afghanistan not only equipped Darul Islam cadres with military expertise but also changed their ideology. It was in Afghanistan that some of the Darul Islam cadres adopted ideas and religious doctrines that would come to be known as Salafi Jihadism. The change in thinking started at the al-Ittihad al-Islamy military academy, where the Indonesians were given religious instruction in addition to military training. The religious teachers came from Camp Khalden, an al-Qaeda training facility set up by bin Laden near Khowst. They included Abdullah Azzam.

One key shift in Darul Islam thinking related to *jihad*. In the understanding of Kartosuwirjo, Darul Islam's founder, *jihad* did not always mean *qital* or war. *Jihad* had a wider meaning: namely, all genuine efforts to do good deeds that accorded with Islam's teachings.[50] Kartosuwirjo came to this conclusion after studying all the verses of the Qur'an that were handed down in Mecca and which contained the word *jihad*. In these verses, the meaning of the word *jihad* was not always war. Indeed, the first Darul Islam Imam, like most orthodox Muslims, was convinced that war was the lesser *jihad*, whereas the greater *jihad* was the *jihad* to resist worldly desires.[51]

In Afghanistan, Darul Islam cadres were taught that the correct understanding of *jihad* was war (*qital*). They were also taught different categories of *jihad*. There was offensive *jihad*, which was *fard al-kifaya* – that is, a collective rather than an individual obligation, meaning that as long as the goals could be achieved with a particular number of fighters, it was not obligatory for each and every Muslim to join in. And there was defensive *jihad*, which was *fard al-ain* – obligatory for all Muslims. Defensive *jihad* was necessary when unbelievers attacked or occupied Muslim lands. There were also two types of occupation: by foreign unbelievers and by local unbelievers. Afghanistan and Palestine, for example, were under the control of foreigners, whereas Indonesia and other Muslim countries were controlled by local unbelievers – namely, the nominally Muslim rulers who in the jihadist view were apostate because they did not implement Islamic law.

There were several reasons why Darul Islam cadres were quick to adopt the Salafi Jihadi concepts. First, many of Darul Islam's own ideas were not that distant from Salafi Jihadi thinking. Second, Darul Islam cadres had great respect for the personal integrity and authority of the people teaching them, such as Abdullah Azzam. Third, the ideas they were taught were seen to have very practical applications. Concepts of *jihad*, for example, were directly applied on the battlefield, while conviction and faith were strengthened under conditions where death and injury were constant risks. Finally, there was even something of a mystical element. A number of Darul Islam members claim to have witnessed miracles in Afghanistan. One such miracle related to the death of Abdullah Azzam. As one Darul Islam member recounted:

> There was a strange occurrence for a week ... the site of the explosion always smelled of flowers and musk oil, which one could smell for a radius of one kilometre. I was the person who witnessed this. I believe that Abdullah Azzam achieved the ambition that he wished for, to die as a martyr. What happened to him was exactly the same as is told in the book *Ayatur Rahman*, which recounts the miracles that accompanied the deaths of the Afghanistan *mujahideen*, that were always accompanied by the scent of musk oil.[52]

If Afghanistan strengthened the belief among Darul Islam cadres that the one and only path to overthrow Indonesia's New Order government was through *jihad*, it also led to divisions within the movement. Not all the Afghan alumni, imbued with Salafi Jihadi ideas, were warmly welcomed by their colleagues in Indonesia when they returned. The result would be the formation of a new movement – Jema'ah Islamiyah.

6
Jema'ah Islamiyah

As Darul Islam cadres trained in Afghanistan, the movement was attempting to regroup yet again in Indonesia. In 1987 Ajengan Masduki became its new leader and Imam. Sungkar continued to play a central role in the movement, given the importance of the Afghan training. That same year, Sungkar accompanied Masduki on a visit to Afghanistan to meet with Abdul Rasul Sayyaf. But the relationship between Sungkar and Masduki soon fell apart. One cause was Sungkar's strong criticism of Masduki's religious practices. Tensions between the two leaders culminated in Sungkar's decision in 1992 to leave the movement and form a new organisation, Jema'ah Islamiyah.

The group was modelled closely on the radical Egyptian group al-Gama'ah al-Islamiyah, with which Darul Islam cadres had co-operated closely in Afghanistan. Its aim, like that of its Egyptian counterpart, was to wage *jihad* against the apostate government at home. But the group would take on other enemies as well. It would take part in sectarian conflict against Christians in Indonesia, and a section of the movement would eventually take up Osama bin Laden's call to wage war against America and its allies. It was this determination to attack the West that would culminate in the 2002 Bali bombings.

• • •

A new Imam

While the Darul Islam cadres in Afghanistan were busy undertaking military training, in Indonesia Darul Islam was in disarray yet again. Key leaders had been arrested or were in exile. In 1986 and 1987 the movement's *usroh* network in Jakarta had been broken up by the security forces. But as the movement had shown repeatedly throughout its history, it was more than capable of regrouping.

Starting in 1986 several Darul Islam members outside of the *usroh* network had been attempting to reconsolidate the movement's remaining forces. These were mostly old Darul Islam members from the Komando Jihad days who had been released from prison. Ujang Bahrudin, a Darul Islam figure from Lampung, was one of the main drivers of this project. He was a close friend of Warman, the legendary Darul Islam robber. Bahrudin had been arrested in 1978.[1] After his release he moved to a village in Bumi, Lampung. Several former members of the Warman-led Darul Islam special forces joined him, including Lukman (alias Banban).[2] There they opened a contracting business. Their reputation as former members of Warman's gang seemed to help them in their business venture. The local government awarded them road development projects and they were soon able to buy a house and furniture, a car, and around a dozen trucks. They also used some of the proceeds from this business to help other Darul Islam members. The success of Bahrudin's business in Bumi made the city a new centre for the Darul Islam movement in Lampung.³

At the end of 1986, Darul Islam Lampung circles began thinking about reforming the movement and filling its leadership vacuum. In early 1987 they started to establish communications with fellow members in places such as Medan, West Java, Central Java and South Sulawesi. Bahrudin and his associates also established contact with members of the Jakarta *usroh* network. Ahmad Furzon was the leader of the Jakarta *usroh* movement at the time.

Bahrudin consulted with Syarifudin Gozin, a Darul Islam elder in Lampung. He said they needed to fill the Imam position after the arrest of Adah Djaelani. They ignored Syahirul Alim's tenure as Imam, because older Darul Islam members had not been not consulted regarding Syahirul's appointment, and so had not recognised his authority. They then made a list of possible candidates who were not in prison. One name that came up was Abdullah Muhammad Masduki, better known as Ajengan Masduki. In West Javanese culture, the honorific 'Ajengan' refers to a person with deep religious knowledge. Masduki had been with the movement from its early days and had been district head in Tasikmalaya.⁴ He had been a member of the Darul Islam Fatwa Council under Adah Djaelani but was arrested along with Adah. He was released in 1984 and had settled in Cianjur, West Java. Among the older Darul Islam generation, he was considered a prominent religious scholar.

Bahrudin met Masduki in Cianjur and asked if he would be prepared to serve as the movement's new Imam. Masduki answered: 'I am a servant (*abid*) of the *mujahideen*. If the *mujahideen* lose a soldier, I will become a soldier. If the *mujahideen* lose their parents, I will become a father to them. And if the *mujahideen* lose their Imam, I will be prepared to lead – as long as it is done according to proper procedures.' Bahrudin told him that the movement had established a new base in Lampung and asked Masduki if he would be prepared to move there. Masduki replied, 'I am ready to move there today, if the *mujahideen* need me to go.'[5]

Despite this seeming willingness to take on the role, Masduki noted that there was another elder not in prison who should be considered, namely Abu Suja, the former head of the Darul Islam Fatwa Council from Adah Djaelani's era. Bahrudin and Masduki went to see Abu Suja in Bandung. Suja agreed that they needed to fill the Imam vacancy, but refused to take it on himself, for health reasons. Suja instead nominated Masduki but the latter insisted again the procedures must be followed. In 1987, on behalf of the Darul Islam Fatwa Council, he convened a special committee to appoint a new Imam. The five-member committee was led by Mia Rasyid Ibrahim, from Ciamis, who had been arrested in 1978 on accusations of involvement in Komando Jihad. Masduki and Bahrudin were also included.[6]

The committee brought Masduki's nomination to a meeting of Darul Islam's consultative council, the Majelis Syura, on 4 November 1987 in Lampung. Two other candidates were discussed: Abdul Fatah Wiranagapati and Abdullah Sungkar. Abdullah Sungkar was the proposal of Khoer Affandi, a Darul Islam elder who was also the head of the Miftahul Huda Islamic boarding school in Manonjaya, Tasikmalaya. Affandi felt the movement needed a younger leader.[7] In the end, however, Masduki was appointed Imam of the Islamic state of Indonesia. A cabinet was also appointed that included Abu Bakar Ba'asyir as Justice Minister, Abdullah Sungkar as Supreme

Commander for Foreign Affairs, and Ujang Bahrudin as Supreme Commander for Home Affairs.

Masduki's cabinet focused on two main tasks: foreign relations and rebuilding military capabilities. Its members believed that one weakness of the Darul Islam struggle had been its lack of foreign support. One of Sungkar's new responsibilities was to lobby for international backing. The job of managing military affairs was entrusted to Ahmad Furzon, who was appointed to the staff of the Java–Madura Greater Regional War Command (KPWB – Komandemen Perang Wilayah Besar). One of his tasks was to recruit and send more Darul Islam cadres to Afghanistan.[8]

In 1988, Masduki and Sungkar travelled to Afghanistan and met Abdul Rasul Sayyaf. At the meeting, Masduki asked for Sayyaf's help to send weapons to Indonesia. The al-Ittihad al-Islamy leader said that he had no means of transporting the weapons to Indonesia. He agreed, however, to continue financing the training of Indonesian *mujahideen* at his military academy. He also promised to help the Darul Islam struggle once Afghanistan regained its independence.[9]

Infishol

It was not long, however, before relations between Masduki and Sungkar deteriorated. The trigger was Masduki's instruction to Sungkar to open Darul Islam embassies in a number of Islamic countries, as if the movement was a state. Sungkar refused. For him, it was wrong to see the Darul Islam movement as somehow equivalent to an Islamic state in Indonesia. He and his followers held to the Salafi view that an Islamic state had to control territory and uphold Islamic law in that territory and this had not been the case for Darul Islam since 1962. Masduki, however, took the position that although Darul Islam did not control territory, the Islamic state of Indonesia still existed. It was simply the case that the enemy, namely the Republic of Indonesia, had seized its territory.[10]

The dispute sharpened after Sungkar criticised Masduki's religious beliefs. A key source of tension was the new Imam's adherence to some Sufi beliefs, since Sufism was frequently targeted by Salafis as a deviant sect. One Afghan alumnus said of Masduki:

> He once said that he possessed *ilmu laduni* (magical knowledge).[11] Using this power, he was able to memorise the Qur'an in three days. The funny thing was that he had not memorised the Qur'an. He was also convinced that he could see the Prophet Muhammad when he was awake, whereas in Salafi teachings the Prophet Muhammad who had already passed away, could only appear in dreams. He was also convinced that he could receive divine inspiration from Allah, which he called *khitab*. The funny thing was that if there was a meeting, Ajengan Masduki never based his decisions on what was agreed there. He would be quiet during the meeting, then suddenly would say he had received a *khitab*, and would use this to decide the outcome. He would simply ignore the outcomes of meetings that had lasted for hours.[12]

Sungkar repeatedly warned Masduki to abandon Sufi teachings, but Masduki refused, and remained firm in his convictions. The dispute worsened when students of Sungkar who were Afghan alumni criticised the religious understanding of several Darul Islam elders. The elders accused Sungkar of rebelling against the Imam, and of demeaning the religious understanding of the Darul Islam membership. Led by Masduki, they eventually moved to sideline him. Masduki formed a financial investigation team to look into the funds being used to send cadres to Afghanistan. Sungkar's limited financial management skills meant he was not able to adequately address all the questions posed by the investigators. Rumour spread that Sungkar had misused funds. In fact, a Darul Islam cadre who had knowledge of the investigation admitted that 'actually it was not misuse like corruption. It was just that [Sungkar's] management was still very traditional and unprofessional.'[13] These disputes culminated in a schism between Sungkar and Masduki which became referred to as the *infishol*. In 1992, Sungkar and his followers officially left Darul Islam.

The birth of Jema'ah Islamiyah

Abdullah Sungkar immediately began work to build a new movement in Malaysia with several of his associates, including Ba'asyir and Thoriqudin. The movement – or as they saw it, the community – that they formed followed Salafi ideas, with the aim of upholding Islamic law through *jihad fisabilillah*.[14] They studied and discussed the ideas of a number of Islamic thinkers in deciding upon a frame of reference for their group. Three books were particularly influential: *At Thoriq ila Jama'atil Muslimin* (*The Path to an Islamic Community*) by Hussain bin Muhammad bin Ali Jabri;[15] *Al Manhaj Al Haraki Li Sirah An Nabawiyah* (*The Method of Struggle According to the History of the Prophet's Struggle*, usually shortened to *Manhaj Haraki*) by Sheikh Munir Muhammad Al Ghadhban;[16] and *Mitsaq*

Amal Al Islamy (*Guide to Islamic Deeds*) by Najih Ibrahim, Ashim Abdul Majid and Ishamudin Darbalah.[17]

At the time, *At Thoriq ila Jama'atil Muslimin* was the only book that discussed a Muslim community in detail. It argued that the true understanding of community was an Islamic caliphate or a government that covered the entire Islamic world. But because there was no such caliphate, contemporary Islamic groups such as the Muslim Brotherhood, Hizbut Tahrir and Darul Islam effectively served as *Jama'atul Minal Muslimin* – communities composed of Muslims striving for the establishment of a caliphate. Based on this understanding, Sungkar and his associates frequently called the community that they had formed Jama'atul Minal Muslimin (JMM).[18]

Manhaj Haraki impressed Sungkar and his associates. The author, who at the time was a lecturer at Umm al-Qura University in Mecca, in Saudi Arabia, was able to offer a method (*manhaj*) for Islamic community struggle in modern times by referring back to the history of the Prophet Muhammad's struggle. The book discussed that struggle stage by stage, and used it as a base for examining the contemporary reality of the Muslim world.[19] It looked at the tactics and strategies that the Prophet employed to disseminate Islam, then discussed how a community could put these tactics and strategies into practice under current conditions. One strategy that Sungkar and his associates adopted was to 'preach openly but organise in secret'. The Prophet Muhammad had applied this strategy when he was preaching in Mecca.

Sungkar did not agree with everything in the book, however. For example, the author praised democracy as a political system, while admitting that it was a non-Islamic system. He argued that democracy was better for the Islamic movement than a dictatorial or tyrannical system. Sungkar, however, saw democracy as an un-forgivable manifestation of idolatry because power rested in the hands of the people, whereas in Sungkar's view true power rested only in the hands of God.[20]

Mitsaq Amal Islami (*Guide to Islamic Deeds*), written by key figures in the radical Egyptian movement al-Gama'ah al-Islamiyah, became the key reference for Sungkar's new community.[21] This book outlined nine basic principles for Islamic struggle:

> Our aim, God's blessings by purifying our sincerity to Him and realising the example of His Prophet.
> Our faith, the faith of the *Salaf as-Salih* [Pious Predecessors].
> Our interpretation, the understanding of Islam comprehensively in the manner of the trusted religious scholars and we follow the Prophet's *Sunnah* and the *Sunnah* of the Rightly Guided Caliphs.
> Our objective, for humans to be servants only to Allah and to uphold his caliphate through the method of the Prophet.
> Our path, preach, embrace virtue and reject vice and *jihad* in the path of God, through a community disciplined in movement, following the Hanafi Islamic law, not compromising or deviating, and learning from past experiences.
> Our resources, piety and knowledge, conviction and resignation, gratitude to God and patience, renouncing worldly pleasures and prioritising the hereafter.
> Our loyalties, to Allah, the Prophet and to the faithful.
> Our enemies, tyrants.

153

> Our association, one aim, based on one faith and under the
> banner of one pattern of thought.[22]

Sungkar and his associates adopted all of these principles,
although they made changes to several and added a new principle
to make it ten in all. For example, they changed principle five to
become: 'Our path is faith, flight [*hijrah*] and *jihad* in the path of
God', which reflected the continuing influence of Darul Islam on
Sungkar's thinking. The tenth principle they added read: 'Our
experience of Islam is pure and comprehensive, with a system of
community and then statehood, then a Caliphate.'[23]

These ten principles became the main method (*manhaj*) of struggle. The new community was forbidden to use parliamentary means
to uphold Islamic law. The adoption of the principles of struggle
from *Mitsaq Amal Islam* made the new community, in the words of
Abu Bakar Ba'asyir, 'of the same form' as the Egyptian al-Gama'ah
al-Islamiyah.[24] Sungkar even used the same name – Jema'ah Islamiyah (JI). In the 1970s, he had used it as a generic term for his small
group of followers in Java. This time it was a direct nod to the radical Egyptians, and its ambitions were far broader.[25]

Immediately after the new community was officially established, Sungkar sent trusted individuals to meet with Darul Islam
members. Their aim was to invite them to join the new community.
Nasir Abbas recounted his experience:

> On one occasion when I was in Torkham in Afghanistan,
> around January 1993, Zulkarnaen summoned me to
> Peshawar, where I was then informed that Ust. Abdul
> Halim [Abdullah Sungkar] and Ust. Abdus Somad [Abu

Bakar Ba'asyir] had separated themselves from the NII
(Darul Islam) Community. Consequently I was given the
opportunity to choose one leader as the leader I would
follow, namely Ust. Abdul Halim or Ajengan Masduki. It
was also explained that if I chose Ust. Abdul Halim then
I would have the opportunity to remain in Afghanistan,
but if I chose Ajengan Masduki my return to Malaysia
would be promptly arranged. Zulkarnain said that all of
our friends would be asked and offered the same thing. So
that each person's stance was not influenced by the others,
Zulkarnaen would only give the explanation and offer to
each of them individually, as was always the practice of
the leaders of the NII Community and of Al-Jamaah Al
Islamiyah [another form of Jema'ah Islamiyah: ed.]. And
he reminded me not to tell any of our friends about the
decision that I had made. Because I wanted to remain in
Afghanistan and I was not too inclined to ask more about
the conflict at the upper leadership level, I thus chose Ust.
Abdul Halim. I had indeed also known him for a long time.
I then also asked to take an oath to my new leader, namely
to Ust. Abdul Halim represented by Zulkarnaen, and so I
was no longer a member of the NII Community. In other
words I had become a member of a new community under
Ust. Abdul Halim [Sungkar].[26]

As with Nasir Abbas, the majority of Darul Islam cadres in
Afghanistan chose to join Sungkar's community. Some refused
and some were hesitant. Dadang (alias Mughiroh), an instructor at
the military academy, refused to join and chose to remain loyal to

Masduki. Imam Samudera was also hesitant, but was convinced by Hambali to choose Jema'ah Islamiyah.[27] In Indonesia, the majority of the Afghan alumni chose to join Sungkar, with only a small proportion of veterans remaining loyal to Masduki.[28]

Preparations for *jihad*

Sungkar and his associates set about establishing an organisational structure, revising it several times before finalising it in 1995. They also wrote a constitution for the movement – the General Guidelines for the Jema'ah Islamiyah Struggle (PUPJI – Pedoman Umum Perjuangan Jamaah Islamiyah). According to the PUPJI, Jema'ah Islamiyah's highest leader was the Amir Jema'ah (Community Commander), a position initially held by Abdullah Sungkar. He was assisted by the Central Leadership Council (Majelis Qiyadah Markaziah) the Consultative Assembly (Majelis Syuro), the Fatwa Council (Majelis Fatwa) and the Internal Discipline Council (Majelis Hisbah). Under the headquarters (Markaziah) there were Regional Leadership Councils (Majelis Qiyadah Mantiqi). By 1997, Jema'ah Islamiyah had established four *mantiqi*, namely: Mantiqi Ula (I), which covered peninsular Malaysia and Singapore. This Hambali-led *mantiqi* was designated as an economic support area. According to Nasir Abbas, these countries 'had better economic potential than other countries in Southeast Asia ... there were many business opportunities and opportunities for individuals to work.'[29] Many Jema'ah Islamiyah members had successful businesses in Malaysia and Singapore. For example, Hambali and some of his friends had established a company exporting palm oil to Afghanistan. Another Jema'ah Islamiyah member owned a chemicals company. Jema'ah

Islamiyah often received up to 10 per cent of the profits of these companies.

Mantiqi Tsani (II) covered Indonesia, minus parts of Kalimantan and Sulawesi, Ambon and Papua. Ibnu Thoyib led this *mantiqi*, which was often called the main work area or the *jihad* region. In this region, Jema'ah Islamiyah planned to wage *jihad* to establish an Islamic state (Daulah Islamiyah). It covered the same territory as Darul Islam's Negara Islam Indonesia (Indonesian Islamic State). It also contained the largest number of Jema'ah Islamiyah members.[30] By 1999, there were some 2000 members of this *mantiqi*, as well as 5000 potential members in various stages of recruitment.[31]

Mantiqi Tsalis (III) covered Sabah in Malaysia, East Kalimantan, North Sulawesi, Central Sulawesi and Mindanao, in the southern Philippines. Imron Baihaqi (alias Musthopa, alias Abu Tholut) led this *mantiqi*, which was designated as a supporting area for *jihad*. This meant, 'a region that can be used for a military training academy and short-term military courses, as well as an area that can become a source of military strength.'[32] Jema'ah Islamiyah established a military training camp (*muaskar tadrib*) in Mindanao called Camp Hudaibiyah.

Mantiqi Ukhro (literally, 'the other *mantiqi*' – it never had a number) covered Australia and Papua. Abdurrahim Ayub led this *mantiqi*, which was designated a supporting economic area.[33]

Within each *mantiqi*, Jema'ah Islamiyah's structure resembled that of a military organisation. The largest subunit, called *wakalah*, might cover a country, such as Singapore, or just one city, such as Solo in Central Java. The *wakalah* was equivalent to a major battle unit such as a brigade. Beneath the *wakalah* was the *katibah*, which was the equivalent of a company, then the *kirdas*, equivalent to a platoon, and beneath the *kirdas* a *fiah*, which was equivalent to a squad.[34]

This battle unit–like organisational structure was designed for what JI called *jihad musholah* – armed *jihad* against Indonesia. In the eyes of JI members, Indonesia was a country on which war must be waged because it was governed by an apostate ruler, President Suharto, who governed with man-made rather than Islamic laws. Indeed, not only did Suharto forbid any portion of Indonesian territory from being regulated by Islamic law, he also arrested those who advocated its implementation.

In Jema'ah Islamiyah's view *jihad* was obligatory for all Muslims in Indonesian (*fard al-ain*). Nonetheless, the movement did not formally declare *jihad*, because its community was not ready: it lacked human resources, funds and weapons. It also lacked a secure base (*qoidah aminah*). Its first priority was, therefore, to prepare for *jihad*. This was planned along two main lines: territorial instruction (*binter*) and personal instruction (*binper*). The first was training for Muslims outside of the JI community, with the goal of recruiting new members. Personal instruction was for community members.[35]

Territorial education and MTI (*Manhaj Taklimat Islamiyah*)

From the outset, Jema'ah Islamiyah had been aware that it would be impossible to wage *jihad* without the support of the Muslim community. It viewed the Muslim community in terms of a series of concentric circles. At the centre were inducted members. Beyond it were the supporters, who backed the movement's aims and were prepared to help with manpower and funds. Next were the sympathisers. And the final, largest circle contained the neutrals, the largest part of the Muslim community. Jema'ah Islamiyah hoped that at the very least, they would not be enemies of the movement and oppose the imposition of Islamic law.[36]

Territorial instruction aimed to recruit new members from among supporters of the movement, and to promote understanding of its aims within the broader Muslim community members, so that they would move from being neutral to active sympathisers.[37] To support that instruction, Jema'ah Islamiyah composed a book: *Manhaj Taklimat Islamiyah* (MTI – *Islamic Briefing Material*). This book contained basic material on JI's version of Islam. It was also used as a basic text for potential members. Salafi Jihadi ideology coloured all of the religious material in this book. For example, one part of the book explained that Islam did not recognise a division between faith and Islamic law. It read 'whoever divides them and takes only one of them is deviant, an unbeliever and apostate.'[38] The material also explained that upholding Islamic law was a pillar of the Islamic faith. Those who did not do so were unbelievers. Material in the book defined *jihad* as *qital fisabilillah* (war in the path of Allah) and said that *jihad* at the time was obligatory (*fard al-ain*). It read: 'Thus the obligation of the Islamic community is to oppose the enemy who is currently occupying and oppressing their states, thus it is clear that *jihad* at present is *fard al-ain* until Islamic rule can be re-established.'[39]

One of those who contributed most to the development of the MTI book was Muhaimin Yahya, better known as Ustadz Ziad, an Afghanistan alumnus from the second class in 1986. From 1995 until 1996 Yahya was also given the task of disseminating the MTI materials to members. He was assisted by a number of others, including

Ahmad Syaifullah, Bambang Sukirno and Imtihan Syafi'i, all seen as among the intellectuals of JI, based in and around Solo. Jema'ah Islamiyah also organised special MTI training. Every *wakalah* was required to send two or three preachers to take part.[40]

Territorial instruction: *dakwah* and *pesantren*

Religious outreach or *dakwah* in the wider community was the spearhead of JI's territorial instruction. To that end, it provided preachers to lead religious study sessions. An example was the ar-Rosikhun Foundation, in Duren Sawit in Jakarta. Muhaimin Yahya led this foundation, which provided preachers to send to various mosques and religious study groups in the capital.[41] There were four phases to JI's *dakwah* campaign:

Tabligh, or preaching to the public at large: there was no restriction on participants, and this could take the form of public religious study sessions, Friday prayer sermons, Idul Fitri sermons or large public religious meetings.[42]

Taklim, or preaching in the form of religion courses to a small number of students: for example, a course in reading and writing the Qur'an, a course on the Arabic language, and so forth. *Taklim* differed from the *tabligh* stage in having more specific material and more carefully screened participants.[43]

Tamrin, or preaching in closed religious study sessions: in this case the participants were usually already known and had already participated in *tabligh* and *taklim*. The participants were limited to five to ten people. The religious study sessions were held once a week, were led by JI teachers and involved deeper study of the MTI materials.[44]

Tamhish, a follow-on stage from *tamrin*: only participants of the religious study sessions in the previous stage could take part in *tamhish*. As with *tamrin*, *tamhish* comprised closed religious study sessions. At this stage, the guiding teacher would be asked to study the participants' backgrounds. If a student was considered to fulfil the membership criteria and understood all of the MTI materials, he or she would be asked to join Jema'ah Islamiyah. It would normally take one to one and a half years to finish the *tamrin* and *tamhish* stages.[45]

Territorial instruction was also conducted in *pesantren*. One JI teacher claimed that the 'biggest supplier of Jema'ah Islamiyah members (were) Jema'ah Islamiyah *pesantren*.'[46] By 2000, Jema'ah Islamiyah operated more than twenty such schools and many more were opened in the years to come.[47] Among the best known were Al Mukmin at Ngruki, the Lukmanul Hakiem school in Johor, Malaysia; the al-Mutaqien school in Jepara, north central Java; and the Darusyahadah school in Boyolali, Solo. At these schools, JI *ustadz* freely taught Salafi Jihadi ideas. This long education process, lasting from three to twelve years, helped the movement implant its doctrines in a new generation.

This was also reinforced by the *pesantren* environment, which was deliberately made to resemble what was termed 'a miniature Islamic government' (*Hukumah Islamiyah Mushoghiroh*).[48] In this environment, students were conditioned to live as if in an Islamic state. As far as possible they implemented all religious teachings and abandoned everything Islam proscribed. This included all temptations such as television, mass media, music and singing. There were also sanctions for all forms of vice, and even for failure to perform actions that were considered meritorious but not obligatory, such as not performing communal prayers.[49] As one Ngruki graduate recalled:

> It was in this Islamic boarding school environment that I
> began to train myself to love Allah, his Prophet and Islam
> above all else. From the *pesantren* my fanatical feelings towards
> Muhammadiyah, NU and so forth faded and disappeared –
> praise be to God – and changed into fanaticism for Islam. At
> the *pesantren* I also reconsolidated the message that my father
> had always given me that this life is faith and *jihad*.[50]

It should be noted, however, that not all students were recruited as JI members. Only high-achieving students with a family background that would not endanger the community would be considered. It was rare, for example, for anyone from a police or military family to be invited to join. JI leaders hoped that the students who did not join would still become supporters. Usually, the selection process would take place when the students were at the senior high school level. Students considered to have potential would be invited to special religious study sessions. The study sessions were based on the MTI. After they had studied all of the material, a religious course would be held to reinforce what they had learned. This course was usually held on the final ten days of Ramadan. This was the final stage in the education of a potential member.[51] A Ngruki graduate said:

> I became a member of the Jema'ah Islamiyah organisation
> in 1994, when I was still in sixth class at the Al Mukmin
> Islamic Boarding School in Ngruki, Solo. At the time my

friends and I took part in the MTI studies taught by Ustad
Abdul Rohim, Ustadz Joko and Ustad Mukhlis for around
ten days. When it was over Ustadz Joko invited my friends
and me to take an oath as members of Jema'ah Islamiyah. In
response to the offer I said I was prepared to join Jema'ah
Islamiyah to apply the knowledge that I obtained in the
MTI lessons. Ustadz Joko then arranged a time for the
oath and I was sworn in as a member of Jema'ah Islamiyah
at Ustadz Abdul Rohim's house. From that time I officially
became a member of the Jema'ah Islamiyah Organisation.[52]

Personal education and military training

The aim of personal training was to develop members in the religious and military spheres. There were two main activities: *tarbiyah*, or religious education, and *tajnid*, or military education. Every
member was required to participate in both. *Tarbiyah* was similar to
usroh education. The aim was to ensure Jema'ah Islamiyah members
had a deep understanding of Salafi Jihadism.

In contrast to *tarbiyah*, *tajnid* aimed to produce an army from
Jema'ah Islamiyah cadres.[53] *Tajnid* was usually packaged as sports
activities like long-distance running, playing soccer, swimming,
climbing mountains and so forth. The movement also held camps
for two to three days on a mountain, at the beach, or on the banks
of a river. Participants were taught survival techniques, war tactics,
map-reading and self-defence. These camps also included religious
study sessions. Usually, the instructors were Afghanistan alumni.[54]

Jema'ah Islamiyah's best cadres were also selected to take part in
military training in Mindanao in the Southern Philippines. Jema'ah

Islamiyah had its own military training camp there called Camp Hudaibiyah. This was established by Nasir Abbas and others in 1994 and was initially a training location for MILF (Moro Islamic Liberation Front) elite forces. From 1997, however, MILF handed over Hudaibiyah to Jema'ah Islamiyah.[55] From that point, Jema'ah Islamiyah opened an express training program lasting only a few weeks, similar to the short *takhasus* programs in Afghanistan. The first Jema'ah Islamiyah cadres to participate in the program included men who would go on to be some of the group's most notorious figures, including Noordin M. Top, Dr Azahari Husein and Ali Fauzi, the adopted younger brother of Ali Ghufron (alias Mukhlas). The instructor was Faturrahman Al Ghozi (alias Saad), an Afghanistan alumnus from the 9th batch in 1990.

In 1998 Jema'ah Islamiyah established more formal military training programs – *Kuliyah Harbiyah* (war college) and *Daurah Asasiyah Askariyah* (basic military training course). The first program lasted three semesters, or one and a half years. The second program was a six-month course. The instructors were drawn from Afghanistan alumni including Nasir Abbas, Imron Baihaqi, Thoriqudin, and Muhaimin Yahya. Between 1998 and 2000 some 170 cadres from Malaysia, Singapore and Indonesia graduated from these two programs.[56]

The Mindanao alumni also gained direct military experience. As Nasir Abbas recounted:

> The biggest martialling of Camp Hudaibiyah residents
> was when they were involved in defending the territory of
> the Bangsa Moro fighters from the 'all out war operations'
> launched by the Philippine military (AFP) in July 2000.

The experience of [fighting] together with the Bangsa
Moro fighters provided a new spirit of struggle to the
al-Jamaah al-Islamiyah members and to other groups of
Indonesians.[57]

From the late 1990s Jema'ah Islamiyah also sent cadres to
Afghanistan to participate in military training (*tadrib askary*) at
al-Qaeda's Camp al-Faruq. There they undertook various military courses, ranging from a basic military course called *daurah
ta'sisiyyah* to one for trainers (*mudarrib*, plural *mudarribin*). For
the final course, participants required special qualifications. From
hundreds of applicants only thirty people were chosen to take part.
After ten months of education, the ten best graduates were selected
as *mudarribin*.[58] A Jema'ah Islamiyah member recounted his experience of this training:

> I also started training in the *mudarribin* course. The
> training that I was to undertake was an extension of the
> *daurah ta'sisiyyah*. Each stage was taught in greater detail
> so that we would truly master the material. We were
> also provided with additional training such as sniper
> and urban warfare tactics. We were also given access to
> shooting facilities with unlimited ammunition. The course
> I undertook lasted for about four months. I began to feel
> the benefits from it. I became convinced and confident
> that I could teach new participants in the *daurah ta'sisiyyah*.
> Several people were unable to continue with the course
> because they were injured during the Urban Warfare
> Tactics training.[59]

In four months I undertook four stages of lessons. The first stage was an extension of [training on] light arms and anti-aircraft weapons such as Grenov, Dashaka, Zukoyak and Shalaka, taught by Huzaifah (a *mudarrib* from Yemen). The second stage was an extension of topography lessons, taught by Abu Faroj (a *mudarrib* from Libya). The third stage was an extension of lessons on explosives, taught by Abu Toha (a *mudarrib* from Algeria). The final stage was lessons on Sniper and Urban Warfare Tactics taught by Sawad (a *mudarrib* from Yemen).[60]

Over a two-year period (1999–2001), around twenty Jema'ah Islamiyah members took part in military training at Camp al-Faruq. Most of them were cadres from Malaysia, including Wan Min Wan Mat and Dr Azahari Husein.

Laskar Khos

Jema'ah Islamiyah was aware that an armed *jihad* to seize power in Indonesia was a long-term project. By 1999, many of the requirements for such a *jihad* remained unfulfilled. In the eyes of Jema'ah Islamiayah's leaders, the Muslim community in Indonesia continued to have a poor understanding of religion and still believed in the separation of religion and state. Moreover, the group still had too few members in the main work area, Mantiqi II. Members had uneven military skills, the group's overall numbers were still low, and it had minimal funds and weapons.[61]

Against this background, Jema'ah Islamiyah's strategy, as an initial step towards seizing power, was to form a *qoidah aminah* – a secure base. This was closely related to their idea of launching what they termed *jihad abnaul haraqah* – a *jihad* waged by a small part of society who were aware of the obligation to uphold Islamic law. They drew inspiration from the history of the Prophet, who had waged a similar struggle at the beginning of his efforts to spread the faith. They hoped that by 2025, Jema'ah Islamiyah would have strong base areas in Indonesia from which to mount an armed *jihad* in all of the country.[62]

Apart from preparing a *qoidah aminah*, Jema'ah Islamiyah also formed a commando force or Laskar Khos (special forces) in early 1998. Its members, between ten and twenty, were recruited from among the Afghanistan alumni who were considered to possess superior military skills.[63] Zuhroni was appointed as the lead officer, assisted by Asep Darwin as the head of its secretariat. Members included Edy Setiono (alias Usman), Farihin (alias Ibnu), Suhail, Sarjiyo (alias Sawad), Abdul Ghoni (alias Umeir), Ali Imron and Iqbal (alias Muktib).[64]

Laskar Khos members undertook short courses to refresh their military knowledge. They also began to survey centres of business in Jakarta, including two malls, Plaza Indonesia and Ratu Plaza; the World Trade Centre; and the Marriott Hotel. The surveillance focused first on the form and position of the buildings – for example, the direction the building faced, whether it faced directly onto the main road, or inwards. The Laskar Khos also surveyed the number of floors, the number of entry and exit doors, and the position of the doors. Second, they surveyed building security, including the number of personnel guarding the location, how many people worked inside and outside, how many people were guarding the lobby, how many people were guarding each floor, and usually also what security equipment they were using, whether firearms or just clubs. Third, they assessed the neighbouring streets, checking when traffic was congested and when it was flowing smoothly, as well as testing routes from Jema'ah Islamiyah's *maktab* (office) in Duren Sawit in Jakarta to the location. Usually two different people would survey each building and then give the results to Zuhroni, who would conduct the final survey before sending a final report to Zulkarnaen, head of military affairs for the organisation.[65]

Another of the Laskar Khos activities was to seek weapons and explosives. Ali Imron was given this task. He was an appropriate choice, because he was known in Jema'ah Islamiyah circles for being fond of gathering explosive materials and conducting bomb-making experiments. He also looked for various types of poison. He planned to mix the poison with explosives to make a chemical bomb, and actively experimented with the chemical materials that he gathered. He was able to make detonators, detonating cord and the liquid explosive nitroglycerine.[66]

The Laskar Khos was formed at a moment when Indonesian politics was heating up. In 1998, a wave of protests demanding that Suharto resign swept Indonesia. The Laskar Khos switched from surveying buildings in Jakarta to surveying the political situation in the field. They were ordered to infiltrate anti-Suharto movements, such as the labour movement. Their task was to provide daily reports on the latest political situation to Muhaimin Yahya, who at the time was head of the Jakarta *wakalah*.

On 21 May 1998, President Suharto stepped down and Vice-President B.J. Habibie became president. Jema'ah Islamiyah decided to support Habibie, whom they thought represented the aspirations of the Muslim community. They joined with KISDI (Komite

Indonesia Solidaritas Dunia Islam – Indonesian Committee for Islamic World Solidarity), which was led by Ahmad Sumargono. This choice was easy to understand, as KISDI was closely affiliated with DDII, Abdullah Sungkar's old organisation. The efforts to infiltrate KISDI were made easier by the fact that the Laskar Khos member Usman (alias Abas) was Ahmad Sumargono's personal driver. Through Abas, money from people who supported Habibie ended up going to Jema'ah Islamiyah members.

Suharto's fall created new opportunities for political activism, but also challenged the movement's principles, as illustrated by its involvement with Partai Bulan Bintang (PBB – the Star and Crescent Party). This party, which was established by DDII activists, offered Abdullah Sungkar positions on its board. Sungkar turned them down, because using parliamentary means violated the principles of Jema'ah Islamiyah's struggle. The Jema'ah Islamiyah upper echelons thought that if they accepted the offer it would mean they accepted democracy, which they considered to be akin to idolatry. But Jema'ah Islamiyah's leadership also appeared to be torn on this question. While it refused to join PBB, it allowed those cadres who so desired to become active in the party. For example, Muhammad Zainuri, a member of Jema'ah Islamiyah's East Java *wakalah*, was permitted to become a PBB candidate in Madiun district. Zainuri, who had been imprisoned for his involvement in Komando Jihad, was elected as a member of the local district council.[67]

Some within Jema'ah Islamiyah even wanted to turn the movement into a formal organisation. On the one hand, the idea violated one of the principles of Jema'ah Islamiyah's struggle, namely that it be a secret organisation. On the other hand, Jema'ah Islamiyah saw that its *dakwah* would be more effective if it were to be conducted openly. The idea sparked controversy within Jema'ah Islamiyah. Some in the upper echelons agreed with the idea, and at one point discussed a plan to hold a declaration of the Jema'ah Islamiyah organisation in Jakarta's main sports stadium in Senayan. The idea failed in the end, however, when other Jema'ah Islamiyah leaders objected that it could endanger the organisation.[68]

As Jema'ah Islamiyah in Indonesia adapted to the changing political situation there, activists in Mantiqi I, covering Malaysia and Singapore, were quietly changing the orientation of their struggle. On 23 February 1998 Osama bin Laden issued a *fatwa* stating that it was 'the obligation of every Muslim to kill Americans and their allies in whatever country when possible.'[69] The *fatwa* was issued in the name of the World Islamic Front, and signed by Osama bin Laden, Ayman al-Zawahiri (Islamic Jihad, Egypt), Rifa'i Ahmad Taha (al-Gama'ah al-Islamiyah, Egypt), Syeikh Mir Hamzah (the secretary of Jamiat ul Ulama, Pakistan) and Fazlur Rahman (a *jihadi* activist in Bangladesh).

Bin Laden invited *jihadi* groups in various countries to join the World Islamic Front, including Jema'ah Islamiyah. In 1998, Abdullah Sungkar and Abu Bakar Ba'asyir were invited to meet directly with bin Laden in Afghanistan. At the meeting, bin Laden explained that it was the most important obligation of the Islamic community, apart from faith, to wage *jihad* to liberate the Arabian peninsula from the enemies of Allah, namely America and its allies. He added:

> If the Arabian Peninsula, as the origin of Islam (*masdaru diinil Islam*) and land of Islam's holiest places is successfully liberated, both its land and its wealth, from the grip of the American unbeliever, then God willing it will be able to

smooth the struggle to uphold the Islamic faith all over Allah's earth. It is highly probable that one of the reasons for the stagnation and difficulty in upholding the Islamic faith everywhere at present is because the American *kuffar* (unbelievers) are still treading on the Arabian peninsula.[70]

Bin Laden's message to Sungkar and Ba'asyir was an invitation for Jema'ah Islamiyah to shift from a local *jihad* (to establish Islamic law in Indonesia) to an international *jihad* targeting America – although the two struggles were seen as connected. America was seen to be controlling the apostate governments that controlled Muslim countries and if it could be overthrown, then automatically America's puppets in the Muslim world would be left in disarray. One result would be that a *jihad* to uphold Islamic law in Muslim countries would be easier.[71]

After the meeting, on 3 August 1998, Sungkar and Ba'asyir wrote a letter to Darul Islam figures in Indonesia with a message from Osama bin Laden to join the front that he had formed. Sungkar and Ba'asyir's letter was delivered to Gaos Taufik, the old Darul Islam leader in Medan, to pass on to others. Darul Islam leaders in West Java rejected the idea, partly out of fear.[72] On 7 August 1998, suicide bombers struck the United States embassies in Kenya and Tanzania, killing more than 200 people and injuring hundreds of others. Most of the casualties were Kenyan and Tanzanian civilians. America acted swiftly. On 17 August 1998, it attacked locations suspected to be al-Qaeda military camps in Khowst, Afghanistan. American missiles killed thirty-four of bin Laden's followers, although bin Laden himself escaped injury. The US response greatly influenced Darul Islam's consideration of the letter. As Gaos Taufik commented: 'At present only crazy people want to fight America. [We] aren't able to fight anti-Islamic forces in our own country, let alone fight America.'[73]

Between the far enemy and the near enemy

It was not only Darul Islam members who rejected bin Laden's *fatwa*, however. There were also arguments for and against it within Jema'ah Islamiyah. Many senior members in Mantiqi I, such as Hambali and Mukhlas, supported this *fatwa*. But Mantiqi II officials like Ibnu Thoyib, Achmad Roihan and Thoriqudin rejected it. A debate emerged between the two factions. Hambali and his associates saw *jihad* against the United States and its allies as the main priority. In their eyes, the United States was not just occupying Muslim lands, but through its military presence in Saudi Arabia, it had occupied Islam's holiest sites. Roihan and his associates refuted this argument, saying that the priority was to fight against the apostate Indonesian government. Even in Salafi Jihadi teachings, they argued, waging war on the near enemy was a greater priority than fighting the far enemy: the Prophet liberated his own country first before expanding outside the Arabian Peninsula. Mantiqi II members gained backing for this view from Salamat Hashim, then head of the Moro Islamic Liberation Front (MILF) in the Philippines. He conveyed his opinion in discussion with several Mantiqi II leaders, including Muhaimin Yahya, who had expressly gone to meet with the MILF leadership to seek their advice on the *fatwa*. In a 1999 meeting, MILF's highest leader said: 'The contents of this *fatwa* are good, but it is impossible to carry out in Mindanao because the situation and conditions do not allow.'[74]

These debates were set aside in 1999 after serious communal conflict exploded in Ambon in Maluku province and Poso in Central Sulawesi. In Ambon the conflict began on 19 January 1999, on the day of Idul Fitri, the feast day marking the end of the Muslim holy month of Ramadan. That afternoon Muslim youths from the village Batu Merah Atas clashed with Christian youths from Batu Merah Bawah. The conflict quickly spread to the entire province, building on tensions that had accumulated for years between the two communities, which were more or less equal in size. Muslims called the first day of violence the Bloody Idul Fitri Tragedy. Dozens of people were killed and injured, thousands of Muslims were driven from their villages and around 20 mosques were burned.[75] The conflict was to continue for several years, with thousands dead on both sides.

Meanwhile, in Poso there had already been several episodes of communal conflict from late 1998. These peaked on 28 May 2000, when Christian militia attacked Muslim villages throughout Poso. The worst incident took place at the Walisongo Islamic boarding school located to the south of Poso town. Christian militia killed around 80 unarmed people taking refuge in the yard of a mosque. This incident came to be known as the Walisongo Massacre.[76] Both the Bloody Idul Fitri Tragedy and the Walisongo Massacre became major causes of mobilisation for Muslims in Indonesia. The press played a key role in stoking anger, particularly the widely read hardline religious magazines like *Sabili*.

The conflict between the Muslim and Christian communities generated a new discourse in Jema'ah Islamiyah circles. The debate about whether to wage war first against far enemies or near enemies became irrelevant; Muslims were being attacked and it was important to come to their defence. The debate over whether to wage *jihad* now or to delay also became academic. In the eyes of Jema'ah Islamiyah's leaders, communal conflict in Indonesia had opened the door to *jihad*. As one Jema'ah Islamiyah member noted:

> Even if our group (Jema'ah Islamiyah) had not interfered in the emergence of the conflict, the events provided new hope for us. Namely, it gave us a path to obtain a field of *jihad* and raised our spirits to wage a *jihad* that we had waited for and desired. The events also gave us new hope to be able to send out associates to conduct *i'dad* (training and preparations for war) as well as an opportunity to take to the field of war directly. I was also able to use these events as a medium for Islamic propagation to make society understand the concept of *jihad fi sabilillah* and as a tool to raise the spirit of *jihad* among Muslims.[77]

Jema'ah Islamiyah discussed preparations for the Ambon *jihad* at a meeting in Solo in June 1999. The attendees at the meeting were the Mantiqi II chair, Ibnu Thoyib, Zulkarnaen and the members of Laskar Khos including Zuhroni, Asep Darwin, Abdul Ghoni (alias Umaer), Sawad (alias Sarjiyo), Ali Imron and Mubarok. Zulkarnaen was responsible for the Ambon *jihad* project as the head of Jema'ah Islamiyah's military organisation. Each attendee was assigned tasks to prepare for the conflict. Some were charged with looking for weapons and explosives, others with recruiting people or preparing military training in Maluku. They also agreed that Jema'ah Islamiyah would conduct territorial instruction with the aim of forming a *wakalah* that would in the future become part of Mantiqi Ukhro, based in Australia.[78]

Jema'ah Islamiyah's financial resources were far from sufficient to implement the project. Nor was it easy to raise funds from the public, given that Jema'ah Islamiyah was not a well-established and trusted organisation. To solve the problem, Ibnu Thoyib sought the help of KOMPAK (Komite Aksi Penanggulangan Akibat Krisis – the Action Committee for Crisis Management), a social organisation under the auspices of DDII. The aim was to receive funds through KOMPAK from the public to allocate to *jihad*. DDII did not object to the arrangement as long as the activity was not harmful to it.[79]

Not long afterwards, branches of KOMPAK were established in Semarang, Surabaya and Solo. Jema'ah Islamiyah members occupied almost all of the board positions. KOMPAK Semarang and Surabaya turned out to be poor fundraisers. KOMPAK Solo, under the leadership of Aris Munandar, a Ngruki graduate and an Afghanistan alumnus from the ninth batch in 1991, was very active, however. Aris Munandar's older brother, Muzayin Abdul Wahhab, was active in DDII's foreign relations bureau. With Muzayin's help, KOMPAK Solo was able to gain funds from sources in the Middle East.

Money raised by KOMPAK was used to buy weapons and explosives. Several Jema'ah Islamiyah members such as Mubarok, Usaid (alias Zainal) and Sarjiyo went back and forth to Mindanao in the Philippines, where they obtained dozens of M16 firearms, FN .45 and Beretta pistols, as well as explosives, and distributed these weapons in Maluku.[80] KOMPAK money also financed military training in Waimorat village on Buru Island. There were twelve participants in this military training, which began in October 1999. They included Asep Jaja and Abdullah Sunata, both of whom were students of Muzayin Abdul Wahhab. The instructor for the three-month-long training course was Pak De (alias Ilyas, alias Muchtar), an Afghanistan alumnus from the eighth class in 1990, who was originally from Kudus. Pak De was known as a reliable instructor, and had been an instructor at Camp Hudaibiyah in Mindanao between 1995 and 1997. In Waimorat he provided everything from weapons training to training in tactics, map-reading and field engineering. He also taught various Salafi Jihadi doctrines of *jihad*.

Some of the alumni of the Waimorat training became important figures in the communal conflict in Ambon. Abdullah Sunata was one of them. Originally from Jakarta, Sunata was appointed as head of KOMPAK Maluku, managing various humanitarian assistance programs. The combination of his religious and military knowledge made him a natural leader among *jihadi* volunteers who came from outside Maluku. He attained even more authority because his position as KOMPAK head gave him great access to funds. Sunata ran a group called Laskar Mujahidin, an organisation that later came to be known as Mujahidin KOMPAK. In one Laskar Mujahidin operation the group attacked a police mobile brigade weapons depot in Tantui, Ambon in June 2000. 'Shadow forces' – military and police who took off their uniforms and fought on the Muslim side – assisted Sunata and his men. They were able to seize more than 800 weapons in the raid.[81]

This caused tension with Jema'ah Islamiyah, however. It had been agreed that KOMPAK would focus on fundraising and managing humanitarian assistance, but it was now playing an active role in the fighting, which was meant to be the preserve of Jema'ah Islamiyah. These tensions were exacerbated by the poor personal relationship between Aris Munandar, the KOMPAK Solo chairperson, and Jema'ah Islamiyah's military head, Zulkarnaen. In the end, KOMPAK decided to operate on its own, separate from Jema'ah Islamiyah.

This division was evident when the two organisations became involved in *jihad* in Poso. Both KOMPAK and Jema'ah Islamiyah had similar military programs. KOMPAK trained locals in the neighbourhood of Poso town called Kayamanya; Jema'ah Islamiyah worked with the residents of two other neighbourhoods, Tanah Runtuh and Gebangrejo. KOMPAK formed the Mujahidin Kayamanya militia, most of whose members were former thugs. Not wanting to be outdone, Jema'ah Islamiyah gathered former thugs in the Mujahidin Tanah Runtuh organisation.[82] KOMPAK's actions made Jema'ah Islamiyah members increasingly angry. They issued a ban on Abdullah Sunata and other KOMPAK members from entering territory controlled by Jema'ah Islamiyah members.[83]

The conflict with KOMPAK notwithstanding, Jema'ah Islamiyah's efforts were relatively successful. In these two locations, Jema'ah Islamiyah succeeded in producing new members who adhered to Salafi Jihadi teachings. Its territorial instruction program was a particular success in Poso. Before the Poso conflict there were only three Jema'ah Islamiyah members in Palu, Central Sulawesi. After the conflict was underway, Jema'ah Islamiyah's ranks swelled to hundreds. The movement formed a new *wakalah* in Palu, the provincial capital, and by 2003, there were two new *wakalah* in Poso – Wakalah Khaibar, covering Poso town and surrounds, and Wakalah Tabuk, covering Pendolo. Jema'ah Islamiyah was even able to persuade Haji Adnan Arsal, the most influential traditionalist Islamic figure in the area, to become a member.[84]

Within Jema'ah Islamiyah, it was not only Mantiqi II that was busy with *jihad* in Maluku. In Malaysia, Mantiqi I also campaigned about the conflict there. They published a book under the title *Peristiwa Ambon* (*The Ambon Incident*) which contained pictures of the Maluku riots, including damage done to mosques and photographs of dead and wounded Muslim victims. They also established a charitable organisation called al-Ihsan to raise funds from Malaysian Muslims. One of the cadres Mantiqi I sent to Maluku was Dr Azahari Husein, a Jema'ah Islamiyah bomb expert. Dr Azahari was a lecturer at the Universiti Sains Malaysia (USM) and taught at the training camp in Waimorat on Buru Island.[85]

al-Immatul Kuffar

At the end of 1999 Abdullah Sungkar died of heart failure, having returned to Indonesia following the downfall of the Suharto regime. His death had a major impact on the movement, not least because it left in charge a figure that many Jema'ah Islamiyah figures considered to be a weak leader – Abu Bakar Ba'asyir. One consequence was that it allowed some figures in the movement to begin planning their own operations without any recourse to the leadership's decisions. Chief among these was the head of Jema'ah Islamiyah's Mantiqi I, Hambali.

Hambali and his associates had been deeply influenced by a Jordanian Palestinian jihadist living in London who was known to be close to Bin Laden and al-Qaeda, Omar Mahmoud Othman – better known by his alias, Abu Qatada al-Filistini. Abu Qatada had written about the *thoifah mansyurah* – the group that will be saved on Judgement Day. One of the main characteristics of this group was that they continued to wage *jihad* even when other Muslims were reluctant to do so – even without permission from the leadership of the community, if necessary. Abu Qatada referred to the actions of Abu Bashir, companion of the Prophet Muhammad, who waged *jihad* on his own without an order from the Prophet, who at the time was entering into a peace agreement with the Muslim community's opponents in Mecca.[86] Members of Mantiqi I became obsessed with becoming part of the *thoifah mansyurah*.

In late 1999 Hambali began planning a secret operation to target priests and other members of the Christian community who were considered to have played a prominent role in the communal violence in Poso and Ambon. The operation was given the name *al-Immatul Kuffar*. In effect, it was an operation to assassinate Christian leaders.[87] The operation was also spurred by rumours and claims that the Christian community was planning to widen the communal conflict beyond the Maluku Islands. Hambali tasked Imam Samudera with coordinating the operation, and appointed Enjang Nurjaman, alias Jabir, as field commander. A close friend of Jabir's from Tasikmalaya, Akim Akimudin, assisted them.

To implement the project, Imam Samudera formed a small team that he called the Tentara Islam Batalyon Badar (TIBB – Badar Battalion Islamic Army). Their first attack was planned for Medan, the capital of North Sumatra province. The TIBB members surveyed all the churches in the city and found out the names of their priests.[88] On Sunday 28 May 2000, just as communal conflict was peaking in Poso, a bomb exploded at the GKPI church (Gereja Kristen Protestant Indonesia – Indonesian Protestant Christian Church) on Jamin Ginting Street in Padang Bulan, Medan. It wounded more than twenty congregation members as they attended a service.

Several hours later the security forces defused two other bombs at the HKBP church (Huria Kristen Batak Protestan – Batak Protestant Christian Church) on Imam Bonjol Street and the Kristus Raja church on M.T. Haryono street. Several days later TIBB issued statements on the internet claiming responsibility for the bombings.[89] As one of these statements explained:

> The bombing that we perpetrated was also an initial
> warning to you that this time the Islamic Community
> is more vigilant and prepared compared with when you
> perpetrated your sly crimes against our brothers in Ambon.
> Nor is it possible that we will give up our reconnaissance
> of you and your priests who are clearly using churches
> for war indoctrination. We know 100% that behind the
> words 'love' and 'worship' you have prepared thousands
> of machetes, bullets and even bombs! You have done all
> of this in churches. So our attacks on your churches are
> attacks on your defences! They are not merely churches.
> And we truly know that your priests and pastors have
> been sworn in by the Vatican and Pope Paul II to spark
> and continue a Holy war operation using the name the
> Richard I Operation.[90]

The religious conflict that Imam Samudera suspected would break out in Medan never happened, but TIBB continued to mount attacks on Christians. In August 2000, it attacked the GKII church on Bunga Kenanga Street in the Padang Bulan neighbourhood of Medan, and also started to attack priests. On 27 August, members put a bomb in front of the house of Reverend M.J. Sitorus. On 17

September, they fired at the car of a GKII pastor, critically wounding the driver. On 29 October, they shot and seriously injured Reverend J.K. Surbakti.

Their biggest attack came on Christmas Eve, 2000. TIBB mounted a coordinated attack in eleven cities throughout Indonesia, with twenty-five bombs causing twenty deaths and injuring around 120 people. Targets included churches and residences of priests. Another twenty-five bombs were placed, but failed to explode. In Bandung, one bomb exploded as it was being put together, killing TIBB field commander Jabir and his deputy Akim Akimudin. In Ciamis, a bomb exploded when the motorcycle the bombers were riding hit a bump on the way to the church they had chosen as a target.[91]

By conducting bombings outside of the conflict areas of Ambon and Poso, Hambali, Ali Imron and their associates hoped that Christians would take revenge and conflict would spread throughout Indonesia. Indeed, Jema'ah Islamiyah members believed that Christians were well prepared to strike back, based on their belief that they had stockpiled weapons in churches. The advantage of sparking this wider conflict was clear. Areas of communal conflict had become excellent locations for recruitment, and if the movement was able to expand its membership it would be able to proclaim a more general armed *jihad* (*jihad musholah*) against the Indonesian government.[92] This is what Hambali meant in his discussions with Jema'ah Islamiyah members in Malaysia, when he said bombings such as the Christmas Eve bombings were intended to smooth the path to establishing an Islamic state.[93]

But the Christmas Eve bombings did not have the desired impact. Rather than Christians and Muslims coming into conflict, the opposite occurred. Muslims and Christians united in criticising the bombings in various cities. As a reaction to the bombings, the Forum Indonesia Damai (FID – Peaceful Indonesia Forum) was established, bringing together various Muslim, Catholic and Protestant figures such as Nurcholis Madjid (Paramadina), Said Agil Siradj (Nahdlatul Ulama), Hidayat Nur Wahid (head of the Justice Party, later the Prosperous Justice Party, PKS), Mudji Sutrisno and Frans Magnis Suseno (both Catholic scholars), and Soritua A.E. Nababan (a Protestant church leader). All worked hard to prevent any backlash from the bombings. Rather than being seen as *mujahideen*, the perpetrators – who at this point were largely unknown – were accused of being terrorists.

In response to these accusations, TIBB posted a long explanation on the internet of the Christmas Eve bombings.[94] TIBB was aware that the campaign had provoked criticism from Indonesian Muslims who felt that Islam forbade attacks on churches, priests and civilians, even in times of war. In response it argued:

> [Regarding] priests who mix with the community
> and even become provocateurs and lead activities that
> contain elements of waging war against Islam and
> Muslims and converting Muslims, it is permissible
> and even obligatory to murder them because they are
> *immatul kufar* (leaders of unbelievers). So said the *ahlul
> ilm* [scholars] based on the *hadith* narrated by Imam
> An-Nasa'i which means, 'Kill the leaders among the
> idolators'. Their opinion was based on At-Taubah
> (9) verse 14. It is clear that today almost all priests in
> Indonesia and elsewhere are part of the second group as
> explained above, both directly and indirectly.[95]

The *bayan* (explanation) also argued that attacking churches in Indonesia was justified because churches had been used as bases to attack the Muslim community:.

> We have received [...] information from several trusted sources that churches outside conflict areas, meaning not in the Maluku archipelago and Poso, but in places that at the moment are still secure, have been made into warehouses to stockpile weapons that they can use whenever they decide the time right to slaughter Muslims as they have done before in the Maluku archipelago and Poso. Thus it is permissible to destroy churches like these and even obligatory for Muslims to do so.[96]

Concerning civilian casualties, TIBB explained:

> According to several *hadith* and the opinions of *ahlul ilm*, it is forbidden to murder women, children, the elderly, those in places of worship and Muslims. But if they are in a location that has become a lair of the *mujahidin*'s enemies, with the result that the *mujahidin* have made it a target, then it is permissible, [as long as it is] with the intention of killing the enemies and not with the intention of killing people whom it is forbidden to kill as mentioned above. The Prophet flung his rockets at the population of Thaif when there were children, women and the elderly among them.[97]

TIBB's actions generated controversy even within Jema'ah Islamiyah. According to Ali Imron, many of the Afghanistan and

Moro alumni disagreed with their actions.[98] This was not just because TIBB had attacked places of worship, which Islamic teachings clearly forbade.[99] The claim that Christians had stockpiled weapons and were planning attacks on the Islamic community was also seen by some Jema'ah Islamiyah members as hollow. One of the perpetrators of the Christmas Eve bombing in Batam, Hasyim Abas, admitted that in surveying churches there for several days he had not found any weapons, nor heard any words that indicated enmity towards the Muslim community. Although this information was conveyed to Hambali, the Mantiqi I leader insisted on continuing with the attacks.[100]

These criticisms did not stop TIBB. In July 2001, it bombed a church in the army and navy housing complex in Duren Sawit, East Jakarta. It then bombed the Bethel church in Semarang, Central Java. In September 2001, TIBB planned to bomb a Sunday service being held at the Atrium Senen mall in Central Jakarta. The bomb exploded prematurely and a Malaysian TIBB member, Taufik Abdul Halim (alias Dani), was arrested as a result. This in turn led to the arrest of Edy Setiono (alias Usman), a Laskar Khos member. Fearing further arrests, many TIBB personnel fled.

The Bali bombings

On 11 September 2001, al-Qaeda attacked America. Its attacks on the World Trade Center in New York and on the Pentagon in Washington killed thousands. The attacks increased the confidence of Hambali and his colleagues, and increased their desire to perpetrate similar attacks in Southeast Asia. Just days after the 11 September attacks, Hambali and his associates in Mantiqi I began making their own plans. An al-Qaeda representative by the name of Mansour Jabarah came to Malaysia to consult with Hambali. He also went to Singapore, Malaysia and the Philippines to search out possible targets. After his tour, Jabarah and Hambali settled on a plan to use bomb-laden trucks to attack the American, Israeli, British and Australian diplomatic missions in Singapore, as well as American companies there. The plan called for at least 17 tonnes of ammonium nitrate and nine tonnes of TNT. They planned to carry out the attacks between December 2001 and May 2002. Faturrahman Al Ghozi, Jema'ah Islamiyah's top operative in the Philippines, was to make the truck bombs.

The plan failed, however, when the Singaporean security services caught wind of it in late 2001. They arrested many of Jema'ah Islamiyah's top Singapore members. A wave of arrests in Malaysia also netted several top leaders, forcing many Mantiqi I members to flee. Some went to Indonesia; Hambali, Mukhlas, Dr Azahari Husein and Noordin Top fled to Thailand. But even there, the fugitives continued their plans for a major terrorist attack. In early 2002, they met and agreed they would undertake a major attack in Indonesia, without determining the target. The meeting also transferred command of Mantiqi I from Hambali to Mukhlas; Hambali was too high on the wanted list of security forces in the region for him to lead any attack.

Mukhlas returned to Indonesia in April 2002. When he arrived at the Al-Islam *pesantren*, the school his family ran in his home town of Tenggulun in Lamongan, he was actually hesitant to continue with the attack plans. He gathered his relatives and friends on the Al-Islam board and asked them to concentrate on managing the school. The Malaysian government had closed JI's Lukmanul

Hakiem *pesantren* in Johor, which Mukhlas had founded. This was a great blow, as he had built the school from nothing at Abdullah Sungkar's behest. Mukhlas did not want the Al-Islam school to suffer the same fate.[101]

But his desire to carry out a major attack was rekindled after he met old friends in Indonesia like Imam Samudera. He contacted Zulkarnaen and asked his permission to use Laskar Khos members for the operation.[102] Zulkarnaen agreed, and Mukhlas accordingly brought in Dulmatin, Umar Patek, Abdul Ghoni and Sarjiyo. In May 2002, he organised a meeting in Solo to discuss the plans with his brother Amrozi, Imam Samudera and Dulmatin. They agreed to focus on attacking America and its allies. Mukhlas suggested that they bomb the Australian school in Jakarta. The others objected that this would just result in schoolchildren and the Indonesian school guards falling victim. Instead, they agreed to attack a large mine in Lombok run by the American-owned Newmont mining company. Dulmatin and Amrozi were asked to conduct a survey.[103]

As with the Christmas Eve bombing, Mukhlas did not tell the Mantiqi II leaders of his plan, as he knew they would not support it; indeed, he knew that most of the Afghanistan alumni would reject the idea. In early August 2002, however, the plan to bomb the Newmont mine was cancelled when the plotters realised that the majority of the workers were Muslims. This decision was taken in a meeting in Solo attended by Dulmatin, Amrozi, Mukhlas and Abdul Ghoni. It was at this point that Mukhlas suggested that they shift the target to Bali and focus on foreign tourists. The participants agreed.

The Bali plan developed further after a meeting in Solo in mid-August, as set out in detail by Ali Imron in his 2007 book, *Ali Imron*

Sang Pengebom (Ali Imron the Bomber). Imam Samudera, Mukhlas, Dulmatin, Ali Imron, Amrozi, Umar Patek and Sarjiyo attended the meeting. Imam Samudera suggested that they carry out the bombings on 11 September 2002 to commemorate the anniversary of the 9/11 attacks. But time was too tight.

The group agreed to an attack using three bombs. The first bomb would be a car bomb, the second a smaller motorcycle bomb and the third an individual suicide bomber with a bomb vest. Imam Samudera as attack coordinator insisted that these be suicide bombings:

> The aim of these suicide bombs is to add to the fear in the
> hearts of unbelievers and the hearts of those we consider
> enemies [and] to give enthusiasm to Muslims to struggle for
> Islam. [We] want them to be brave like the courage of the
> individuals who perpetrate the suicide bombings.[104]

Of the meeting participants, Ali Imron was most hesitant about the plan. He had rejected the idea half a year earlier, when Imam Samudera had first proposed it. He felt that there was little use in bombing public places outside of communal conflict zones, and he wanted to focus on *jihad* in Maluku and Poso. He suggested to his older brother that if they wanted to attack American interests, they should, where possible, avoid attacks on civilians. He said:

> ... if we want to wage jihad against America and its allies
> then we should go after their warships which sometimes
> dock at large ports in Indonesia. Then we bomb the
> warship using a suicide bomber on a speedboat that we fill

with explosives. I made this recommendation so that there would not be bombings in public places that could affect innocent people.[105]

But Mukhlas and Imam Samudera took no heed of his suggestion. They insisted on attacking foreign tourists in Bali. For Imam Samudera, an attack in Bali would be revenge for what American troops had done in Afghanistan, where he argued the American invasion had caused more than 200 000 deaths of innocent children, women and weak men.[106] In his view, if the enemies of Islam (unbelievers) killed women and children, then Muslims were permitted to retaliate in kind.[107] Samudera said of Bali visitors in particular that 'there is not a single Western tourist who comes without at a minimum a mission to destroy morals and character ...'[108]

In late August several young protégés of Imam Samudera from a Darul Islam faction in Banten known as the Ring Banten robbed a gold shop in Serang, Banten, ostensibly to fund the planned attack although, as it later turned out, Hambali had already arranged funding from al-Qaeda. Some of these men later joined their mentor in Bali.

The bombing team prepared intensively throughout September and October. Amrozi bought a Mitsubishi L300 with Bali number plates to use as the car bomb. They scratched out the chassis and engine numbers. They sent the explosives that they had gathered in Lamongan to Bali. In Bali, Ali Imron surveyed various tourist sites from Nusa Dua to Kuta, to choose the target of the attack. They also prepared five candidates to be suicide bombers. They constructed the bombs in Bali, finishing the task at the end of September. All of Jema'ah Islamiyah's bomb-making experts, including

Ali Imron, Umar Patek, Dulmatin, Sarjiyo and Abdul Goni, were involved in making the car bomb. Dr Azahari, who had fled Malaysia after the crackdown there, also joined in. On 11 October, all of the preparations were complete. The car bomb, containing around 1 tonne of explosives, the bomb vest with 5 kilograms of TNT and the motorbike bomb with 50 kilograms of TNT were all ready.[109]

They had chosen as targets two of the most popular nightspots in Kuta, the Sari Club and Paddy's Cafe, as well as the American Consulate.[110] They would use the bomb vest and car bomb at the two entertainment venues, whereas they planned to attack the American Consulate with the suicide bomber on the motorbike. But a problem arose – the men they had chosen as suicide bombers did not know how to drive a car or ride a motorcycle. Consequently, they decided to use an ordinary motorbike bomb that they would position in front of the Consulate and detonate using a mobile phone. The attacks on the Sari Club and Paddy's remained to be finalised. Ali Imron was given the task of taking the van containing the bomb close to the target. From there the suicide bomber would drive the vehicle forward. The car attack would be preceded by the attack by the suicide bomber wearing the explosive vest.[111]

On Saturday night, 12 October 2002, bombs exploded at the Sari Club and Paddy's Cafe on their busiest night, burning both to the ground. Shop windows shattered along the length of Legian Street and the roofs of houses flew into the air, damaging dozens of shops and residences. Two hundred and two people died, eighty-eight of them Australian and thirty-eight Indonesian, and more than 300 people were wounded.

The Indonesian police investigated the Bali bombings with the help of police forces from around the world. For more than ten days they patiently examined the objects left at the crime scene. Their efforts produced results. From a piece of metal from the body of the Mitsubishi L300 van they were able to retrieve the inspection number, indicating that it had been a public transport vehicle in Bali. It was that number that led the security forces to the Bali bombers. On 5 November 2002, the police arrested Amrozi in Lamongan. After that, the police arrested the others one by one, including Imam Samudera, Mukhlas, Ali Imron and Mubarok.

The Bali bombings dealt a serious blow to Jema'ah Islamiyah. The arrests of the perpetrators were just the beginning of a broader crackdown. The police did not just hunt the perpetrators – they pursued anyone who had played any role at all in meeting the bombers, helping them flee or failing to report their whereabouts to the police. The arrests eventually enabled the police to uncover and disrupt the broader network. A number of Jema'ah Islamiyah's members acknowledged the damage that the bombing had done to their cause. As one noted:

> *Jihad* in Allah's path, which should have served as
> protection for Islam and Muslims, caused disruption
> instead. *Jihad* in Allah's path, which should have promised
> glory, instead caused the bombers and those who assisted
> them to be vilified, because they had to be hunted, pursued
> and imprisoned. And *jihad* in Allah's path, which should
> have been a tool to get rid of blasphemy, instead caused a
> rise of blasphemy. All of this was caused because [we were]
> wrong in carrying out and applying the obligation of *jihad*
> in Allah's path.[112]

The damage done to Jema'ah Islamiyah as a movement did not bring an end to terrorism in Indonesia, or undermine the spread of Salafi Jihadi ideas. The Marriott bombing in 2003, the Australian Embassy bombing in 2004, the second Bali bombing in 2005 and the Marriott and Ritz-Carlton hotel bombings in 2009, in which new individuals and groups beyond Jema'ah Islamiyah took part, underlined the fact that Salafi Jihadi ideas remained alive and well in Indonesia.

Epilogue:
Jihad after the Bali bombings

The broader crackdown on Jema'ah Islamiyah after the Bali bombings saw even leading members of the movement who had been opposed to the bombings arrested, including Achmad Roihan, Hamzah, Musthopa and Nasir Abbas. This generated considerable resentment towards the perpetrators within the movement. Many Jema'ah Islamiyah members argued that the benefits of the attack were far outweighed by the cost. They also criticised the view of Mukhlas and his associates that it was a greater priority to wage war against the far enemy them the near enemy.

Mukhlas's followers rejected all of these arguments. They argued that their *jihad* was based on Islamic law, which certainly could not be annulled on the basis of calculations of cost and benefit. They also insisted that there could be no delay in waging war on the far enemy such as America and its allies, because these enemies of Islam were, in their view, occupying the heart of the Islamic community's territory – a reference to the US presence in Saudi Arabia and neighbouring Gulf countries. They were convinced that for as long as America and its allies controlled the oil-rich Arabian Peninsula, then the fall of other Muslim countries was only a matter of time. In their view, *jihad* against America had to be prioritised and waged immediately.[1]

No compromise could be reached to bridge this divide within Jema'ah Islamiyah. Each side chose its own path. This did not mean, however, that those in the movement opposed to the bombings were averse to engaging in violence. After the Bali bombings, the continuing communal conflict in Poso became the main focus of Jema'ah Islamiyah activities. They continued the Uhud Project, which had commenced in 2000.[2] This project had initially aimed to help local Muslims wage war on Christians. After the Malino Peace Agreement in December 2001, the aim of the project changed. The new goal was to establish a *qoidah aminah*, or secure base, in Poso, which would precede the establishment of an Islamic state.[3] Poso seemed perfect terrain for these goals. Geographically, the hilly and mountainous terrain with its fast-flowing river made for good defences. Additionally, the mountains, sea and river provided abundant supplies. Demographically, Poso's Muslim community strongly supported the presence of Jema'ah Islamiyah, whom they felt protected them. Supporters of Jema'ah Islamiyah also dominated the community leadership. One of the most influential Muslim figures in Poso, Haji Adnan Arsal, even joined Jema'ah Islamiyah.[4]

In 2003, Jema'ah Islamiyah formed the Wakalah Khaibar in Poso and the Wakalah Tabuk in Pendolo. Its leader was Hasanudin, an alumnus of Moro. To strengthen Jema'ah Islamiyah's influence in Poso, Hasanudin married one of Adnan Arsal's daughters. Jema'ah Islamiyah organised various programs, such as an Islamic propagation program with the task of organising religious study sessions in various locations and recruiting members from among the participants. The preachers for these sessions were brought in from Java, and typically were graduates of Jema'ah Islamiyah schools there. Jema'ah Islamiyah also organised various military training programs (*tadrib askary*) for its members. They recruited some of the alumni for Jema'ah Islamiyah's Tim Askary (Military Team), whose task it was to provide security for the Muslim community in Poso.[5]

Between 2003 and 2006 the Team was responsible for dozens of attacks against the Christian community in Poso, including beheadings, shootings and bombings. Among these attacks were the beheading of three Christian schoolgirls in October 2005, and the fatal shooting of Reverend Irianto Kongkoli, Secretary-General of the Central Sulawesi Christian Church (GKST – Gereja Kristen Sulawesi Tengah) in October 2006. The team was also responsible for the bombing of the Tentena market in May 2005, which killed twenty-two people and wounded around seventy people. Another bombing attack targeted a pork market in Palu in December 2005. This attack killed eight people and wounded fifty-six others.

The continuing communal violence in Poso was fuelled by the feelings of injustice that continued to be held by parts of the Muslim community even after the Malino accord. For example, some pointed to the fact that not all of the perpetrators of a May 2000 massacre of Muslims at the Walisongo *pesantren* in Poso had been brought to justice. These feelings caused some in the Muslim community to join with the jihadists in perpetrating various acts of violence. Jema'ah Islamiyah itself portrayed Malino as an act of sabotage against the Muslim community's victory over local Christians.[6]

The local security forces found it difficult to gain control of the situation. They repeatedly arrested the wrong people. After the 2005 schoolgirl beheadings, national police headquarters formed a CID Task Force for Poso. Some of its personnel were recruited from the police Bomb Task Force and from the highly capable anti-terrorist unit, Detachment 88. The team still faced many difficulties. The local Muslim community tended to protect and defend the perpetrators of terror attacks. Many in the community saw the *jihadi*s as their sole means of defence against attacks from Christians.

It was this situation that eventually forced the Poso CID Task Force to launch a large-scale assault on Jema'ah Islamiyah's base area in the Tanah Runtuh neighbourhood on 22 January 2007. Two hundred and ten police personnel from the Mobile Brigade, Detachment 88 and other units were deployed for this operation. The police were only able to occupy Tanah Runtuh after an almost 10-hour shootout. Thirteen *jihadi*s and one police officer were killed. The police then continued their pursuit of those who fled Poso. As a result of the operation, the police were able to make arrests in at least thirty-seven outstanding cases of violence, including many of the major cases already mentioned. Some sixty-four Jema'ah Islamiyah members were picked up by police.[7]

The success of the police in uncovering Jema'ah Islamiyah's network in Poso was a telling blow. Following on from the Poso sweep, the police captured Jema'ah Islamiyah's interim commander (*Amir*) Zuhroni (alias Zarkasih, alias Nuaim), as well as Abu Dujana, Jema'ah Islamiyah's military chief in June 2007. Jema'ah Islamiyah was crippled as an organisation, and subsequently shifted its attention away from militancy towards Islamic propagation.

In contrast to Jema'ah Islamiyah's activities in Poso, Mukhlas's followers continued their *jihad* against America, led by Dr Azahari Husein and Noordin M. Top, two Jema'ah Islamiyah members from Malaysia. Although the pair were members of Jema'ah Islami-yah, they did not coordinate with the organisation's leadership. They were influenced by the concept of an individual jihad (*jihad fardiyah*), which had been popularised by Abu Qatada al-Filistini, a Palestinian *jihadi* religious scholar living in London. They considered that *jihad* did not require the permission of their organisation because it was a defensive *jihad* (*jihad difai*), which was obligatory for all Muslims (*fard al-ain*).

Azahari and Noordin's group carried out regular bombings against foreigners and symbols of the interests of America and its allies. Despite continued arrests by police of the perpetrators of each successive bombing, the group managed to sustain their attacks from 2003 until 2005. On 5 August 2003 they detonated a car bomb containing around 150 kilograms of explosives at the Marriott Hotel in Jakarta, killing twelve people and wounding around 150 people. On 9 September 2004, Noordin's group bombed the Australian Embassy in Kuningan in Jakarta. This car bomb used hundreds of kilograms of explosives: nine people were killed and more than a hundred were injured. A year later, on 1 October 2005, the group attacked Bali for a second time. They bombed three restaurants, killing twenty-three people and wounding almost 200 people.

Noordin and Azahari repeatedly eluded raids, and always succeeded in reorganising their group. The key to their success was the structure of the organisation. They established a *jihadi* cell rather than a *jihadi* movement, with just ten to fifteen members. If the cell's members were arrested after a bombing, the pair immediately recruited new members and prepared them to perpetrate the next act of terror.[8] The annual acts of terror ceased temporarily only after Azahari was killed by police in November 2005.

In late 2006, Noordin Top's group's ideas regarding *jihad fardi-yah* faced a rival discourse. At the time, a photocopy of a translation of a treatise by Abu Muhammad al-Maqdisi circulated in *jihadi* circles. Titled *Waqafaat Ma'a Tsamaraati Jihad* (*A Correction of the Results of Jihad to Date*), the treatise contained al-Maqdisi's reflections on the *jihadi* movement globally.[9] Al-Maqdisi himself is a Jordanian–Palestinian *jihadi* religious scholar and the teacher of Abu Musab al-Zarqawi, the infamous Jordanian jihadist who fought in Iraq. Al-Maqdisi criticised bombings that caused Muslim casualties. In his view, bombings in public places brought greater cost than benefit. Rather than killing unbelievers, they instead claimed innocent Muslim victims such as women, children and the elderly. Al-Maqdisi emphasised that only in truly emergency conditions was it permitted to spill the blood of Muslims. In his view, such emergency conditions did not presently exist.[10]

Al-Maqdisi criticised the views of some *jihadi*s who ignored consideration of cost and benefit in *jihad* operations. He held that it was not sufficient to discuss *jihad* only in terms of whether or not a particular deed was permissible. It was also obligatory to consider which actions would be beneficial to the *jihad* and the Islamic community and which actions would cause the greater loss for the enemy. Al-Maqdisi focused in particular on the tendency of the *jihadi* movement to only undertake *qital nikayah*, or fighting to weaken the enemy. In his view *qital tamkin*, or fighting to seize territory and uphold Islamic law within it, was more important.[11]

This book provided ammunition to opponents of Noordin's group. The respective merits of *qital tamkin* versus *qital nikayah* were hotly debated throughout 2007. As the popularity of *qital tamkin* grew in *jihadi* circles, the idea of a *jihadi* organisation – a *tanzim jihad*, as opposed to just *jihadi* cells – revived in popularity. This shift also saw a refocusing back toward local issues. For a movement focused on *qital tamkin*, the main enemy was the Indonesian government, which would obstruct their goal of establishing an Islamic polity within Indonesia. In 2008, Abu Bakar Ba'asyir, former Amir of Jema'ah Islamiyah, and his followers formed Jamaah Ansharut Tauhid (JAT), to pursue *qital tamkin*.

The debates over the virtues of *qital tamkin* versus *qital nikayah* did not dissuade Noordin's groups from continuing their attacks on the West. On 17 July 2009, bombs exploded at the Marriott and Ritz-Carlton hotels in Jakarta, killing nine people and injuring fifty-three. This would be Noordin's final act of terror, however. Precisely two months later, on 17 September 2009, the police shot dead Noordin and several of his accomplices, including Ario Sudarso (alias Aji) and Urwah, in a raid in Solo.

Meanwhile, the adherents of *qital tamkin* made preparations in Aceh. They chose the province for several reasons. Aceh was seen to be very suitable for a *qoidah aminah* (a secure base that would be the forerunner of an Indonesian Islamic state). Islamic law was already in force in Aceh, and pro-Islamic groups such as Front Pembela Islam Aceh (FPI Aceh – the Aceh Islamic Defenders Front) were active in the province. Additionally, there were many weapons in Aceh left over from the conflict between the Gerakan Aceh Merdeka (GAM – Free Aceh Movement) and the Indonesian government, while Aceh's geography was conducive to a guerrilla campaign. The terrain was hilly and covered by tropical forest, with rivers flowing in the valleys, providing a perfect place of refuge. GAM itself had waged a long guerrilla war without ever being defeated by the Indonesian military. Aceh was also located close to Southern Thailand, meaning it would be easy to forge relations with the Patani *mujahi-deen*, to gain weapons and cooperate in each other's *jihad* struggle.[12]

The Aceh project was the initiative of several *jihadi* organisations, including JAT (Jamaah Ansharut Tauhid), Mujahidin KOMPAK and Darul Islam Ring Banten (Banten Ring of Darul Islam). Accordingly, it is often called the Aceh Inter-Organisation Project (Proyek Lintas Tanzim Aceh). The project's leader was Dulmatin, a Bali bombings fugitive who fled to Mindanao, but managed to return to Indonesia in 2007. They adopted the concept of Imaroh Islam, namely that *jihadi* movements in a country would enter into an alliance, then establish a *qoidah aminah* together. Afterwards, they would declare an Imaroh Islam – an Islamic emirate. They hoped various *jihad* movements in other countries would be able to do the same, and eventually all the Imaroh Islam would unite and form an Islamic caliphate.

The plans of Dulmatin and his associates in Aceh failed midstream, however. Security forces uncovered the group's military training on 21 February 2010. The police immediately surrounded the training location. The training broke up and the participants fled. Some escaped, some were arrested and some were shot dead. Dulmatin himself was killed in a police raid in Pamulang, Tangerang in March. The police also arrested several JAT leaders such as Lutfi Haidaroh (alias Ubaid), Haris Amir Falah, Abu Tholut and, most significantly of all, Abu Bakar Ba'asyir.

The failure of the Aceh enterprise was a major blow for the *jihadi* movement in Indonesia. Various *jihadi* organisations who joined the Aceh project were crippled because their leaders were shot or arrested – for instance, the Darul Islam Ring Banten group lost its leader, Pura Sudarma (alias Jaja, alias Akdam), who was shot dead.

It was JAT, though, that suffered the greatest damage. Alongside Abu Bakar Ba'asyir, the police arrested several senior JAT figures in August 2010 because they were involved in funding the Aceh project. Apart from Jema'ah Islamiyah, which refused to join the exercise from the outset because it wanted to focus on Islamic propagation, all other *jihadi* movements were left in a state of disarray.

The failure of the Aceh project helped to once again revive the idea of individual *jihad* (*jihad fardiyah*). This coincided with the emergence of translations of the book *Dakwah Al-Muqowamah*, written by the Syrian jihadist Abu Musab al-Suri.[13] Various *jihad fardiyah* groups began to emerge, promoting anew the idea of *qital nikayah*. These groups were responsible for various acts of terror from 2010 to 2012. For example, one group in Medan, led by Sabar, a former member of Majelis Mujahideen Indonesia, robbed several banks and internet cafes in North Sumatra in 2010 to raise funds for *jihad*. Another group in Medan was Toni Togar's group, whose members were involved in the CIMB Niaga bank robbery in August 2010, as well as the attack on the Hamparan Perak Sector Police Station in September 2010. In Jakarta, an example is Pepi Fernando's group, which carried out the book bombings in March 2011. Still in Jakarta, the Kemayoran group, under the leadership of Ali Miftah, planned to poison police in 2011. Sofyan's group, meanwhile, was involved in the Beji bomb in Depok in October 2012. In Cirebon, the Ashabul Kahfi group, under Yadi Al Hasan's leadership, was connected to the Cirebon bombing in 2011, which targeted a police mosque. Farhan Mujahid's group in Solo, meanwhile, was responsible for various shooting attacks on police in August 2012.

The strengthening of this *jihad fardiyah* ideology was not, however, accompanied by a return to America as the main enemy. *Jihad fardiyah* groups were consistent in making the Indonesian government their principal enemy. There was a particular focus on the police, driven by their success in fighting terrorism. Between the Aceh case and the end of 2012, the police arrested more than 200 suspects and fatally shot more than twenty people, including many who were central figures in the *jihadi* movement.

The spate of recent terrorist attacks targeting police demonstrates the extraordinary resilience of the contemporary *jihadi* movement in Indonesia. Between the 2002 Bali bombings and 2012, the police arrested more than 700 suspects and shot dead more than sixty people. Yet the *jihadi* movement has remained active even if it has been weakened. It is true that some *jihadi* movements like Jema'ah Islamiyah have laid low because of police repression, but new *jihadi* groups have taken over where they left off.

The resilience of the Indonesian *jihadi* movement is impressive. It has survived under varied political circumstances, from authoritarian to democratic rule. The movement's resilience reflects the persistence within sections of the Islamic community in Indonesia of the idea of upholding Islamic law. Some of these Muslims are readily receptive to *jihadi* ideology such as Salafi Jihadism when their desire is very strong and they are frustrated with the situation in Indonesia, which they perceive to be un-Islamic. This ideology legitimates their disappointment and provides them with an alternative path to realise their ambitions. This path is *jihad fisabilillah*, alias *qital* (war). Salafi Jihadism justifies this violent path as the most noble form of worship apart from recognising the oneness of God, and promises the reward of heaven for those who die waging *jihad*. Once exposed to *jihadi* ideology, these disaffected Muslims then join *jihadi* groups, who are able to mobilise them to wage war on the unbelievers whom they hold responsible for blocking their ambition to uphold Islamic law in Indonesia. This is the reason why *jihadi* ideology remains attractive to sections of the Islamic community in Indonesia, and why the *jihadi* movement continues to develop and regenerate.

Notes

Introduction

1　Ali Ghufron explains the bombing as *jihad* in his unpublished manuscript, *Jihad Bom Bali*, written in 2003. See also Imam Samudera, *Aku Melawan Teroris* (Solo: Al Jazeera, 2004).

2　Ali Ghufron, *Risalah Iman dari Balik Terali* (no location: Khafilah Syuhada, 2009), 128–129.

3　Muhammad bin Abdul Wahhab, *Penjelasan Tentang Pembatal Keislaman* (Solo: At Tibyan, 2000), 9.

4　Richard Bonney, *Jihad: From Qu'ran to Bin Laden* (New York: Palgrave Macmillan, 2004), 111.

5　Abdullah Azzam, *Bergabung Bersama Kafilah* (Jakarta: Ahad, 2001), 71

6　Qamarudin Khan, *Pemikiran Politik Ibn Taymiyyah* (Bandung: Pustaka Bandung, 2001), 10.

7　Kamil Muhammad Uwaidah explains the influence of Ibn Taymiyyah on Muhammad bin Abdul Wahhab in *Muhammad bin Abdul Wahhab dan Gerakan Wahhabi* (Malang: Penerbit Madinah, 2004).

8　Khaled Abou el Fadl, *Selamatkan Islam dari Muslim Puritan* (Jakarta: Serambi, 2006), 68.

9　Oliver Roy and Mariam Abou Zahab, *Islamist Networks: The Afghan–Pakistan Connection* (New York: Columbia University Press, 2004), 14.

10　Quinten Wiktorowicz, 'The New Global Threat: Transnational Salafis and Jihad', *Middle East Policy*, vol. VIII no. 4, 2001.

11　Abdullah Azzam, *Bergabung Bersama Kafilah*, 11–20.

12　Jason Burke discusses the arrival of foreign *mujahideen* in Afghanistan in *Al Qaeda: The True Story of Radical Islam* (London: Penguin Books, 2004).

13　Abdullah Azzam, *Tarbiyah Jihad Jilid 12* (Solo: Pustaka Al Alaq, 2002), 56.

14　Abdullah Azzam, *Prinsip-Prinsip Jihad* (Klaten: Kafayeh, 2007), 95.

15　Abdullah Azzam, *An Nihayah Wal Khulashoh* (no location: Pustaka Irhaby, no date), 4.

16　Abdullah Azzam, *Di Bawah Naungan Surat At Taubah* (Solo: Pustaka Al Alaq, 2005), 12.

17 Rasul Sayyaf also believed this version. Ali Imron recounts that Sayyaf once addressed Darul Islam cadres in Afghanistan regarding America's involvement in the assassination of Abdullah Azzam: see Ali Imron, *Ali Imron Sang Pengebom* (Jakarta: Penerbit Republika, 2007).
18 Muhammad Abbas, *Bukan Tapi Perang Terhadap Islam* (Solo: Wacana Ilmiah Pers, 2004), 277.
19 Concerning the dispute between the Saudi regime and the opposition, see International Crisis Group, *Saudi Arabia Backgrounder: Who are The Islamists?* (Amman/Riyadh/Brussels: International Crisis Group, 2004).
20 Anonymous, 'The World Islamic Front' in Bruce Lawrence (ed.), *Osama Bin Laden: Messages to The World* (New York: Verso, 2005), 61.

1 Darul Islam

1 Christine Dobbin, *Islamic Revivalism in a Changing Peasant Economy* (London: Curzon Press, 1983), 128.
2 For further discussion of the Padri movement, see Christine Dobbin, *Islamic Revivalism in a Changing Peasant Economy*.
3 Dobbin discusses the conflict between the Padris and Dutch troops: see Christine Dobbin, *Islamic Revivalism in a Changing Peasant Economy*.
4 Muhammadiyah was founded by K.H. Ahmad Dahlan. Ahmad Dahlan was strongly influenced by the thinking of Ibn Taymiyyah, Ibn Qayyim, Muhammad bin Abdul Wahhab, Jamaluddin Al Afghani, Muhammad Abduh and Muhammad Rasyid Ridho: see Syaifullah, *Gerak Politik Muhammadiyah Dalam Masyumi* (Jakarta: Grafiti Press, 1997).
5 Al Irsyad was founded by Ahmad Surkati Al Sudani, a Sudanese religious scholar who preached in Indonesia. Ahmad Surkati was greatly influenced by the thinking of Ibn Taymiyyah, Ibn Qayyim, Muhammad bin Abdul Wahhab, Muhammad Abduh and Muhammad Rasyid Ridho: see Bisri Afandi, *Ahmad Surkati (1874–1943): Pembaharu dan Pemurni Islam di Indonesia* (Jakarta: Pustaka Al-Kautsar, 1999).
6 Persis was founded by Haji Zamzam and Muhammad Yunus. The Singaporean Hasan bin Ahmad, better known as A. Hasan, was an important figure in the organisation who joined Persis in 1925. Hamka said it was A. Hasan who spread Muhammad Abduh's thinking in Indonesia. Wahhabi thought was another influence on A. Hasan. This influence arose because his father, who was one of A. Hasan's religious teachers, was a Wahhabi sympathiser: see A. Latief Muchtar, *Gerakan Kembali Ke Islam: Warisan Terakhir* (Bandung: Rosda Karya, 1998), 159–66.
7 In modern Salafi circles, Muhammad Abduh is not considered an adherent of Salafism. Indeed, he is considered to engage in unwarranted innovation. Although Abduh recommended a return to the Qu'ran and the *Sunnah*, and rejected blind faith in the legal interpretations of the four schools, he also recommended independence of thought and the use of reasoning. Consequently, Abduh was frequently considered an adherent of rational

thinking (*mutazilah*): see Jafar Umat Thalib, 'Para Penipu Ummat Yang Bermuka Dua', 2008.

8 See Howard M. Federspiel, *Labirin Ideologi Muslim* (Jakarta: PT Serambi Ilmu Semesta, 2004), 74. The Wahhabis' victory in Saudi Arabia was another reason for the establishment of NU. Traditionalists worried that Wahhabis would ban their mode of worship when on the *hajj*, including making pilgrimages to the tombs of the Prophet Muhammad and his companions: see Deliar Noer, *Gerakan Modern Islam di Indonesia 1900–1942* (Jakarta: LP3ES, 1996), 242–44.

9 Howard M. Federspiel, *Labirin Ideologi Muslim*, 69.

10 Howard M. Federspiel, *Labirin Ideologi Muslim*, 69.

11 Japan formed BPUPKI in April 1945 to prepare a constitution for an independent Indonesia. BPUPKI members represented various groups, including nationalist, Christian and Islamic groups.

12 Syaifullah, *Gerak Politik Muhammadiyah Dalam Masyumi* (Jakarta: Grafiti Press, 1997), 124.

13 On the Jakarta Charter, see H. Endang Syaifuddin Anshari, MA, *Piagam Jakarta 22 Juni 1945 Sebuah Konsensus Nasional Tentang Dasar Negara Republik Indonesia* (1945–1959) (Jakarta: Gema Insani Pers, 1997).

14 Holk Dengel, *Darul Islam dan Kartosuwirjo* (Jakarta: Pustaka Sinar Harapan, 1986), 8.

15 S.M. Kartosuwirjo, *Sikap Hijrah PSII 2* (Majelis Tahkim Partai Syarikat Islam Indonesia, 1936), as appended in Al Chaidar, *Pemikiran Politik Proklamator Negara Islam Indonesia SM Kartosuwiryo* (Jakarta: Darul Falah, 1999), 424. Sukarno also mentioned PSI's aim to establish an Islamic government or an Islamic state in a session in Bandung in 1930: see Anhar Gonggong, *Abdul Qahhar Mudzakkar, Dari Patriot Hingga Pemberontak* (Jakarta: Ombak, 2004), 242.

16 Deliar Noer, *Gerakan Modern Islam di Indonesia 1900–1942* (Jakarta: LP3ES, 1996), 153.

17 See C. Van Dijk, *Rebellion Under the Banner of Islam* (The Hague: Martinus Nijhoff, 1981). See also Deliar Noer, *Gerakan Modern Islam di Indonesia 1900–1942* and Hiroko Horikoshi, 'The Darul Islam Movement in West Java (1948–62): An Experience in the Historical Process', *Indonesia*, 1975.

18 Iraqi religious scholar Abdul Qadir Djaelani founded this *tarekat*: see Hendra Gunawan, *M Natsir dan Darul Islam* (Jakarta: Media Dakwah, 2000), 21. Many books mention Kartosuwirjo as an adherent of *tasawuf*: see C. Van Dijk, *Rebellion Under the Banner of Islam*; Deliar Noer, *Gerakan Modern Islam di Indonesia 1900–1942*; and Hiroko Horikoshi, 'The Darul Islam Movement in West Java (1948–62): An Experience in the Historical Process'.

19 Holk Dengel, *Darul Islam dan Kartosuwirjo*, 111.

20 See S.M. Kartosuwirjo, *Daftar Oesaha Hidjrah*, as appended in Al Chaidar, *Pemikiran Politik Proklamator Negara Islam Indonesia SM Kartosuwiryo*, 465.

In the book Kartosuwirjo does not use the term 'Islamic state', but he speaks of an Islamic community identical with a Darul Islam. However, when he states that Darul Islam is a community that implements Islamic law, both personal and social, we can conclude that by Darul Islam he means an Islamic state.

21 S.M. Kartosuwirjo, *Daftar Oesaha Hijrah*, as appended in Al Chaidar, *Pemikiran Politik Proklamator Negara Islam Indonesia SM Kartosuwiryo*, 466.
22 Suradi, *Haji Agus Salim dan Konflik Politik Dalam Sarekat Islam* (Jakarta: Sinar Harapan, 1997).
23 Deliar Noer, *Gerakan Modern Islam di Indonesia 1900–1942*, 166.
24 Deliar Noer, *Gerakan Modern Islam di Indonesia 1900–1942*, 166.
25 Holk Dengel, *Darul Islam dan Kartosuwirjo*, 25.
26 Holk Dengel, *Darul Islam dan Kartosuwirjo*, 41.
27 Sabilillah was an Islamic militia formed by Masyumi specifically to defend Indonesian independence from enemy attack.
28 M. Arsjad Lubis, *Penuntun Perang Sabil* (Medan: Madju, 1957), 23.
29 S.M. Kartosuwirjo, *Sikap Hijrah PSII 2*, 413.
30 S.M. Kartosuwirjo, *Sikap Hijrah PSII 2*, 417–18.
31 Holk Dengel, *Darul Islam dan Kartosuwirjo*, 73.
32 M.C. Ricklefs, *Sejarah Indonesia Modern 1200–2004* (Jakarta: Serambi, 2008), 457.
33 *Kitab Undang-Undang Hukum Pidana Negara Islam Indonesia*, Vol. No. II, Article 2 (1–4) and Article 3 (1–4).
34 *Kitab Undang-Undang Hukum Pidana Negara Islam Indonesia*, Chapter VIII, Article 21.
35 Holk Dengel, *Darul Islam dan Kartosuwirjo*, 75–76.
36 *Kitab Undang-Undang Hukum Pidana Negara Islam Indonesia*, Chapter III, Article 10.
37 For an account of the conflict between Kartosuwirjo and Kyai Yusuf Taudjiri and the attack on the Cipari *pesantren*, see Hiroko Horikoshi, 'The Darul Islam Movement in West Java (1948–62)'.
38 S.M. Kartosuwirjo, *Sikap Hijrah PSII 2*, 402.
39 S.M. Kartosuwirjo, *Sikap Hijrah PSII 2*, 413–18.
40 S.M. Kartosuwirjo, *Sikap Hijrah PSII 2*, 411.
41 Holk Dengel, *Darul Islam dan Kartosuwirjo*, 75.
42 For a discussion of the legend of Kartosuwirjo's mystical powers, see Holk Dengel, *Darul Islam dan Kartosuwirjo* and Hiroko Horikoshi, 'The Darul Islam Movement in West Java (1948–62)'.
43 Hiroko Horikoshi, 'The Darul Islam Movement in West Java (1948–62)'.
44 This section draws extensively on Holk Dengel, *Darul Islam dan Kartosuwirjo*. This book is the only work that provides a complete and detailed explanation of Darul Islam during the period from 1949 until 1962.
45 Aminullah Al Mahady, *Sejarah Masuk dan Berkembangnya Islam di Indonesia* (no publisher, no date). This is an internal Darul Islam history document.

Aminullah also states that sympathy for Darul Islam outside of West
Java first arose in Central Java, prior to South Sulawesi, Aceh and South
Kalimantan responding to the DI movement. In January 1950, Hizbullah
troops under the leadership of Amir Fatah Wijaya Kusumah and the Majelis
Islam Mujahidin under Abas Abdullah joined Darul Islam. They also
stated that Central Java was a part of the Negara Islam Indonesia (NII –
Indonesian Islamic State).

46   On the Darul Islam rebellions in Aceh and in South Sulawesi, see C. Van
     Dijk, *Rebellion Under the Banner of Islam*. See also Anhar Gonggong, *Abdul
     Qahhar Mudzakkar, Dari Patriot Hingga Pemberontak*.

47   C. Van Dijk, *Rebellion Under the Banner of Islam*, 124.

48   Hendra Gunawan, *M. Natsir dan Darul Islam* (Jakarta: Media Dakwah,
     2000), 36. M. Natsir and his party Masyumi wanted a resolution at the
     negotiating table for three reasons. First, the obligation in Islam to bring
     peace between fellow Muslims. Second, Darul Islam and Masyumi's
     common goal to establish an Islamic state. Finally, Masyumi wished to
     attract Darul Islam supporters to vote for Masyumi in the 1955 election.
     They hoped that if Masyumi won, then an Islamic state could be established
     without the need for bloodshed.

49   Holk Dengel, *Darul Islam dan Kartosuwirjo*, 146.

50   Holk Dengel, *Darul Islam dan Kartosuwirjo*, 153. A Darul Islam document,
     Laporan Berita Kemenangan, reports all of these armed robberies and acts of
     terror in detail.

51   Anhar Gonggong, *Abdul Qahhar Mudzakkar, Dari Patriot Hingga
     Pemberontak*, 393.

52   Holk Dengel, *Darul Islam dan Kartosuwirjo*, 191.

53   This section extensively uses data from an NII internal document: I. Z.,
     Shulhul Hudaibiyah (no location: no publisher, 2002), 53–62.

54   I. Z., *Shulhul Hudaibiyah*, 60.

55   I. Z., *Shulhul Hudaibiyah*.

56   Holk Dengel, *Darul Islam dan Kartosuwirjo*, 194.

57   Holk Dengel, *Darul Islam dan Kartosuwirjo*, 206.

58   Holk Dengel, *Darul Islam dan Kartosuwirjo*, 207.

59   Author's interview with Zaenal Hutomi, Jakarta, January 2005. Ahmad
     Sobari claimed that Kartosuwirjo had bequeathed the reins of an interim
     government to him. He said the Imam had made this bequest to him
     prior to being sentenced to death. The claim was based on the testimony
     of Zaenal Hutomi, a Darul Islam figure who had been detained with
     Kartosuwiro. In a conversation in prison, he said, Kartosuwirjo had
     given him the message that Ahmad Sobari should continue the Darul
     Islam struggle. According to Zaenal, Kartosuwirjo also expressed his
     disappointment in the Darul Islam figures who had made the Joint
     Pledge, which stated that Darul Islam's struggle was iniquitous. Whereas
     Kartosuwirjo himself had never called the movement iniquitous. He said

that the form of Darul Islam's *jihad* struggle must be changed because the conditions for *jihad* were not met.

60 The police subsequently captured Ahmad Sobari in 1978. They also arrested his followers in Cianjur and Tasikmalaya. After the arrests, no further news was heard of this group.

61 See Chapter 2.

2 Komando Jihad

1 For a discussion of these events, see Harold Crouch, *The Army and Politics in Indonesia* (Jakarta: Equinox, 2007).

2 Kejaksaan Agung R.I., Interrogation Depositon of Adah Djaelani, Jakarta, 19 August 1982.

3 International Crisis Group, *Recycling Militants in Indonesia* (Jakarta/Brussels: International Crisis Group, 2005).

4 Laksus Pangkopkamtib Jawa Barat, Interrogation Deposition of Haji Ateng Djaelani Setiawan bin Muhammad Husen, 12 April 1977.

5 Defence plea of Adah Djaelani, Pengadilan Negeri Bandung, 16 March 1983.

6 Author's interview with a Darul Islam activist, Bekasi, November 2006; author's interview with Uci Enong, a Darul Islam *fillah* figure, Bogor, December 2004.

7 I.Z., *Shulhul Hudaibiyah* (no location: no publisher, 2002), 3.

8 Aminullah Al Mahadi, *Sejarah Masuk dan Berkembangnya Islam Indonesia* (no publisher, no date), 43. This internal NII document mentions ten names and erroneously mentions the names 'Sambas' and 'Suryana' as two different people, whereas they refer to one person called Sambas Suryana. More than five sources confirmed that Ir. Ageng and Mamin were among Aceng Kurnia's first cadres.

9 Author's interview with Ridwan, a PRTI figure, Ciparay, November 2004.

10 Author's interview with Ridwan, a PRTI figure, Ciparay, November 2004.

11 The text of the second Joint Pledge, which was addressed to Indonesian President Suharto, included a statement of the loyalty of former Darul Islam members to the Indonesian government, and a commitment not to affiliate with political parties. The four signatories of the 28 October 1970 pledge were Danu Muhammad Hasan, Haji Zainal Abidin, Ateng Djaelani and Tahmid Rahmat Basuki.

12 Author's interview with Ridwan, a PRTI figure, Ciparay, November 2004.

13 Author's interview with Ridwan, a PRTI figure, Ciparay, November 2004.

14 Heru Cahyono, *Pangkopkamtib Jenderal Soemitro dan Peristiwa 15 Januari '74* (Jakarta: Sinar Harapan, 1998), 195.

15 Laksus Pangkopkamtib Jawa Barat, Interrogation Deposition of Haji Ateng Djaelani Setiawan bin Muhammad Husen, 12 April 1977.

16 Komando Operasi Pemulihan Keamanan dan Ketertiban Daerah Jawa Timur, Interrogation Deposition of Gaos Taufik, Surabaya, 15 November 1977.

17 See Laksus Pangkopkamtib Jawa Barat, Interrogation Deposition of Haji Ateng Djaelani Setiawan bin Muhammad Husen, 12 April 1977 and Laksus Pangkopkamtib Jawa Barat, Interrogation Dossier of Dodo Muhammad Darda, Bandung, 18 April 1977. Additionally, he also succeeded in recruiting Acip Suyud, former Regiment Commander of Darul Islam in Garut; Abdul Wahhab, former Salawu Tasik Batallion Commander; and Mahmud Basya, former Darul Islam Batallion commander in South Garut.

18 Laksus Pangkopkamtib Daerah Jawa Barat, Interrogation Dossier of Dodo Muhammad Darda, Bandung, 18 April 1977.

19 Laksus Pangkopkamtib Daerah Jawa Barat, Interrogation Dossier of Dodo Muhammad Darda, Bandung, 18 April 1977.

20 Laksus Pangkopkamtib Daerah Jawa Barat, Interrogation Dossier of Dodo Muhammad Darda, Bandung, 18 April 1977.

21 Laksus Pangkopkamtib Daerah Jawa Barat, Interrogation Dossier of Dodo Muhammad Darda, Bandung, 18 April 1977.

22 Laksus Pangkopkamtib Daerah Jawa Barat, Interrogation Dossier of Dodo Muhammad Darda, Bandung, 18 April 1977.

23 Laksus Pangkopkamtib Daerah Jawa Barat, Interrogation Dossier of Dodo Muhammad Darda, Bandung, 18 April 1977.

24 See Laksus Pangkopkamtib Daerah Jawa Barat, Interrogation Dossier of Dodo Muhammad Darda, Bandung, 18 April 1977 and Kejaksaan Agung RI Jakarta, Interrogation Deposition of Gaos Taufik alias Muchlis, 7 October 1982.

25 Laksus Pangkopkamtib Daerah Jawa Barat, Interrogation Dossier of Dodo Muhammad Darda, Bandung, 18 April 1977 and Kejaksaan Agung RI Jakarta, Interrogation Deposition of Gaos Taufik alias Muchlis, 7 October 1982.

26 Kejaksaan Agung RI Jakarta, Interrogation Deposition of Gaos Taufik alias Muchlis, 7 October 1982.

27 Author's interview with Gaos Taufik, Jakarta, November 2004.

28 Author's interview with Gaos Taufik, Jakarta, November 2004. Gaos Taufik is the author's sole source for Daud Beureueh's motives. The author has been unable to find another source, written or otherwise, to corroborate this information.

29 Kejaksaan Agung RI, Interrogation Deposition of Timsar Zubil alias Sudirman, Jakarta, 7 October 1982.

30 Kejaksaan Negeri Jakarta Pusat, Interrogation Deposition of Muhammad Jabir Abu Bakar alias Gandi alias Dedy, Jakarta, 6 May 1985.

31 Kejaksaan Agung RI, Interrogation Deposition of Timsar Zubil alias Sudirman, Jakarta, 7 October 1982.

32 Kejaksaan Agung RI, Interrogation Deposition of Maktub alias
    Muhammad Rifa'i Ahmad, Jakarta, 7 October 1982.
33 Kejaksaan Agung RI, Interrogation Deposition of Maktub alias
    Muhammad Rifa'i Ahmad, Jakarta, 7 October 1982.
34 Kejaksaan Agung RI, Interrogation Deposition of Maktub alias
    Muhammad Rifa'i Ahmad, Jakarta, 7 October 1982.
35 Laksus Pangkopkamtib Daerah Jawa Barat, Interrogation Dossier of Haji
    Ateng Djaelani Setiawan, Bandung, 12 April 1977.
36 Laksus Pangkopkamtib Daerah Jawa Barat, Interrogation Dossier of Haji
    Ateng Djaelani Setiawan, Bandung, 12 April 1977.
37 Author's interview with a Darul Islam activist, Jakarta, November 2006.
    Several months prior to the Malari incident, the special operations team had
    already heated up the political situation in Jakarta with various clandestine
    leaflets, of which one of the most famous was the Ramadi document. At the
    same time they consolidated and gathered together a group of people to
    carry out a riot at a certain moment. They drew upon thugs, the urban poor
    and former Darul Islam members. These were the three main forces that
    the special operations team marshalled for Malari, and which subsequently
    carried out the riot in Jakarta. See also Heru Cahyono, *Pangkopkamtib
    Jenderal Soemitro dan Peristiwa 15 Januari '74.*
38 Kejaksaan Negeri Bandung, Sentencing Request in the Case of Abdul
    Fattah Wiranagapati, Bandung, 23 February 1982.
39 Laksus Pangkopkamtib Daerah Jawa Barat, Interrogation Dossier of Dodo
    Muhammad Darda.
40 This estimate was obtained after the 1997 arrests of Darul Islam members.
    It is estimated more than 800 people were arrested that year, even as many
    others eluded capture: see Chapter 3.
41 Author's interview with a Darul Islam activist, Bogor, December 2004.
42 Komando Operasi Pemulihan Keamanan dan Ketertiban Daerah Jawa
    Timur, Interrogation Deposition of Timsar Zubil alias Sudirman, Surabaya,
    13 November 1977.
43 Kejaksaan Agung RI, Interrogation Deposition of Timsar Zubil alias
    Sudirman, Jakarta, 7 October 1982.
44 The bombing of the Immanuel Hospital was indeed part of a scenario to
    provoke unrest. In addition, though, Timsar purposefully detonated the
    bomb that he had made as a protest against the misuse of the hospital as
    a tool for Christianisation. He had received information that conversions
    were taking place in the hospital, and that several people had changed
    religion.
45 Kejaksaan Agung RI, Interrogation Deposition of Timsar Zubil alias
    Sudirman, Jakarta, 7 October 1982.
46 See Komando Operasi Pemulihan Keamanan dan Ketertiban Daerah Jawa
    Timur, Interrogation Deposition of Timsar Zubil alias Sudirman, Surabaya,
    13 November 1977. Apart from the aim of pitting different groups against

each other, they also bombed the Nurul Imam mosque because it was perceived as a mosque that was being used to cause division in the Islamic community (*mesjid dhiror*). In the history of the Prophet Muhammad, such mosques had been destroyed. Timsar and his associates perceived that the mosque had been used for purposes beyond the interests of the Islamic community, such as for the Golkar campaign in 1971.

47 Kejaksaan Agung RI, Interrogation Deposition of Timsar Zubil alias Sudirman, Jakarta, 7 October 1982.

48 Kejaksaan Agung RI, Interrogation Deposition of Timsar Zubil alias Sudirman, Jakarta, 7 October 1982.

49 Laksus Pangkopkamtib Daerah Jawa Barat, Interrogation Deposition of Ules Sujai, Bandung, 9 September 1981.

50 Laksus Pangkopkamtib Daerah Jawa Barat, Interrogation Deposition of Haji Ateng Djaelani Setiawan bin Muhammad Husen.

51 Komando Operasi Pemulihan Keamanan dan Ketertiban Daerah Jawa Timur, Interrogation Deposition of Haji Ismail Pranoto, Surabaya, 6 June 1977.

52 International Crisis Group, *Recycling Militants in Indonesia.*

53 For an account of the arrest of these two figures, see Kejaksaan Negeri Bandung, Sentencing Request in the Case of Abdul Fattah Wiranagapati, 23 February 1982.

54 Laksus Pangkopkamtib Jawa Barat, Interrogation Deposition of Haji Ateng Djaelani Setiawan bin Muhammad Husen, Bandung, 12 April 1977.

55 Kejaksaan Agung RI, Berita Acara Pemeriksaan Toha Mahfud alias Rizal, Jakarta, 19 August 1982; see also Kejaksaan Agung RI, Interrogation Deposition of Ules Sujai alias Makruf alias Ahmad Said, Jakarta, 20 August 1982.

56 Kejaksaan Agung RI, Interrogation Deposition of Tahmid Rahmat Basuki, Jakarta, 19 August 1982

57 Kejaksaan Agung RI, Interrogation Deposition of Toha Mahfud alias Rizal, Jakarta, 19 August 1982.

58 Kejaksaan Agung RI, Interrogation Deposition of Haji Adah Djaelani alias Kyai Solihin, Jakarta, 4 August 1982.

59 This information on Warman and Darul Islam in Lampung is drawn from various sources, namely Komando Operasi Pemulihan Keamanan dan Ketertiban Daerah Jateng dan D.I. Yogyakarta, Interrogation Deposition of Abdul Kadir Baraja, 8 April 1980, 9 April 1980, 18 May 1980; Kejaksaan Agung RI Jakarta, Interrogation Deposition of Maktub alias Muhammad Rivai Ahmad, 7 October 1982. The information is also drawn from the author's interview with a former member of DI Lampung in Tangerang, October 2004 and an interview with a former member of the special forces in Bogor, November 2004.

60 Kejaksaan Agung RI, Interrogation Deposition of Opa Mustopa, 19 August 1982.

61 See Chapter 4.

62 Kejaksaan Agung RI, Interrogation Deposition of Adah Djaelani, Jakarta, 16 August 1982.

63 Kejaksaan Agung RI, Interrogation Deposition of Toha Mahfud alias Rizal, 19 August 1982.

64 Kejaksaan Agung RI, Interrogation Deposition of Toha Mahfud alias Rizal.

65 Pengadilan Negeri Bandung, Decision in Case No. 1/83 Pid. Subversi/13-02/Bdg of Gustam Efendi alias Oni, 7 September 1983.

66 Author's interview with a former member of the Special Forces, Bogor, November 2004.

67 Pengadilan Negeri Bandung, Decision in case of Gustam Efendi alias Oni, 7 September 1983.

68 Kejaksaan Agung RI, Interrogation Deposition of Opa Mustopa.

69 'Gembong Teror Warman Tertembak Mati di Bandung', Suara Karya, 24 July 1981.

3 New ideology and new recruits

1 Kejaksaan Agung RI, Interrogation Deposition of Tahmid Rachmat Basuki alias Maksum alias Ihsan alias Sukron, Jakarta, 19 August 1982.

2 Author's interview with a Darul Islam member in Bekasi, November 2006, and author's interview with a former member of Jamaah Pemuda Mujahidin, Bandung, October 2007.

3 S.M. Kartosuwirjo, 'Perjalanan Suci Isra' dan Mi'raj Rasulullah', which was written on 7 Rajab 1374 Hijriah, as appended in Al Chaidar, *Pemikiran Politik Proklamator Negara Islam Indonesia SM Kartosuwiryo* (Jakarta: Darul Falah, 1999), 512.

4 Author's interview with a former member of Jamaah Pemuda Mujahidin, Bandung, October 2007.

5 Author's interview with a former member of Jamaah Pemuda Mujahidin, Bandung, October 2007.

6 Author's interview with a former member of Jamaah Pemuda Mujahidin, Bandung, October 2007.

7 Author's interview with a former member of Jamaah Pemuda Mujahidin, Bandung, October 2007.

8 Author's interview with a former Darul Islam member, Bekasi, November 2006. This information on the emergence of a *takfiri* characteristic within DI circles is also consistent with Laksus Pangkopkamtib Daerah Jawa Barat, Interrogation Deposition of Djaja Budi Raharja alias Edi Raidin alias Heru, Bandung, 15 February 1982.

9 Robert W. Hefner, *Civil Islam* (Jakarta: Institut Studi Arus Informasi, 2000), 178–79.

10 M.C. Ricklefs, *Sejarah Indonesia Modern 1200–2004* (Jakarta: Serambi, 2008), 586.

11 This suggestion encountered stern opposition from parts of the Islamic community, however. The government eventually softened its stance and only recognised traditional spiritual movements as a cultural phenomenon and not as a religion.

12 The reaction to this draft legislation was very stern. A group of Muslim students and youths engaged in open confrontation. They invaded the parliament building during discussion of the draft legislation and forced the government to withdraw the draft. The government softened its stance, the controversial articles were erased and the marriage law was eventually ratified in December. See Robert W. Hefner, *Civil Islam* and Andree Feillard, *NU vis a vis Negara* (Yogyakarta: Lembaga Kajian Islam dan Sosial, 1999).

13 Anonymous, *Risalah Singkat Gerakan Fundamentalis Islam di Indonesia*, Darul Islam internal document (no location: Madinah Indonesia, 1 Syaban 1401 H).

14 Pengadilan Negeri Sukoharjo, Defence plea of Abdullah Sungkar, 10 March 1982.

15 Recording of unknown person's interview with Sunarto and Abu Bakar Ba'asyir, discussing the biography of Abdullah Sungkar. The interview was conducted in the Cipinang prison in April 2006. This recording has circulated in *jihadi* circles and was obtained by the author.

16 Recording of unknown person's interview with Sunarto and Abu Bakar Ba'asyir.

17 Recording of unknown person's interview with Sunarto and Abu Bakar Ba'asyir.

18 Recording of unknown person's interview with Sunarto and Abu Bakar Ba'asyir.

19 Recording of unknown person's interview with Sunarto and Abu Bakar Ba'asyir.

20 Recording of unknown person's interview with Sunarto and Abu Bakar Ba'asyir.

21 Defence plea of Abdullah Sungkar, as read out at Sukoharjo District Court, 10 March 1982.

22 Muh. Nursalim, *Faksi Abdullah Sungkar dalam Gerakan NII Era Orde Baru*, Islamic Studies Masters Thesis, Universitas Muhammadiyah Surakarta, 2001, 54.

23 Recording of unknown person's interview with Sunarto and Abu Bakar Ba'asyir.

24 Recording of unknown person's interview with Sunarto and Abu Bakar Ba'asyir.

25 Kejaksaan Negeri Sukoharjo, Sentencing Request in the Case of Abdullah Sungkar and Abu Bakar Ba'asyir, 6 March 1982.

26 This was the Central Java Regional Special Administrator for the Restoration of Law and Order Command (Pelaksana Khusus

Pangkopkamtib Daerah Jawa Tengah). This command, usually known as Kopkamtib, was established in 1965 and given broad powers to restore stability after the coup attempt in September 1965. It had the authority to coordinate all security and intelligence agencies, including the Indonesian military, and became the main agency for curbing political dissent.

27 Recording of unknown person's interview with Sunarto and Abu Bakar Ba'asyir.

28 Recording of unknown person's interview with Sunarto and Abu Bakar Ba'asyir.

29 Muh. Nursalim, *Faksi Abdullah Sungkar dalam Gerakan NII Era Orde Baru.*

30 Recording of unknown person's interview with Sunarto and Abu Bakar Ba'asyir.

31 Defence plea of Abdullah Sungkar, 10 March 1982.

32 Komando Operasi Pemulihan Keamanan dan Ketertiban Daerah Jateng dan DI Yogyakarta, Interrogation Deposition of Abdul Kadir Baraja alias Abu Hasan alias Syaifullah, Yogyakarta, 14 April 1980.

33 Komando Operasi Pemulihan Keamanan dan Ketertiban Daerah Jateng dan DI Yogyakarta, Interrogation Deposition of Muhammad Yusuf Latif alias Iskak alias Ahyar, 26 March 1980, 23 December 1980 and 8 April 1981.

34 Komando Operasi Pemulihan Keamanan dan Ketertiban Daerah Jateng dan DI Yogyakarta, Interrogation Deposition of Muhammad Yusuf Latif alias Iskak alias Ahyar.

35 Komando Operasi Pemulihan Keamanan dan Ketertiban Daerah Jateng dan DI Yogyakarta, Interrogation Deposition of Muhammad Yusuf Latif alias Iskak alias Ahyar.

36 As of early 1979 they had been able to recruit 86 students of the Institut Agama Islam Negeri (IAIN – State Islamic Institute).

37 Kejaksaan Negeri Sukoharjo, Sentencing Request in the Case of Abdullah Sungkar and Abu Bakar Ba'asyir, 6 March 1982.

38 Komando Operasi Pemulihan Keamanan dan Ketertiban Daerah Jateng dan DI Yogyakarta, Interrogation Deposition of Muhammad Yusuf Latif alias Iskak alias Ahyar.

39 Komando Operasi Pemulihan Keamanan dan Ketertiban Daerah Jateng dan DI Yogyakarta, Interrogation Deposition of Muhammad Yusuf Latif alias Iskak alias Ahyar.

40 Author's interview with a former Special Forces member, Bogor, November 2004; see also Komando Operasi Pemulihan Keamanan dan Ketertiban Daerah Jateng dan DI Yogyakarta, Interrogation Deposition of Muhammad Yusuf Latif alias Iskak alias Ahyar.

41 Recording of unknown person's interview with Sunarto and Abu Bakar Ba'asyir.

42 Hasan Al Banna, Usroh serta Pedoman Penyelenggaraan Grup Studi dan Diskusi Usroh, compiled in Indonesian by Ahmad Djuwaeni (no location, no year of publication).

43 Subsequently, this institute changed its name to Lembaga Ilmu Pengetahuan Islam dan Arab (LIPIA – Arab and Islamic Science Institute).

44 Recording of unknown person's interview with Sunarto and Abu Bakar Ba'asyir.

45 Author's interview with former Pesantren Express activist, Bandung, June 2006.

46 Kejaksaan Negeri Jakarta Pusat, Interrogation Deposition of Syahirul Alim, Jakarta, 19 March 1985.

47 Kejaksaan Negeri Jakarta Pusat, Interrogation Deposition of Syahirul Alim.

48 Kejaksaan Negeri Jakarta Pusat, Interrogation Deposition of Syahirul Alim.

49 Kejaksaan Negeri Jakarta Pusat, Interrogation Deposition of Syahirul Alim.

50 Kejaksaan Negeri Jakarta Pusat, Interrogation Deposition of Syahirul Alim.

51 Kejaksaan Negeri Jakarta Pusat, Interrogation Deposition of Syahirul Alim.

52 Kejaksaan Negeri Jakarta Pusat, Interrogation Deposition of Syahirul Alim.

53 In Syahirul Alim's telling, he also met with Abdullah Sungkar. It is possible Syahirul Alim's statement is incorrect, because in March 1982 Sungkar was still in detention and on trial.

54 Recording of unknown person's interview with Sunarto and Abu Bakar Ba'asyir.

55 Kejaksaan Negeri Jakarta Pusat, Interrogation Deposition of Ageng Sutisna Hadiredja, Jakarta, 8 April 1985.

56 Kejaksaan Negeri Jakarta Pusat, Interrogation Deposition of Ageng Sutisna Hadiredja.

4 Revolution

1 Mohd. Musa Al Galih, 'Pembunuhan Wewenang Penguasa', *Buletin Al Ikhwan*, Vol. 1. No. 9, Jumadil Awal 1405 H.

2 See Chapter 3.

3 Kejaksaan Negeri Jakarta Selatan, Indictment of Sahroni alias Amat Himat bin Abbas, Jakarta, August 1987.

4 Kejaksaan Negeri Jakarta Selatan, Indictment of Sahroni alias Amat Himat bin Abbas.

5 Mohd. Musa Al Galih, 'Pembunuhan Wewenang Penguasa'.

6 Defence plea of Abdullah Sungkar, as read out in Sukoharjo District Court, 10 March 1982.

7 Rifki Rosyad, *A Quest for True Islam* (Canberra: ANU E Press, 1995), 22–23.

8 Rifki Rosyad, *A Quest for True Islam*, 22–23.

9 Abdul Qadir Djaelani, *Menyatakan Kebenaran di Hadapan Penguasa Zalim adalah Perjuangan Terbesar* (Jakarta: Yayasan Pengkajian Islam Madinah Al Munawarah, 2001), 21.

10 Abdul Qadir Djaelani, *Menyatakan Kebenaran di Hadapan Penguasa Zalim adalah Perjuangan Terbesar*, 21.

11 Lukman Hakiem, *Perjalanan Mencari Keadilan dan Persatuan, Biografi Dr. Anwar Harjono*, S.H. (Jakarta: Media Dakwah, 1993), 374.

12 On actions opposing CSIS in 1978, see Abdul Qadir Djaelani, *Menyatakan Kebenaran di Hadapan Penguasa Zalim adalah Perjuangan Terbesar.*

13 Tim Lembaga Ilmu Pengetahuan Indonesia, *Militer dan Politik Kekerasan Orde Baru* (Bandung: Mizan, 2001), 172.

14 Tim Lembaga Ilmu Pengetahuan Indonesia, *Militer dan Politik Kekerasan Orde Baru*, 174.

15 Lukman Hakiem, *Perjalanan Mencari Keadilan dan Persatuan, Biografi Dr. Anwar Harjono*, S.H., 368–74.

16 Lukman Hakiem, *Perjalanan Mencari Keadilan dan Persatuan, Biografi Dr. Anwar Harjono*, S.H., 390.

17 M.C. Ricklefs, *Sejarah Indonesia Modern 1200–2004* (Jakarta: Serambi, 2008), 605–607.

18 Vedi Hadiz and David Bourchier (eds.), *Pemikiran Sosial dan Politik Indonesia Periode 1965–1999* (Jakarta: PT Pustaka Utama Grafiti dan Freedom Institute, 2006), 158–61.

19 Kejaksaan Negeri Jakarta Pusat, Interrogation Deposition of Mursalin Dahlan, Jakarta, 7 May 1985.

20 Author's interview with a former Pesantren Express participant, Jakarta, November 2004.

21 Author's interview with a former Pesantren Express participant, Jakarta, November 2004.

22 Kejaksaan Negeri Jakarta Pusat, Interrogation Deposition of Nuriman, Jakarta, 8 April 1985.

23 Kejaksaan Negeri Jakarta Pusat, Interrogation Deposition of Syahirul Alim, Jakarta, 4 April 1985.

24 This was the phrase the perpetrators always used.

25 Kejaksaan Negeri Jakarta Pusat, Interrogation Deposition of Mursalin Dahlan.

26 Kejaksaan Negeri Jakarta Pusat, Interrogation Deposition of Syahirul Alim, Jakarta, 11 April 1985.

27 Kejaksaan Negeri Jakarta Pusat, Interrogation Deposition of Syahirul Alim, Jakarta, 25 March 1985.

28 Kejaksaan Negeri Jakarta Pusat, Interrogation Deposition of Nuriman.

29 Kejaksaan Negeri Jakarta Pusat, Interrogation Deposition of Muhammad Jabir Abu Bakar alias Gandi alias Dedy.

30 Kejaksaan Negeri Jakarta Pusat, Interrogation Deposition of Marwan Ashuri, Jakarta, 8 May 1985.

31 See Kejaksaan Negeri Jakarta Pusat, Interrogation Deposition of Muhammad Jabir Abu Bakar alias Gandi alias Dedy, and Kejaksaan Negeri Jakarta Pusat, Interrogation Deposition of Marwan Ashuri.

32 Saleh Amin was one of Jabir's underlings who was a true expert in bomb-making. Saleh had trained Sumatran Komando Jihad members, including Timsar Zubil and his associates, in bomb-making, and the bombs were then used for Komando Jihad operations.

33 Anonymous, 'Undangan Apel Akbar Wihdatul Islam', 19 February 1983.

34 Author's interview with a former Pesantren Express member, Bandung, June 2006.

35 Kejaksaan Negeri Jakarta Pusat, Interrogation Deposition of Syahirul Alim, Jakarta, 11 April 1985.

36 Sinar Pagi, 26 February 1983.

37 Kejaksaan Negeri Jakarta Pusat, Interrogation Deposition of Syahirul Alim, Jakarta, 25 March 1985.

38 Kejaksaan Negeri Jakarta Pusat, Interrogation Deposition of Syahirul Alim, Jakarta, 25 March 1985.

39 Aos Firdaus was recruited by West Java Darul Islam leader Opa Mustopa. Aos fled to Jakarta when Opa and other Darul Islam leaders were arrested, and was then inactive for almost three years. He turned to petty trade and by chance met Aceng Kurnia's son, Encep Syaifullah, after Friday prayer one time. Encep was staying at Jabir's house, and invited Aos to meet him, after which Aos also took part in a religious study session at Muchliansyah's residence. Aos then became active again and was an *ustadz* in the Condet group.

40 Ustadz Wahyudin was a friend of Aos Firdaus. When the security forces pursued him on charges that he masterminded the dissemination of pamphlets in Rengasdengklok in the case of the government *jilbab* ban, Aos invited him to flee to Jakarta, where he joined the *usroh* group.

41 Author's interview with former Usroh Condet activist, Jakarta, June 2010.

42 Kejaksaan Negeri Jakarta Selatan, Sentencing Request in the Case of Abdullah Anshori alias Ibnu Thoyib. Among Indonesian Muslims this term is frequently used to denote Nahdlatul Ulama, whereas in the Middle East, the term also refers to Salafis or Wahhabis. Additionally, they also frequently called themselves the Generasi 554 (554 Generation) community. This referred to Al Maidah 54 (the fifth chapter of the Qu'ran), which discusses a generation which loves and is loved by Allah.

43 Many *hadith* discuss the division of the Islamic community into 73 groups, including the *hadith* narrated by Imam Tarmizi, which says that the Islamic community will be divided into 72 groups which will all enter hell, and one group that follows the Prophet and his companions. Salafis often call those who follow the Prophet and his companions Ahlul Sunnah Wal Jama'ah.

44 Kejaksaan Negeri Jakarta Selatan, Sentencing Request in the Case of Abdullah Anshori alias Ibnu Thoyib.

45 Pengadilan Negeri Malang, Decision in Case No. 438/Pid.Sus./1990/PN Malang of Husein bin Ali Al Habsyi, Malang, 31 January 1991.

46 Kejaksaan Negeri Malang, Interrogation Deposition of Lutfi Ali, Malang,
    22 March 1990 and 30 April 1990.
47 Kejaksaan Negeri Malang, Interrogation Deposition of Lutfi Ali, Malang,
    30 April 1990.
48 The massacre was the culmination of a sequence of events over five days,
    which started when a member of the security forces asked an Islamic prayer
    house to take down a pamphlet he felt was anti-government. The prayer
    house refused, eventually leading to the arrest of two members of the prayer
    house board, its head, and a member of the public. They were arrested
    after rumours had spread that the security forces had defiled the prayer
    house, and a crowd had burned a security forces' motorbike at a gathering
    to discuss the incident. These arrests led a crowd of over 1000 Muslims
    to march on the local police and military headquarters in protest, and the
    massacre occurred when the security forces opened fire on the marchers.
    The crowd had damaged and burned churches and Chinese-owned houses
    along the way. When troops opened fire, army trucks stood ready to collect
    the injured and killed and take them all to the army hospital. The figure of
    more than 100 killed cited in the text is drawn from *Tempo*, 24 November
    2002.
49 Janet Steele, *Tempo Wars Within* (Jakarta: Dian Rakyat, 2007), 113.
50 Kejaksaan Negeri Malang, Interrogation Deposition of Lutfi Ali, Malang,
    22 March 1990.
51 Kejaksaan Negeri Malang, Interrogation Deposition of Lutfi Ali, Malang,
    22 March 1990
52 Kejaksaan Agung RI, Interrogation Deposition of Muhammad David alias
    Frits Willem Davids Frans, Jakarta, 19 February 1985.
53 Kejaksaan Negeri Malang, Interrogation Deposition of Basirun Sinene,
    Malang, 1 May 1990.
54 Pengadilan Negeri Malang, Decision in Case No. 438/Pid.Sus./1990/PN
    Malang of Husein bin Ali Al Habsyi.
55 Pengadilan Negeri Malang, Decision in Case No. 2/PTS/Pid.B/PN Malang
    of Abdul Kadir Ali Al Habsyi, Malang, 24 March 1986.
56 Pengadilan Negeri Malang, Decision in Case No. 2/PTS/Pid.B/PN Malang
    of Abdul Kadir Ali Al Habsyi.
57 Kejaksaan Negeri Malang, Interrogation Deposition of Achmad
    Muladawila, Malang, 9 April 1990.
58 Pengadilan Negeri Malang, Decision in Case No. 2/PTS/Pid.B/PN Malang
    of Abdul Kadir Ali Al Habsyi.
59 Kejaksaan Negeri Malang, Interrogation Deposition of Sadiq Musawa,
    Malang, 9 April 1990.
60 Pengadilan Negeri Malang, Decision in Case No. 2/PTS/Pid.B/PN Malang
    of Abdul Kadir Ali Al Habsyi.
61 Pengadilan Negeri Malang, Decision in Case No. 2/PTS/Pid.B/PN Malang
    of Abdul Kadir Ali Al Habsyi.

62 Pengadilan Negeri Malang, Decision in Case No. 438/Pid.Sus./1990/PN Malang of Husein bin Ali Al Habsyi.

5 *Hijrah and jihad*

1 Several months later a similar regulation came into force for community organisations via Law No. 8/1985 on Community Organisations, which the parliament ratified in June 1985.

2 Recording of unknown person's interview with Sunarto and Abu Bakar Ba'asyir, discussing the biography of Abdullah Sungkar. The interview was conducted in the Cipinang prison in April 2006. This recording has circulated in *jihadi* circles and was obtained by the author.

3 See Chapter 4.

4 Recording of unknown person's interview with Sunarto and Abu Bakar Ba'asyir.

5 Recording of unknown person's interview with Sunarto and Abu Bakar Ba'asyir.

6 Kejaksaan Tinggi DKI Jakarta, Interrogation Deposition of Mutahar Muchtar, Jakarta, 8 October 1986.

7 Recording of unknown person's interview with Sunarto and Abu Bakar Ba'asyir.

8 Recording of unknown person's interview with Sunarto and Abu Bakar Ba'asyir.

9 Recording of unknown person's interview with Sunarto and Abu Bakar Ba'asyir.

10 Kejaksaan Negeri Jakarta Selatan, Indictment of Sahroni alias Amar Hikmat bin Abbas, Jakarta, August 1987.

11 Kejaksaan Negeri Jakarta Selatan, Indictment of Sahroni alias Amar Hikmat bin Abbas. This document accords with the author's interview of an Afghanistan alumnus, Jakarta, September 2006.

12 Recording of unknown person's interview with Sunarto and Abu Bakar Ba'asyir.

13 Kejaksaan Tinggi DKI Jakarta, Interrogation Deposition of Muzahar Muchtar, Jakarta, 23 August 1986.

14 Kejaksaan Tinggi DKI Jakarta, Interrogation Deposition of Wiyono Muhammad Sidiq, Jakarta, 6 November 1986

15 Recording of unknown person's interview with Sunarto and Abu Bakar Ba'asyir.

16 Recording of unknown person's interview with Sunarto and Abu Bakar Ba'asyir.

17 Recording of unknown person's interview with Sunarto and Abu Bakar Ba'asyir.

18 Author's interview of an Afghanistan alumnus, Jakarta, September 2006.

19 Pengadilan Negeri Jakarta Selatan, Decision in the Case of Syafki Suarul Huda bin Usman alias Kiki, 12 December 1987; see also Kejaksaan Negeri Jakarta Selatan, Indictment of Sahroni alias Amat Hikmat bin Abbas.

20 Author's interview with a Darul Islam activist, Tangerang, October 2004.

21 International Crisis Group, *Why Salafism And Terrorism Mostly Don't Mix* (Southeast Asia/Brussels: International Crisis Group, 2004).

22 Author's interview of an Afghanistan alumnus, Jakarta, September 2006.

23 Hambali is now in detention at Guantanamo Bay.

24 On the role of Mamin Mansyur, see Chapter 4.

25 On the role of Ahmad Husein, see Chapter 3.

26 Nasir Abbas, *Membongkar Jema'ah Islamiyah* (Jakarta: Grafindo, 2005), 36–37.

27 Ali Imron, *Ali Imron Sang Pengebom* (Jakarta: Republika, 2007), 6.

28 Nasir Abbas, *Membongkar Jema'ah Islamiyah*, 37.

29 Nasir Abbas, *Membongkar Jema'ah Islamiyah*, 49.

30 Nasir Abbas, *Membongkar Jema'ah Islamiyah*, 51.

31 Author's interview of an Afghanistan alumnus, Jakarta, September 2006.

32 Nasir Abbas, *Membongkar Jema'ah Islamiyah*, 50.

33 Author's interview of an Afghanistan alumnus, Jakarta, September 2006.

34 Ali Imron, *Ali Imron Sang Pengebom*, 17.

35 Nasir Abbas, *Membongkar Jema'ah Islamiyah*, 54.

36 Nasir Abbas, *Membongkar Jema'ah Islamiyah*, 58.

37 Nasir Abbas, *Membongkar Jema'ah Islamiyah*, 57.

38 Ali Ghufron, *Pengalaman di Jabbah bersama Usamah* (unpublished, no date), 1–2.

39 Ali Ghufron, *Lingkungan Medan Perang*, unpublished, undated, but probably written around 2003 while in prison, 4.

40 Ali Ghufron, *Pengalaman di Jabbah bersama Usamah*, 4.

41 Ali Ghufron, *Lingkungan Medan Perang*, 4.

42 Author's interview of an Afghanistan alumnus, Jakarta, September 2006.

43 Author's interview of an Afghanistan alumnus, Jakarta, September 2006.

44 Author's interview of an Afghanistan alumnus, Jakarta, September 2006.

45 Author's interview of an Afghanistan alumnus, Jakarta, September 2006.

46 Nasir Abbas, *Membongkar Jema'ah Islamiyah*, 62.

47 Ali Imron, *Ali Imron Sang Pengebom*, 20.

48 See Chapter 1.

49 Ali Imron, *Ali Imron Sang Pengebom*, 38.

50 Kartosuwirjo's complete definition of *jihad*: a serious effort consisting of readiness, serving, preparation or completeness, in the path of Allah heading in the direction of Truth and Reality, for the whole teachings of the Religion of Islam. Kartosuwirjo stated this definition in his book, *Sikap Hijrah PSII 2*, as appended in Al Chaidar, *Pemikiran Politik Proklamator Negara Islam Indonesia SM Kartosuwiryo* (Jakarta: Darul Falah, 1999), 417.

51 S.M. Kartosuwirjo, *Sikap Hijrah PSII 2*, 418.
52 Author's interview of an Afghanistan alumnus, Jakarta, September 2006.

6 Jema'ah Islamiyah

1   See Chapter 3.
2   On the special forces and Warman, see Chapter 3.
3   Author's interview with Darul Islam activist, Bogor, November 2004
4   Author's interview with Darul Islam activist, Tangerang, October 2004.
5   Author's interview with Darul Islam activist, Tangerang, October 2004.
6   Author's interview with Darul Islam activist, Tangerang, October 2004.
7   Author's interview with Darul Islam activist, Tangerang, October 2004.
8   Author's interview with Darul Islam activist, Tangerang, October 2004.
9   Author's interview with Darul Islam activist, Tangerang, October 2004.
10 Recording of unknown person's interview with Sunarto and Abu Bakar
    Ba'asyir, discussing the biography of Abdullah Sungkar. The interview
    was conducted in the Cipinang prison in April 2006. This recording has
    circulated in *jihadi* circles and was obtained by the author.
11 It was believed Allah granted *ilmu laduni* to holy people without their
    needing to undertake study.
12 Author's interview with an Afghanistan alumnus, Jakarta, September 2006.
13 Author's interview with Darul Islam activist, Tangerang, October 2004.
14 Author's interview with a Jema'ah Islamiyah member, Jakarta, November
    2006. This new idea, aim and path (*wasilah*) differed little from Darul
    Islam. The difference was that this new community established Salafism as
    its school. This meant that all Salafi doctrines and teachings became the
    community's doctrines and teachings.
15 This book was the author's masters thesis in the Hadith Faculty, Al
    Jami'ah Al Islamiyah, Medina, Saudi Arabia. The author was also a Muslim
    Brotherhood activist. The book was subsequently translated into Indonesian
    as Hussain bin Muhammad bin Ali Jabri, *Menuju Jamiatul Muslimin*
    (Jakarta: Ar Rabbani Pers, 1992).
16 The author was a lecturer at Umul Qura University, Mecca, Saudi Arabia.
    He was also a Muslim Brotherhood activist. Two Indonesian translations
    have been published: Sheikh Munir Muhammad Al Ghadhban, *Manhaj
    Haraki* (Solo: Pustaka Mantiq, 1994, and Jakarta: Ar Rabbani Pers, 2006).
17 The authors were al-Gama'ah al-Islamiyah figures in Egypt. There are two
    published Indonesian translations: Najih Ibrahim, Ashim Abdul Majid and
    Ishamudin Darbalah, *Mitsaq Amal Islam: Panduan bagi Gerakan Islam dalam
    Memperjuangkan Islam* (Solo: Pustaka Al Alaq, 2000); Najih Ibrahim, Ashim
    Abdul Majid and Ishamudin Darbalah, *Ikrar Amaliah Islami* (Jakarta: Gema
    Insani Pers, 1993).
18 In its early days, Jema'ah Islamiyah members more frequently called the
    community JMM.

19 The book lists five *marhalah* of the Prophet's struggle that every movement
    can use as an example:
    First *marhalah*: *Sirriyatu Ad Da'wah dan Sirriyatu At Tanzhim*. (Propagate
    Islam Secretly and Secrecy in Organisation.)
    Second *marhalah*: *Jahriyatu Ad Da'wah dan Sirriyatu At Tanzim*. (Propagate
    Islam Openly and Secrecy in Organisation.)
    Third *marhalah*: *Iqamatu Ad Daulah*. (Establish an Islamic State.)
    Fourth *marhalah*: *Ad Daulah Wa Tatsbiti Da'amiha*. (The State and
    Strengthening the Pillars of the State.)
    Fifth *marhalah*: *Instisyaru ad Da'wah fi al Ardhi*. (The Political Struggle and
    the Victory of Islamic Propagation.)
20 Author's interview with a Jema'ah Islamiyah member, Jakarta, October
    2007.
21 Author's interview with a Jema'ah Islamiyah member, Jakarta, October
    2007. Al-Gama'ah al-Islamiyah figures wrote this book when they were still
    imprisoned in Liman Turah gaol in Egypt because of their involvement in
    the assassination of Egyptian president Anwar Sadat in 1981. Sungkar and
    his associates obtained the book from Egyptian al-Gama'ah al-Islamiyah
    activists in Afghanistan. Relations between Sungkar and this group were
    indeed quite close. In Afghanistan the two groups frequently worked
    together. Starting in 1990, Darul Islam cadres who had finished at the
    military academy were able to undertake a specialised program in military
    expertise in al-Gama'ah al-Islamiyah's camp. Darul Islam instructors were
    also repeatedly invited to provide military training for foreign *mujahideen* in
    al-Gama'ah al-Islamiyah's camp. Relations between figures from each group
    were also relatively excellent. When the Egyptian al-Gama'ah al-Islamiyah's
    spiritual leader Omar Abdel-Rahman came to Pakistan and Afghanistan in
    1990, he even made time to meet and hold discussions with the Darul Islam
    cadres there. The meeting was held at Abu Bakar Islamic University in
    Karachi in Pakistan.
22 Najih Ibrahim, Ashim Abdul Majid and Ishamudin Darbalah, *Mitsaq Amal
    Islam*, 11–12.
23 Author's interview with a JI member, Jakarta, October 2007; see also
    Anonymous, *Pedoman Umum Perjuangan Jamaah Islamiyah* (PUPJI) (no
    location, 1995).
24 Recording of unknown person's interview with Sunarto and Abu Bakar
    Ba'asyir.
25 Author's interview with a JI member, Depok, December 2007. Editor's
    note: In Egyptian colloquial Arabic the J sound is pronounced with a hard
    G sound (as in 'go') and is therefore most commonly transliterated that way
    in English. The Indonesians, however, appear to have adopted the standard
    Arabic pronunciation using the J sound, and have transliterated it with the J
    sound. Jema'ah Islamiyah is therefore equivalent to Gama'ah Islamiyah, but

we have chosen to transliterate the latter in keeping with the most typical general transliteration used in relation to the Egyptian organisation.

26 Nasir Abbas, *Membongkar Jamaah Islamiyah* (Jakarta: Grafindo Khazanah Ilmu, 2005), 85–86.
27 Author's interview with a JI member, Jakarta, October 2007.
28 Author's interview with a JI member, Jakarta, November 2006.
29 Nasir Abbas, *Memberantas Terorisme, Memburu Noordin M. Top* (Jakarta: Grafindo, 2009), 170.
30 Nasir Abbas, *Membongkar Jamaah Islamiyah*, 126.
31 Anonymous, *Dalam Rangka Menatap Masa Depan Jihad Islamy di Belahan Bumi Asean, Kita Coba Cermati Perkembangan Pergerakan Al Jamaah Al Islamiyah*, JI Internal Report on Seminar in Mindanao, Philippines (no date).
32 Nasir Abbas, *Memberantas Terorisme, Memburu Noordin M. Top*, 173.
33 Nasir Abbas, *Memberantas Terorisme, Memburu Noordin M. Top*, 165.
34 Nasir Abbas, *Membongkar Jamaah Islamiyah*, 121–22.
35 Nasir Abbas, *Membongkar Jamaah Islamiyah*, 126.
36 Nasir Abbas, *Membongkar Jamaah Islamiyah*,
37 Nasir Abbas, *Membongkar Jamaah Islamiyah*,
38 Anonymous, *Materi Taklimat Islamiyah*, 'Al Islam' chapter (no date).
39 Anonymous, *Materi Taklimat Islamiyah*, 'Al Jihad Fie Sabilillah' chapter.
40 Author's interview with a JI member, Jakarta, November 2006.
41 In general the preachers were graduates of Pesantren Al Mukmin, Ngruki. They received training in religious knowledge under the leadership of Ustadz Ziad and Ustadz Farid Okbah, a Jakarta Salafi figure who was also close to Jema'ah Islamiyah. They were required to memorise the Qu'ran and *hadith* and read the texts of Salaf religious scholars such as Ibn Taymiyyah's *Majmu Fatawa* and *Tafsir Ibn Katsir*. Training for these preachers lasted from six months to a year. The cadres were then sent to propagate and to recruit members. Author's interview with a JI member, Jakarta, November 2006.
42 Nasir Abbas, *Membongkar Jamaah Islamiyah*, 99.
43 Nasir Abbas, *Membongkar Jamaah Islamiyah*.
44 Nasir Abbas, *Membongkar Jamaah Islamiyah*.
45 Nasir Abbas, *Membongkar Jamaah Islamiyah*, 100.
46 Author's interview with a JI member, Depok, November 2006.
47 The number of Jema'ah Islamiyah *pesantren* has increased from year to year. By 2009 there were more than 50 *pesantren*.
48 Ali Ghufron, *Lingkungan Pondok Pesantren*, unpublished, 1.
49 Ali Ghufron, *Lingkungan Pondok Pesantren*, 8.
50 Ali Ghufron, *Lingkungan Pondok Pesantren*, 5.
51 Author's interview with a JI member, Jakarta, November 2006.

52 Detasemen Khusus 88, Interrogation Deposition of Ahmad Saifullah Ibrahim alias Hudzaifah alias Abu Masud alias Rojer Santos, Kuala Lumpur, Malaysia, 11 May 2004.
53 Author's interview with a JI member, Depok, November 2006.
54 Author's interview with a JI member, Depok, November 2006.
55 Relations between members of Jema'ah Islamiyah and MILF were long-standing. Cadres of the two groups had trained at the same school in the Afghanistan Mujahidin military academy. The same applied to relations between the groups' leaders. Salamat Hasyim, head of the MILF, was a close friend of Abdullah Sungkar. In 1994, Salamat Hasyim asked for Abdullah Sungkar's help to send Jema'ah Islamiyah cadres to teach the MILF army. Sungkar agreed. Jema'ah Islamiyah then sent Mustopa, Nasir Abbas, Husein alias Abdurrahman, Ukasyah alias Ahmad Dahlan, and Nasrullah to teach. Of these trainers, though, only Nasir Abbas and Qotadah, alias Basyir, were sent to stay: see Nasir Abbas, *Membongkar Jamaah Islamiyah.*
56 Nasir Abbas, *Membongkar Jamaah Islamiyah*, 139–67.
57 Nasir Abbas, *Membongkar Jamaah Islamiyah*, 166.
58 Muhammad Rais, *Perjalanan Spiritual*, unpublished, 26.
59 Muhammad Rais, *Perjalanan Spiritual*, 26–27.
60 Muhammad Rais, *Perjalanan Spiritual.*
61 Anonymous, *Dalam Rangka Menatap Masa Depan Jihad Islamy di Belahan Bumi Asean, Kita Coba Cermati Perkembangan Pergerakan Al Jamaah Al Islamiyah*, JI Internal Report on Seminar.
62 Anonymous, *Laporan Perkembangan Dakwah wal Irsyad Wakalah Jawa Wustho* (Semarang: Jema'ah Islamiyah, 1999).
63 Author's interview with a JI member, Jakarta, October 2005.
64 Author's interview with a JI member, Jakarta, October 2005.
65 Author's interview with a JI member, Jakarta, October 2005.
66 Ali Imron, *Ali Imron Sang Pengebom* (Jakarta: Republika, 2007), 54.
67 Author's interview with a JI member, Jakarta, June 2005. Abu Bakar Ba'asyir also confirms the offer from Partai Bulan Bintang in the recording of unknown person's interview with Sunarto and Abu Bakar Ba'asyir.
68 Author's interview with a JI member, Jakarta, June 2005.
69 Author's interview with a JI member, Jakarta, November 2007.
70 Abdullah Sungkar and Abu Bakar Ba'asyir quoted Osama in their letter, addressed to Islamic figures in Indonesia. They wrote the letter on 3 August 1998.
71 Author's interview with a JI member, June 2005 and October 2007.
72 Author's interview with DI Medan figure Gaos Taufik, Jakarta, May 2005.
73 Author's interview with DI Medan figure Gaos Taufik, Jakarta, May 2005.
74 Author's interview with a JI member, June 2005.
75 On the Maluku conflict, see International Crisis Group, *The Search for Peace in Maluku* (Jakarta/Brussels: International Crisis Group, 2001); see also

Gerry Van Klinken, *Perang Kota Kecil* (Jakarta: Yayasan Obor dan KITLV Jakarta, 2007).

76 On the Poso conflict, see International Crisis Group, *Indonesia Backgrounder: Jihad in Central Sulawesi* (Jakarta/Brussels: International Crisis Group, 2004); see also Gerry Van Klinken, *Perang Kota Kecil*.

77 Ali Imron, *Ali Imron Sang Pengebom*, 56.

78 Author's interview with Jema'ah Islamiyah Laskar Khos member, November 2006.

79 Anonymous, unpublished personal notes of a Jema'ah Islamiyah Solo member on the Ambon *jihad* project.

80 Author's interview with KOMPAK member, Jakarta, February 2005.

81 Author's interview with KOMPAK member, Jakarta, February 2005.

82 International Crisis Group, *Indonesia Backgrounder: Jihad in Central Sulawesi*.

83 Author's interview with KOMPAK member, Jakarta, February 2005.

84 Author's interview with Jema'ah Islamiyah member, Jakarta, November 2006.

85 Badan Reserse Kriminal, Detasemen Khusus 88 Anti Teror, Interrogation Deposition of Purnama Putera alias Usman alias Tikus, 14 July 2005.

86 Abu Qatada al-Filistini, *Rambu-Rambu Thoifah Mansyuroh* (no publisher), 29–30.

87 Author's interview with Jema'ah Islamiyah member, Jakarta, June 2005. Information about this operation is also mentioned in Korps Reserse Kriminal Kepolisian Negara Republik Indonesia, Interrogation Deposition of Hasyim Abas alias Osman alias Rudi, Singapore, 1 November 2002.

88 Author's interview with Jema'ah Islamiyah member, Jakarta, June 2006.

89 Three TIBB statements were circulated on the internet. None of these statements had a title or date, but they circulated on the internet between 1 June and 3 June 2000.

90 Anonymous, *Statemen Tentara Islam Batalyon Badar*, untitled, discusses the Medan bombing.

91 The perpetrator was Dedi Mulyana, alias Unes, an Afghanistan alumnus from the eighth class, which commenced training in 1990.

92 Author's interview with a Jema'ah Islamiyah member, Depok, December 2007.

93 Badan Reserse Kriminal Kepolisian Negara Republik Indonesia, Interrogation Deposition of Fa'iz Abu Bakar Bafana, Singapore, 19 February 2003.

94 Anonymous, *Pernyataan TIBB tentang bom Natal*, undated and untitled. This statement circulated for several days after Idul Fitri 1421 H, or in January 2001.

95 Anonymous, *Pernyataan TIBB tentang bom Natal*.

96 Anonymous, *Pernyataan TIBB tentang bom Natal*.

97 Anonymous, *Pernyataan TIBB tentang bom Natal*.

98 Ali Imron, *Ali Imron Sang Pengebom*, 232–33.

99 Fa'iz Abu Bakar Bafana states in an interrogation depositon that Zulkarnaen told him that Mantiqi Sani did not agree with the bombing operation because it targeted places of worship, which was proscribed in Islam: see Badan Reserse Kriminal Kepolisian Negara Republik Indonesia, Interrogation Deposition of Fa'iz Abu Bakar Bafana, Singapore, 19 February 2003.

100 In an interrogation deposition, Hasyim states: 'I conveyed that we did not find weapons in the churches that we monitored and nor words that indicated hostility towards Islam. Hambali then answered (more or less): We only need to stop the Christians' plan to attack Muslims at Lebaran and it is not a matter of victims but we must show the Christians that we are also capable.' Badan Reserse Kriminal Kepolisian Negara Republik Indonesia, Interrogation Deposition of Hasyim Abas alias Osman alias Rudi, Singapore, 1 November 2002,

101 Ali Imron, *Ali Imron Sang Pengebom*, 256–57. This information accords with the author's interview with a Jema'ah Islamiyah member, Jakarta, June 2005.

102 Author's interview with a Jema'ah Islamiyah member, Jakarta, June 2005.

103 Badan Reserse Kriminal Kepolisian Negara Republik Indonesia, Interrogation Deposition of Abdul Aziz alias Abu Umar alias Ir. Imam Samudera, no location, 23 January 2003.

104 Ali Imron, *Ali Imron Sang Pengebom*, 77

105 Ali Imron, *Ali Imron Sang Pengebom*, 256.

106 Badan Reserse Kriminal Kepolisian Negara Republik Indonesia, Interrogation Deposition of Abdul Aziz alias Abu Umar alias Ir. Imam Samudera.

107 Imam Samudera, *Aku Melawan Teroris* (Solo: Al Jazera, 2004), 135–45.

108 Abul Istimata alias Imam Samudera on www.istimata.com. (This website was closed down in December 2002.)

109 Ali Imron, *Ali Imron Sang Pengebom*, 75–108.

110 The bomb at the US Consulate was a low explosive device and did not cause any casualties.

111 Ali Imron, *Ali Imron Sang Pengebom*.

112 Ali Imron, *Ali Imron Sang Pengebom*, 221.

Epilogue: *Jihad after the Bali bombings*

1   Sulaiman Ibnu Walid Damanhuri alias Yasir Bin Bar, *Menabur Jihad Menuai Teror* (no location: Penerbit Al Qoidun, 2005), 5–58.

2   On the Uhud Project, see Dr M. Tito Karnavian, MA, et al., *Indonesian Top Secret Membongkar Konflik Poso* (Jakarta: Gramedia, 2008), 176–85.

3   See Anonymous, *Pedoman Umum Perjuangan Jamaah Islamiyah* (PUPJI) (no location, 1995).

4   There are three criteria to determine whether an area is suitable to be a *qoidah aminah*. First, its geography – that the location is very conducive to defence, that resources are available, and so forth. Second, demography

– that the majority of the population have answered the call of Islamic propagation and are prepared to make sacrifices. Finally, that movement activists (*abnaul haraqah*) dominate the community's formal and informal leadership.

5   All operations by the Wakalah Khaibar in Poso were locally funded. Sources of funding ranged from members' contributions (*infaq*) to *fa'i*, or the robbery of unbelievers' property. One spectacular act of *fa'i* was the robbery of Rp. 478 million in cash from the Poso district government in broad daylight at the Poso District Head's office. The Jema'ah Islamiyah Askary Team also frequently undertook so-called 'red lip' actions – namely, stealing police or district government owned cars (government cars have red number plates).

6   Author's interview with Farihin alias Ibnu, a Jema'ah Islamiyah member who waged *jihad* in Poso, Jakarta, October 2011.

7   Dr M. Tito Karnavian, MA, et al., *Indonesian Top Secret: Membongkar Konflik Poso*, 293.

8   Author's interview with a former member of Mujahidin KOMPAK, Jakarta, October 2011.

9   Al Maqdisi's book was actually published in 2004, but only became the subject of lively discussion after it was translated in late 2006. The translator was Aman Abdurrahman, a former Salafi religious scholar who graduated from LIPIA Jakarta, and transformed into a *jihadi* through the influence of Al Maqdisi's books. He translated this book in prison, after he and several of his students were arrested in 2004 for training in bomb-making.

10 Abu Muhammad Al Maqdisi, *Waqafaat Ma'a Tsamaraati Jihad (Koreksi Atas Hasil-Hasil Jihad Selama ini)*, (no location: Jamaah Tauhid Wal Jihad, 2006), 7.

11 Abu Muhammad Al Maqdisi, *Waqafaat Ma'a Tsamaraati Jihad*, 51.

12 Markas Besar Kepolisian Negara Republik Indonesia, Detasemen Khusus 88 Anti Teror, Interrogation Deposition of Sofyan Asauri, Jakarta, 22 September 2010.

13 Abu Musab Al Suri's book *Dakwah Muqowamah* was translated chapter by chapter and split into about ten separate treatises. These included: *Nasib Tanzhim Jihad Tradisional: Struktural Perlawanan yang Gagal (The Fate of Traditional Jihad Organisations: A Failed Structure of Resistance)*; *Kekeliruan Pemahaman dan Tindakan Jamaah Jihad Tradisional dalam Baiat dan Asamu wa Thoat (Mistaken Understandings and Actions of Traditional Jihad Movements in Oaths and Obedience)*; and *Madrasah Jihad Fardi dan Sel Jihad (Individual Jihad Schools and Jihad Cells)*.

Index